Performance Modifying Ford Trucks

For Street, Strip and Off-Road

by Rich Johnson

The text, photographs, drawings, and other artwork (hereafter referred to as information) contained in this publication is sold without any warranty as to its usability or performance. In all cases, original manufacturer's recommendations, procedures, and instructions supersede and take precedence over descriptions herein. Specific component design and mechanical procedures — and the qualifications of individual readers — are beyond the control of the publisher, therefore the publisher disclaims all liability, either expressed or implied, for use of the information in this publication. All risk for its use is entirely assumed by the purchaser/user. In no event will CarTech and/or the authors be liable for any indirect, special, or consequential damages, including but not limited to personal injury or any other damages, arising out of the use or misuse of any information in this publication.

This book is an independent publication, and the authors and/or publisher thereof are not in any way associated with, and are not authorized to act on behalf of, Ford®, a division of Ford Motor Company. Ford®, and FoMoCo® are registered trademarks of Ford Motor Company.

The publisher reserves the right to revise this publication or change its content from time to time without obligation to notify any persons of such revisions or changes.

Performance Modifying

Ford Trucks

by Rich Johnson • Layout & Production by Rich Johnson

Copyright © 1996 by CarTech, Inc., 11481 Kost Dam Road, North Branch, MN 55056. All rights reserved. All text and photographs in this publication are the copyright property of CarTech, Inc. It is unlawful to reproduce — or copy in any way — resell, or redistribute this information without the expressed written permission of the publisher. Printed in U.S.A.

OVERSEAS DISTRIBUTION BY:

BROOKLANDS BOOKS LTD.
P.O. Box 146, Cobham, Surrey, KT11 1LG England
Telephone 01932 865051 FAX 01932 868803

BROOKLANDS BOOKS PTY LTD.
1/81 Darley Street, P.O. Box 199, Mona Vale, NSW 2103, Australia
Telephone 2 999 78428 FAX 2 997 95799

Part No. 47
ISBN 1-884089-19-4

Cover photo by Frank Hamilton

CARTECH, INC., 11481 KOST DAM ROAD, NORTH BRANCH, MN 55056

CONTENTS

Introduction	4
About Performance	6
Duty Ratings	9
Performance Engines	11
Induction System	38
Turbocharging vs. Supercharging	48
Nitrous Oxide	56
Exhaust System	59
Ignition System	64
Electrical System	70
Wheels & Tires	76
Axles	84
Suspension	92
Performance Brakes	100
Transmissions & Transfer Cases	106
Interior and Exterior Accessories	112
Body & Paint	123
Sources	126

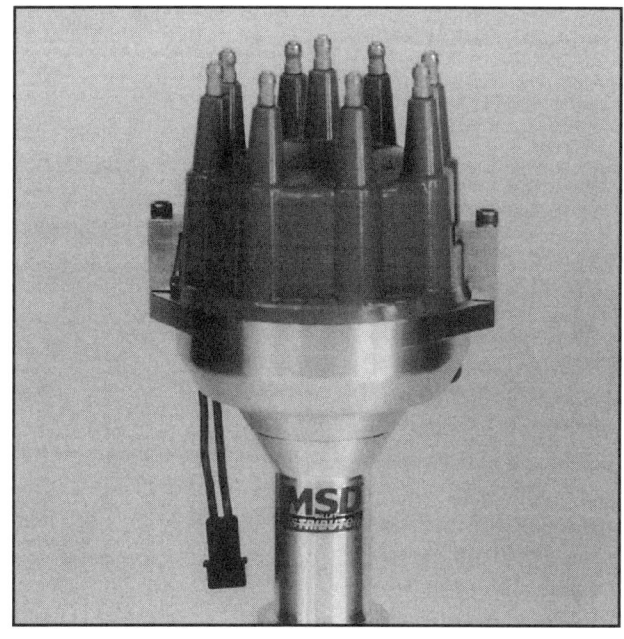

Performance Modifying Ford Trucks

Introduction

There is no question that trucks have become the number one choice among performance-oriented drivers. Pickups are rugged, powerful, sexy, sporty, wild, macho, and cool. Whatever the image that you're trying to portray, there's a truck that will do the job.

Pickups have become the overwhelming favorites for youthful drivers, and the truck divisions of all the vehicle manufacturing companies have grown wildly in the past several years. This has happened for one reason — trucks, regardless of shape or size, are generally more exciting than almost anything else that's being built today. They are fairly affordable, infinitely available, easy to modify, and highly desirable for everything from hauling firewood to hauling the hot dogs to a beach party.

The part about being easy to modify is really important. Trucks are made to be modified, personalized, hopped up, stripped down, jacked up, slammed to the ground, customized, accessorized or otherwise tinkered with. Granted, most of the trucks sold in America will live their entire lives in bone stock condition. Many trucks are purchased to become a work horse on a construction site, or to haul stuff on a farm or ranch, or just to haul the kids to their Little League games and get groceries for the family. So be it.

But a significant number of trucks, especially those in metropolitan areas, are the foundation upon which automotive dreams are built. Some are new pickups that can be fancied up with aftermarket accessories. But many are older models that have been cast aside in favor of a new ride. Along comes a kid with a dream and a wrench and suddenly the old truck becomes something very special.

If any of that sounds familiar, it should. This is the same fuel that has powered the hot rod and custom car interests for decades. Start with whatever you can afford, scour local wrecking yards for desirable "experienced" components, tap into the aftermarket for the latest mail order technology, add a lot of your own ingenuity and garage hours, and drive away in a highly personalized vehicle that is unlike anything else on the highway.

My first pickup was a discarded 1956 farm truck that had outlived its usefulness to the farmer, so he decided that he could part with his pride and joy for $100. Road testing in his field failed to reveal that the steering and brakes were almost non-functional — something I later discovered, much to my dismay, while driving on the freeway toward home. After all, the entire test drive consisted of one looping circle of the field (steering in only one direction), and stopping once at the end. After parting with my hundred bucks and heading home, I discovered that some major work was needed.

Thus began a series of modifications intended to improve performance of this "classic gem" (that's the term I used to convince my wife about the wisdom of owning the old junker). Luckily, I knew another guy who was in the process of upgrading his old truck. He contributed a front axle, complete will all the necessary steering hardware and front brakes. It wasn't new, but it was a whole lot better than mine, because it steered in both directions. After replacing the rear binders, suddenly I could steer and stop, and that was a quantum leap in progress. Later came an engine rebuild, carburetion changes, some body work, rear axle replacement and countless other projects that vastly increase my intimate relationship with Old Betsy (I'm not kidding, that was what the farmer named her).

Years later, I bought another old discarded pickup. This one was worse than the first, in some respects, but at least it had steering and brakes. Of course, that was immaterial because the engine wouldn't run. It was a 1981 4x4 that went for $500. So, what did I get for my five hundred bucks? This pickup had belonged to a couple of guys who obviously needed to file an environmental impact statement before venturing off road. Every body panel and both bumpers had been damaged by rocks, trees and whatever else got in their way. The engine was dead, the interior was torn up, the rear glass was gone, the floor mat was buried beneath some sort of sticky mass that seemed to be a combination of soda pop, dirt and decayed fish bait, and there was a hole in the roof where a CB antenna had once resided. A great truck. Lots of potential ... for a guy who was willing to start from scratch.

A year later, I was driving the truck — all new body and bed, balanced and blueprinted engine, new suspension, 35-inch tires and designer wheels, completely new interior,

---

The secret of building a used truck into a stunning show-and-go rig lies in recognizing where there is potential and where there is not.

---

electric sliding rear window, tube grille, roll bar, driving lights, and a bright white paint job with pearl red flames — when I ran into the original owner. He jokingly called me a liar when I told him this was the same truck he had sold me for $500. Then he offered to buy it back for the original price.

The point is that for $500 here was a truck that nobody wanted, but it had a straight frame, good transmission and transfer case, good axles and driveshafts, and something to start with under the hood. I spoke with the local mechanic who had done all the maintenance work on this truck, and he assured me that it was in good mechanical condition, except for the blown engine. From every angle, it looked like Hell was having a bad day, but underneath this pickup had great potential. Lots of time and money and work later, it could run with the best of them.

The secret of building a used truck into a stunning show-and-go rig lies in recognizing where there is potential and where there is not. Often, this is only distinguished by the amount of money, time and energy you are willing to spend in the resurrection process. Naturally, starting with a fairly nice truck that already runs will cut down considerably on the cost of doing the project, both in terms of time and money. But the beauty of working with a Ford truck is that they are everywhere. If you don't already have one, you can pick one up real cheap ... depending upon how much work you are willing to do to make it live again. And if you do already have one, you're ready to roll up your sleeves and get started.

In this book, we'll be discussing performance modification of Ford pickups, both full-size and compact. We'll talk about both street and off-road use, and performance modifications that are most useful in those environments. You'll be exposed to hundreds of techniques and products, and you can pick and choose those that you want to employ for building your project truck into whatever you want it to become.

Performance Modifying Ford Trucks

A Word About Performance

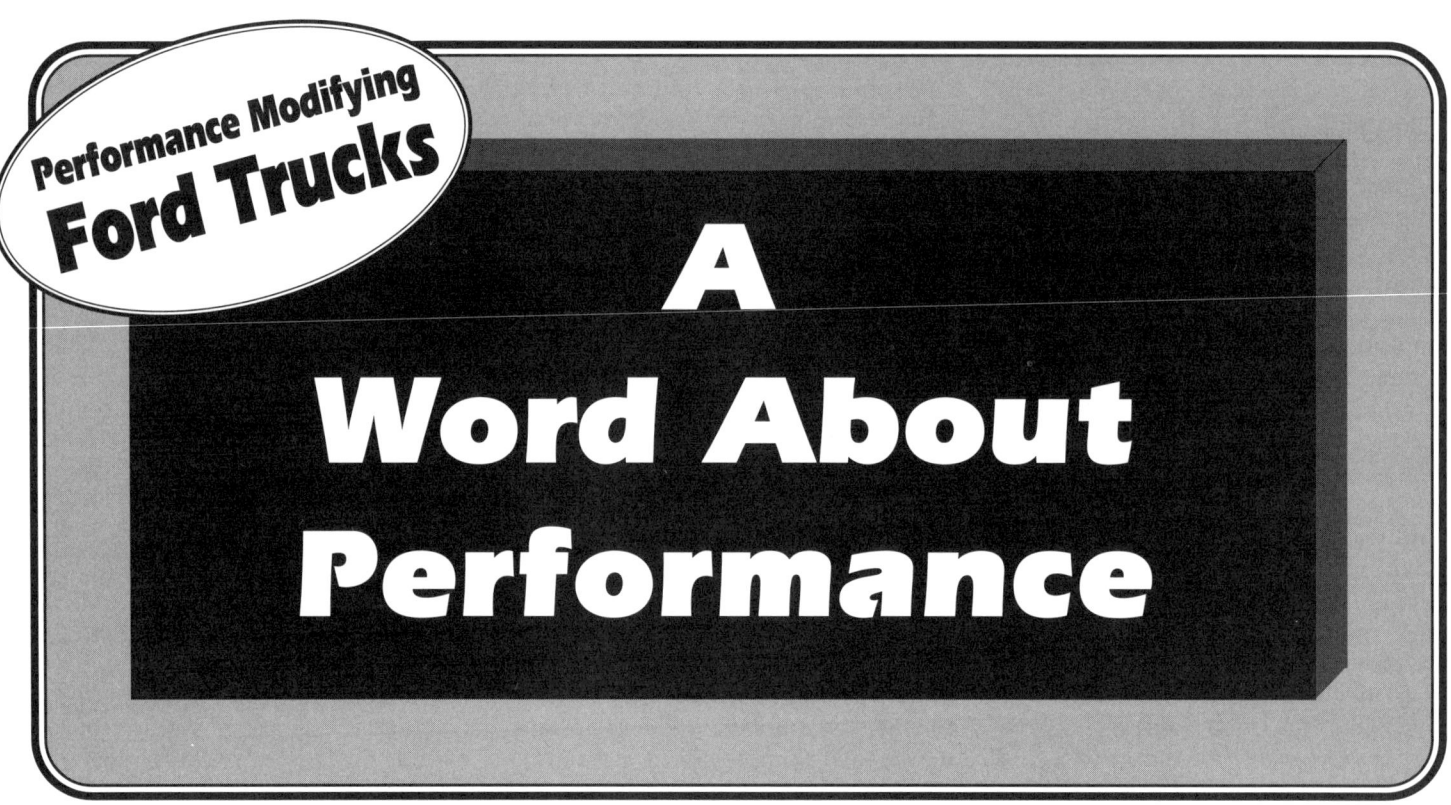

What exactly does the "P" word mean, anyway? Performance — is it pure, raw power? Is it a conglomeration of racing components? What is it that constitutes performance? Unfortunately, there are lots of people who cherish the misconception that the sum total of performance is when their vehicle can beat the vehicle next to them in some particular test of speed. That's all that counts — getting there first, beating the other guy, being king of the hill.

Growing up in Southern California in the Sixties, I managed to stumble into this same misconception. My buddies and I would gather at the designated stretch of deserted highway, conveniently marked with painted lines across the asphalt at quarter-mile intervals. It was run-what-you-brung drag racing in hundred-dollar cars, because that was all any of us could afford. These were the same cars we drove to school and church and on dates. We didn't race for pink slips or money or anything that Hollywood could make a story out of. It was all just for fun. Go fast (but not really very fast) in a straight line. Get your foot on the floor first and hold it there through power shifts and pray that nothing broke. That was my first image of performance.

Then one day, a guy took me for a ride in a 4x4 pickup. Out through the desert we went, driving slowly and carefully, crossing areas of blown sand that could suck an ordinary vehicle out of sight, negotiating an obstacle course of natural obstructions. At one point, we drove to the edge of a near vertical drop-off and stopped. My friend got out to survey the situation, which to me looked completely insane. The ground dropped away steeply for about four feet to the bottom of a sandy washout. The far wall was extremely steep, and I was convinced that if we went down there we would never get the truck out. He got back inside and

6 Performance Modifying Ford Trucks

smiled as he said, "Piece of cake." Then he drove over the edge, across the bottom and up the far side. I was blown away to think that a vehicle could actually cover that kind of terrain, and I came away with a completely different impression of performance.

I have stood track-side and photographed 1000-horsepower trucks tow a weighted sled in truck pull competition that never exceeds 12 miles per hour. I have towed heavy trailers over steep mountain grades, and realized that performance doesn't necessarily have anything to do with speed.

To me, it is obvious that the word "performance" cannot be defined so simply as to say that it involves only speed or power or getting there first or having the biggest engine or anything like that. Performance relates to several aspects of both vehicle and driver, including the proper combination and assembly of components to get the job done, and the ability of the driver to take the vehicle to its fullest potential. It is the successful accomplishment of the goal that defines performance, and the goal may not always have to do with speed.

To get a handle on this concept, let's consider a variety of different types of trucks. We'll start with a category called Street Trucks. Let's assume your truck is never going to be driven off-road or at a drag race or at the Bonneville Salt Flats. A stock truck, right out of the box from Detroit, will easily handle any task in the Street Truck category. But you want a "performance" truck (whatever that means to you) because it will bring more excitement into your life.

At this point, you have to ask yourself a series of questions and be truthful enough to answer them honestly. The questions go like this: 1) What is my definition of a "performance truck?" 2) How big an engine do I really need? 3) Why? 4) Why do I want to make a change in the suspension? 5) If I modify the suspension, am I willing or able to also make the necessary steering geometry and driveshaft modifications? 6) Am I really more interested in cosmetics, or are mechanical modifications absolutely necessary? 7) How much money do I have?

What most Street Truck owners are really interested in is the cosmetic appeal of a modified truck. They may want to look like they're driving a race truck or a big, bad off-road vehicle, but they don't necessarily need to actually build one. That being the case, a substantial portion of the answer to question #7 should be set aside for visible accessories and a custom paint job. Forget upgrading brakes and axle ratios and things that cannot be on display while cruising down Main Street.

Now let's take a look at a truck that's intended for asphalt racing. Detroit's offerings are not sufficient for most racing environments. Depending upon the type of competition intended (straight-line drags vs. road racing or gymkhana), several different types of modifications should be considered. Quicker torque production and higher horsepower will definitely be needed, so modifications will be in order for the engine, intake, exhaust and ignition. The entire drivetrain — transmission, driveshaft, differential, and axle shafts should be beefed up to withstand the trauma of racing. Various suspension modifications may be needed — lowering for increased lateral stability and decreased wind resistance, traction bars to counteract spring wrap-up during violent acceleration, and stronger sway bars. Wide, low-profile tires, and wheels with increased positive offset may be needed to improve traction and stability. Improved brakes, if road racing and gymkhana events are anticipated, will be something to consider. A roll cage that is tied directly to the frame, five-point safety harness, onboard fire suppression system, aftermarket gauges, a fuel cell, and stuff like that may also find its way onto your list. Needless to say, a race truck is a completely different (more expensive) animal than a street truck that just wants to look like a race truck.

Some trucks are pressed into service for heavy towing. Although Detroit tries to address this when the truck is engineered, sometimes a person will need to increase towing performance for one reason or another. Although this category may not seem to be particularly exciting to some folks, it very definitely involves performance modification. No, the truck doesn't become more sexy through this process, but it does become stronger and more capable of producing the increased performance that is needed. This is performance modification for a practical reason, and it is no less valid than performance modification for racing.

Off-road trucks can fall into different categories. There are relatively stock trucks used primarily for trail rides. I call these Street & Trail Trucks because the same vehicle can probe the nether reaches of desert and mountain wildlands on the weekends, then shuttle Mom to the grocery store, Dad to work, the kids to school the rest of the week. Minor modifications can make a stock 4x4 into a great Street & Trail ride. Another category of off-road truck is the 4x4 racer. Nothing about this truck is stock, including parts of the frame, body, or interior. You wouldn't want to drive this thing to work, school or the store — although taking it to church might be a hoot. It would be miserable to drive or ride in because the interior would be spartan to keep the truck light, and other components would be set up for racing and not for comfort or good highway handling.

Well, hopefully the point is well made by now. Performance trucks cannot fit into a single category. Before building a performance truck, you need to define exactly what it is you want the truck to do. Unless you're a serious racer, in which case you will be restricted by rules related to the truck's composition, you are free to choose how you want to build the truck. You can pick a little of this and a little of that until you have the truck you really want. But use a logical plan, and don't slap something on your truck just because you see someone else using it. If it won't work for your purpose, forget it. This is an opportunity to build something unique, so don't necessarily be content to just follow the most recent fads. On the other hand, there may be a very good reason why other people are using certain components. Find out what that reason is, then make up your mind if that will fulfill your needs.

Now, a word about performance drivers. Remember one thing — A performance truck does not a performance driver make. Skill, experience, common sense, self control, understanding the limits, the proper attitude, and finesse make a performance driver. Put an unqualified driver in a high-performance vehicle, and he'll either get himself killed or wreck the vehicle or both. Imagine taking a novice pilot who has only flown a Cessna 150, and turning him loose in a Lear jet. Nothing could be more dangerous or foolish. On the other hand, put a qualified driver in an average vehicle, and he'll take it farther and faster than one might believe possible.

So, performance is a function of driver as well as vehicle. In this book, we'll be talking about the vehicle aspect. There's not much we can do in the context of this book to make you into a competent high-performance driver. But let me impress upon you that just having a hot truck does not result in performance. You need to become a high-performance driver to match the truck you build. Seek out drivers who have experience in the kind of driving you intend to do. Hang around with them, watch what they do, ask to ride along during practice runs. Enroll in high-performance driving schools. Learn to be the kind of driver you need to be in order to take fullest advantage of your truck.

In the meantime, throw out any misconceptions about just putting your foot to the floor and steering between the obstacles. That's not how it's done. A friend who races off-road has a sticker on his dashboard that says, "To finish first, first you have to finish." Finesse is the name of the game, whether you're negotiating rush-hour traffic, running for a land speed record, or racing in Baja. Learn to respect the terrain, the vehicle, and your own abilities.

Performance is an action word. Build the right truck for the right purpose, and become expert in proper driving technique, and you can go where the action is. While you're there, you'll understand precisely what the "P" word is all about.

Performance Modifying Ford Trucks

Duty Ratings

When it comes to a discussion of duty ratings, there are some questions that we need to be able to answer, and here they are: What are GVWR, GAWR, GCWR? What is the significance of having a half-ton or a three-quarter-ton, or a one-ton pickup? Does bigger necessarily mean better? How does all this correlate with performance, payload capacity or tow rating? Lots of questions. And maybe the best question of all — what does any of this have to do with building a performance truck?

Let's answer the last question first. The rated capacities of a truck are directly related to the strength and/or the right combination of components. When building a performance truck, you want to have the strongest parts and pieces possible, because the stresses created by high-performance driving will require rugged hardware. Naturally, you want to build with minimal weight, but at the same time you want all the strength you can get. Starting with an understanding of factory duty ratings will help you decide if you need to upgrade or if you can use stock components.

All of these various capacities can be grouped into a category we will call "Duty Ratings." They refer to the factory's recommendations for maximum payload carrying, towing, and such. It's important to understand that all of these ratings are weight limits imposed on the truck due to engineering safety factors. They are also directly related to warranty coverage. But they are not in any way related to guarantees of driver satisfaction.

In other words, just because a truck is rated to tow as much as 8,500 pounds, doesn't mean that the driver will necessarily be satisfied with the performance level of the truck when towing that much. It also doesn't mean that the truck will only tow 8,500 pounds and anything more than that will cause a meltdown. All the tow rating means is that as long as you don't tow more than the limit, warranty coverage for problems caused by towing will still be in effect. Tow more than the limit, and you're on your own. Use the warranty to wipe up spills, because it won't be good for anything else. And this is because the engineers who designed the truck have decided that this particular assemblage of components can safely tow only as much as 8,500 pounds.

The same concept applies to all duty ratings. Violate them at your own risk. It might be good to realize that the warranty paper isn't the only thing at risk here. If you disregard the duty ratings, things like brakes, axles, bearings, suspension, steering components, frame and other stuff may fail. The spill they'll be wiping up with your warranty paper may be the grease spot on the highway that you become when the truck falls apart.

Okay, so let's get down to definitions. GVWR (gross vehicle weight rating) is the maximum allowable weight of the vehicle, including passengers, fuel, cargo, optional equipment, everything. In other words, the truck should never, under any condition weigh more than the GVWR.

GAWR (gross axle weight rating) is the maximum weight that can is allowed to be placed on an axle. The front axle will probably have a different GAWR than the rear axle, so when you look for this information you should be watching for two GAWRs. To know whether or not you are violating the GAWR, take the truck to a commercial scale and weigh it one axle at a time.

GCWR (gross combination weight rating) is the maximum total allowable weight of a truck and trailer, including passengers, cargo, and all that stuff. Again, never, under any condition should the truck and trailer combination weigh more than the GCWR. Naturally, to be confident that you are within the constraints imposed by the GCWR, you'll have to take the truck and trailer to a commercial scale and have them both weighed.

Tow Rating is kind of flexible. The factory imposes a maximum tow rating, but it's only a place to start. What must be remembered above all is that the GCWR cannot be violated. Even if the trailer itself falls within the weight given as the tow rating, but the truck and passengers and other cargo weigh so much that by the time you hook the trailer up the combination weighs more than is allowed by the GCWR, you're in trouble. When that happens, you have to either leave some of the passengers home, toss out some of the cargo, or lower the tow rating to the point that the whole combination stays below the GCWR.

Payload Capacity is defined as the maximum amount of weight that you are allowed to put in the truck. This isn't just the amount of bricks you can load in the bed, because payload includes passengers, fuel, cargo, optional equipment, etc. Obviously, the remaining payload allowance is a flexible number, depending upon how much stuff you

---

...you have to be careful what you buy. Watch the numbers, study the component combinations, and never assume anything.

---

load on the truck as optional equipment, and how much the passengers weigh, and how much fuel you carry, etc. Knowing the GVWR, drive to a commercial scale and have the truck weighed when it's empty (except for a full fuel tank). The difference between the factory-stated GVWR and the number on the scale is the initial payload capacity. As you add the weight of passengers or accessories like a roll bar, a tool box, a winch, and stuff like that, the remaining payload allowance is reduced.

Now, here's where it gets tricky. You might figure that a big engine will always give you a higher capacity than a smaller engine, or that a one-ton truck would naturally have a higher duty rating in every category than a 3/4-ton truck. But that's not always the case. For example, an F-350 4x2 powered by a 5.8-liter V8 engine, with 3.55:1 axle ratio has a tow rating that is 700 pounds lower than the same truck in an F-250 model. The 3/4-ton beats the 1-ton in this category.

Another example is the F-250 4x2 that is powered by a 5.0-liter V8 beating the same truck powered by a 5.8-liter V8. The GCWR of the truck with the smaller engine is 1,000 pounds higher than the truck with the bigger engine, and the tow rating is 1,100 pounds higher for the smaller engine. The difference is that the truck with the 5.0-liter V8 is equipped with 4.10:1 axle ratio, while the truck with the bigger engine has a 3.55:1 ratio. Little engine beats big engine in this case, because of the axle ratios involved.

Some people think a manual transmission beats an automatic in duty rating, but that is not always the case. Ford rates the GCWR for many of their drivetrain combinations higher for an automatic transmission than for a manual. Tow ratings are sometimes more than twice as high for the same truck equipped with an automatic transmission.

The weak link in a manual transmission is the clutch, and the lower rating is given by the factory because clutches burn out more easily when heavy loads are involved. The factory is reluctant to issue high ratings when doing so might result in a lot of warranty clutch replacement.

The point to be made is that you can't just go out and buy bigger components and think you're automatically getting higher capacity. Bigger is only better when it's the right stuff for the right application. Bigger can sometimes be a disappointment, especially when weight is a concern. So you have to be careful what you buy. Watch the numbers, study the results of various component combinations, and never assume anything.

Performance Modifying Ford Trucks

Performance Engines

The heart and soul of any performance vehicle is to be found under the hood. After all that can be said about suspension, gearing, brakes, handling, and other aspects of performance, if there's no life under the hood all the rest doesn't even matter. In recent years, Ford trucks have been powered by a number of different types of engines, ranging from fuel efficient V6's to gas guzzling big-block V8's. Most popular among all powerplants, however, is the small-block V8. Chances are, if you have a Ford truck, it's powered by a small-block, and most likely a 302 or 351 cid version of this venerable V8.

The small-block Ford V8 is such a popular engine that much attention has been given this powerplant by the aftermarket when designing components for building a performance Ford engine. Employing the best components, it's possible to take a small-block engine and turn it into a real fire breather that's intended for professional competition. Ford NASCAR Supertrucks are based on the small-block V8, so are many off-road race trucks, and so are plenty of hot street trucks.

With the small-block V8 being so readily available, and such a great platform for performance potential, one might ask, "Why bother with anything else?" That's a good question, but it's a fact that many Ford truck owners love their big-blocks, and some performance automotive events are dominated by trucks running big-block engines. And the streets are full of Ford trucks running around with V6's under the hood, and owners wanting to know how to pump these engines up to get more performance.

For performance purposes, it doesn't make much sense to work with a stock V6 in a full-size truck. The factory V6 is a great little engine for the compact trucks, but for the F-series, go with either a small-block or a big-block V8. In fact, in the opinion

Seasoned blocks, and other components, are found in "bone piles" like this one, where experienced engines have been salvaged and set aside for a future day, when someone will come along who is looking for just the right block as a foundation for a high performance engine project. Don't be discouraged by the fact that the block may be sitting in the dirt. After all, if it's the right one and if it's in good condition, it will be cleaned and machined to make it like brand new.

of some performance-minded folks, the V6 should be swapped out of even the compact pickups in favor of a small-block V8. If you really want a V6, and you're looking for maximum performance, look into the 4.5-liter SVO engine.

In this section, we'll introduce you to the 4.5-liter V6 and we'll be discussing some of the basic information you'll need as you consider ways to stuff more performance into your small-block or big-block V8. There are ways to take what you already have under the hood and make it breathe as much fire as you can afford. You can shop the aftermarket for parts and pieces for a totally custom-built powerplant, or Ford can help you out with this project right from the factory. One of the neatest ways to shop for high-performance Ford engine components is through the Ford Motorsports SVO Performance Equipment catalog. Of course, you may also decide to transplant a totally different engine. We'll discuss all these possibilities here.

Entire books have been written about building performance engines, so we aren't going to attempt to repeat that performance in this chapter. What we want to do is give you the basics about making the proper

This salvaged head is being thoroughly washed with a high-pressure spray gun to remove most of the dirt so the piece can be evaluated for possible use. Once all the grease and grime are gone, it can be inspected for cracks or other damage.

12 Performance Modifying Ford Trucks

A fresh bare block can be purchased directly from Ford, through the Motorsports SVO Performance Equipment catalog. Pictured here is a bare small block for building an engine in the 289 to 351-CID size range, although some of these blocks can be over-bored to result in even larger displacement sizes. By referring to the chart on the next page, it becomes evident that beginning with a bare small block, you can build an engine with a displacement of well in excess of 400 cubic inches.

choices when it comes to the powerplant. We also want to discuss some of the different components and building techniques that you will need to be familiar with.

But let's spend a moment exploring what makes a good performance engine in the first place. Performance is a relative thing. The level of desired performance is directly related to the intended use of the engine. Quick response at a moderately low RPM may serve you well, if you want a streetable truck and maybe you're into gymkahna-type events. But if you're planning on running for the world land speed record, or you intend to compete in serious drag

Performance Modifying Ford Trucks

SVO Performance Blocks for Small-Block V8

Part #	Material	Type	Deck Height	Cylinder Design	Overbore Capacity	CID Capacity	Notes
M-6010-A4	Cast Iron	302 SVO	8.206	Non-Siamesed	4.060	355	Wet or dry sump. 4-bolt main bearing caps on number 2, 3, 4.
M-6010-C302	Aluminum	302 SVO	8.206	Ductile Iron Sleeves	4.125	360	4-bolt main bearing caps on all mains. Dry sump only. No passages between cylinders.
M-6010-G351	Cast Iron	351 SVO	9.200	Non-Siamesed	4.030	408	Dry sump. 4-bolt mains on # 2, 3, 4. NASCAR Winston Cup block.
M-6010-H351	Cast Iron	351 SVO	9.500	Non-Siamesed	4.030	434	Dry sump. 4-bolt mains on # 2, 3, 4. NASCAR Winston Cup block. Requries remote oil filter.
M-6010-J351	Aluminum	351 SVO	9.200	Ductile Iron Sleeves	4.125	427	4-bolt main caps on all mains. Dry sump.
M-6010-K351	Aluminum	351 SVO	9.500	Ductile Iron Sleeves	4.125	454	4-bolt main caps on all mains. Dry sump. Smaller 351C mains.
M-6010-M351	Cast Iron	351 SVO	9.200	Non-Siamesed	4.030	408	Wet or dry sump. 4-bolt mains on # 2, 3, 4. Oil pan must be modified.
M-6010-N351	Cast Iron	351 SVO	9.500	Non-Siamesed	4.030	434	Wet or dry sump. 4-bolt mains on # 2, 3, 4. Oil pan must be modified.

SVO Performance Blocks for Big-Block V8

Part #	Material	Type	Deck Height	Cylinder Design	Overbore Capacity	CID Capacity	Notes
M-6010-A460	Cast Iron	460 SVO	10.322	Siamesed	4.625	600+	Accepts production cast iron, SVO wedge or SVO hemi heads.
M-6010-C460	Cast Iron	460 SVO	9.750	Siamesed	4.625	500	351C size main bearing journals to reduce friction.
M-6010-A500	Cast Iron	460 SVO	9.300	Siamesed	4.625	500	351C size main bearing journals. Head bolt locations fit SVO Pro Stock wedge heads.
M-6010-A94	356 T-6 Aluminum	429 SVO	11.700	Ductile Iron Sleeves	4.625	705	351C size main bearing journals. Head bolt locations fit SVO aluminum hemi heads.
M-6010-A600	Cast Iron	460 SVO	10.322	Siamesed	4.625	600	4.600" bore and roller cam bearings.

races, you will want an engine that can continue to produce horsepower well up into the higher RPM range. Not everybody needs or wants one (or more) horsepower per cubic inch, but some folks certainly do. Everything depends upon what kind of driving will be done.

Regardless of performance level, one of the first criteria for an engine is that it hold together well. There's no use having a killer engine if it won't last through the day. The best way to ensure that an engine stays in one piece is to properly select components for the task at hand, and then to balance and blueprint the assembly.

It is best to take a holistic approach to engine building. Rather than just installing a big carburetor or slamming a set of high-compression pistons or a radical cam in the block in search of more horsepower, make sure every component is compatible with every other. Decide in advance just how much performance you need, then choose the parts that will work together to accomplish the task.

Component Selection

Let us draw a line in the sand when it comes to selection of certain components, and that line is defined by intended application. For example, if the engine is never going to run faster than 5000 RPM, you can probably be very secure in using cast pistons. But if the engine will be running more than 5000 RPM, forged pistons are a better choice because they are more durable at high speeds. A similar statement can be made regarding lots of things in an engine.

The point is, don't just go out and buy fancier components to build a more expensive engine because of the mistaken belief that higher cost is always better. Higher cost is sometimes just more expensive, and not necessarily better for your application. When building an engine, use components and techniques that will do the job. But don't fall into the trap of using the stuff that some famous race driver is using, unless you intend to do that kind of driving. Then it might be a good idea to follow the racer's example, if you can actually justify it.

Block

If you are going to rebuild your existing engine, and that engine hasn't suffered some kind of catastrophic event, you probably won't need to go shopping for a block. But, if you have decided to build a totally different engine, block selection is the place to begin.

Not all blocks are created equally. Some were engineered from the beginning to be performance engines, by being made of lightweight aluminum and featuring things like four-bolt main bearing caps for extra strength. That doesn't mean that a two-bolt main cast iron block can't be built to offer more performance than it originally had, but there are limits. If you're looking for a block to build for a street truck that won't be seeing much in the way of serious racing, you can do just fine with a two-bolt main, cast iron block. But, if you're going to build an engine for a true high-performance application, you might want to consider an aluminum four-bolt main block. Again, everything depends on what you intend to do with the engine.

Your first step is going to be settling on exactly which engine you want to build. Some people are tempted to build the biggest engine possible, but remember, bigger isn't always better. You have to decide on the kind of balance you want between horsepower, torque, fuel economy, streetability, and the amount of money you want to invest in the engine. We won't try to make those decisions for you, but we will help you understand how to pick out a good block and how to recognize a bad one as you proceed with your search.

Some people have an aversion to buying used engine components, but buying a used block is not necessarily a bad idea. The word "seasoned" is often used in reference to engine blocks that have been used before, have gone through the change of life, and have settled into their final shape. A new block typically undergoes some dimensional shifting as it is subjected to stress. A seasoned block is stable in its dimensions, so after it has been machined and assembled with all the moving parts, a used block should serve nicely, as long as there are no structural problems.

Checking for structural problems is difficult when the engine is covered with grime. It must be thoroughly cleaned before a complete examination can be made, but there are a few items you can look at even before cleaning. Inspect the cam bore to make sure it is centered in the cam bore boss. Also inspect the lifter bores to see that they are centered in their bosses. If all this checks out, the engine probably didn't suffer much core shift, and the cylinder walls have a better chance of being in good condition. A minor amount of core shift doesn't matter so much for an engine that is built primarily for street use, but for an all-out high-performance engine, you want no core shift at all, if possible.

For more thorough evaluation, it will be necessary to have the block cleaned. Although hot tanking the block does a fair job of cleaning, an even better job is done by a tank with rotating spray jets or a platform that supports the block and rotates to permit the jets to clean the block from all sides.

Once you can see beyond the grease and grime, inspect for cracks, gouges, breaks, scrapes, everything. If the block looks good to the naked eye, have it pressure tested and Magnafluxed to see if there are problems that may have sneaked past your visual inspection.

Regardless of whether you build the engine yourself or you have someone else do the job, once you have settled on the block of your choice, there are a few preliminaries that should be taken care of. First, make certain everything has been removed. All freeze plugs, all accessory brackets, everything. If you're a little nervous about stripping the engine bare for fear you may not remember how to reinstall everything correctly, take some Polaroid photos beforehand to use as a reminder of how things were originally positioned. But get everything off the block so it can be sanitized during and after the machining processes. Organize all the small parts into plastic bags that you label for later identification. This little procedure will help immensely during reassembly.

Next, deburr the entire block. Use a small high-speed grinder and a variety of tips to simply take the cast flashing and sharp edges off of all parts of the block. Stress fractures most frequently occur along sharp edges, so grind them away. Don't go nuts with the deburring process, and be careful to avoid gouging or scarring the block, but gently carve away the sharp edges. During this process, stay out of areas that have been or will be machined. Just work on the exterior.

Now, the block is ready for a visit to the machine shop. And we'll talk about what you want the machine shop to do later in this chapter. But for now, let's take a look at factory available high-performance blocks.

In the V6, small-block and big-block categories, Ford manufactures a selection of blocks that range in design application from street use to full-out professional competition, and everything in between. Following is a rundown of the blocks available through the Ford Motorcraft SVO Performance Equipment catalog.

V6

If you're dead set on using a V6 in your truck, you might as well have one that can really turn the horses loose. Here's the low-down on the high-performance V6 block that is available through the SVO catalog. By the way, engines based on this V6 block are used in NASCAR, Grand National, ASA, All Pro, drag racing and off-road racing trucks. This is no wimp V6!

Part number M-6010-F380 — This is a cast iron 4.5-liter SVO block that can be finish bored and stroked to result in a displacement that ranges from 250 cubic inches to 315 cubic inches.

The block is cast from high-strength gray iron that is alloyed with nickel and chrome. It is stress relieved prior to machining to maintain dimensional stability, and features four-bolt main caps with splayed outer bolts. Main journals measure 2.7468" and deck height is 9.233" nominal. The block comes with semi-finished cylinder bores to 3.900" to permit custom finish boring and the use of standard-bore pistons. It can be bored to a maximum size of 4.060".

Small-Block V8

If your truck is destined to be powered by a high-performance small-block V8, here is the basic information about the SVO offerings in the small-block category.

Part number M-6010-A4 — A cast iron 302 SVO block with a deck height of 8.206" and non-Siamesed cylinder design. Overbore capacity is 4.060" yielding a total displacement capacity of 355 cubic inches. This block features 4-bolt main bearing caps on numbers 2, 3 and 4, and the numbers 1 and 5 main caps are of a new and beefier design. Can be set up to run either wet or dry sump, and will accept stock hydraulic roller lifters. This block has been approved by NHRA as a service replacement for the 302 BOSS block in "Stock" and "Super Stock" classes. Oil pan must be modified to provide clearance for 4-bolt main bearing caps.

Part number M-6010-C302 — This is the aluminum SVO 302 block with a deck height of 8.206" and cylinders that feature ductile iron sleeves. Cylinder configuration is Siamese, with solid metal between cylinders and no cavity for coolant passages. Overbore capacity is 4.125" for a total displacement capacity of 360 cubic inches. The block is set up for 4-bolt main bearing caps on all mains, and is designed for dry sump operation only.

Part number M-6010-G351 — A cast iron 351 SVO block with deck height of 9.200" and overbore capacity of 4.030" to yield a total displacement capacity of 408 cubic inches. This is a NASCAR Winston Cup block with non-Siamese cylinder configuration. The block is designed with 4-bolt main bearing caps at the number 2, 3 and 4 positions, and the main bearing journals are the smaller 351C size (2.749") to reduce friction and heat. Block is intended for dry sump operation, a remote oil filter is required, and the oil pan must be modified to provide clearance for the 4-bolt main bearing caps.

Part number M-6010-H351 — A cast iron 351 SVO block with deck height of 9.500" and overbore capacity of 4.030" to result in a total displacement capacity of 434 cubic inches. This is a NASCAR Winston Cup block with non-Siamese cylinder configuration. The block is designed with 4-bolt main bearing caps at the number 2, 3 and 4 positions, and the main bearing journals are the smaller 351C size (2.749") to reduce friction and heat. Block is intended for dry sump operation, a remote oil filter is required, and the oil pan must be modified to provide clearance for the 4-bolt main bearing caps.

Part number M-6010-J351 — An aluminum 351 SVO block with deck height of 9.200" and overbore capacity of 4.125" to yield a total displacement capacity of 427 cubic inches. The block is designed for dry sump operation and with Siamese cylinder configuration and solid metal between bores for greater strength and rigidity. No cavity for coolant passages exists between cylinders, and ductile iron sleeves line the cylinders. There are 4-bolt main bearing caps on all positions, and the main bearing journals are the smaller 351C size (2.749") to reduce friction and heat.

Part number M-6010-K351 — An aluminum 351 SVO block with deck height of 9.500" and overbore capacity of 4.125" to yield a total displacement capacity of 454 cubic inches. The block is designed for dry sump operation and with Siamese cylinder configuration and solid metal between bores for greater strength and rigidity. No cavity for coolant passages exists between cylinders, and ductile iron sleeves line the cylinders. There are 4-bolt main bearing caps on all positions, and the main bearing journals are the smaller 351C size (2.749") to reduce friction and heat.

Part number M-6010-M351 — A cast iron 351 SVO block with deck height of 9.200" and overbore capacity of 4.030" to yield a total displacement capacity of 408 cubic inches. Non-Siamese cylinder configuration. The block is designed with 4-bolt main bearing caps at the number 2, 3 and 4 positions, and the main bearing journals are the smaller 351C size (2.749") to reduce friction and heat. Block is intended for wet or dry sump operation, and the oil pan must be modified to provide clearance for the 4-bolt main bearing caps.

Part number M-6010-N351 — A cast iron 351 SVO block with deck height of 9.500" and overbore capacity of 4.030" to yield a total displacement capacity of 434 cubic inches. Non-Siamese cylinder configuration. The block is designed with 4-bolt main bearing caps at the number 2, 3 and 4 positions, and the main bearing journals are the smaller 351C size (2.749") to reduce friction and heat. Block is intended for wet or dry sump operation, and the oil pan must be modified to provide clearance for the 4-bolt main bearing caps.

Big-Block V8

If you are on building a high-performance big-block V8 engine, here's what Ford offers in the way of bare blocks through the SVO catalog.

Part number M-6010-A460 — A cast iron 460 SVO block with deck height of 10.322" and overbore capacity of 4.625" to result in a total displacement capacity of 600+ cubic inches. The cylinder configuration is Siamese, with solid metal between bores for added strength and rigidity. No coolant passage cavity exists between the cylinders. Main journal diameter is 3.000". This block accommodates production cast iron, SVO wedge or SVO hemi cylinder heads. Bolt bosses added to accept M-6049-D460 cylinder heads. Approved by NHRA as service replacement for any 429/460 engine block in "Stock" and "Super Stock" drag race classes.

Part number M-6010-C460 — A cast iron 460 SVO block with deck height of 9.750" and overbore capacity of 4.625" to result in a total displacement capacity of 500 cubic inches. The cylinder configuration is Siamese, with solid metal between bores for added strength and rigidity. No coolant passage cavity exists between the cylinders. Main bearing journals are the smaller 351C size (2.749" diameter) to reduce friction and heat when compared with the production 351W or 460 journals (3.000" diameter). Head bolt locations are designed to fit the M-6049-D460 cylinder head.

Part number M-6010-A500 — A cast iron 460 SVO block with deck height of 9.300" and overbore capacity of 4.625" to result in a total displacement capacity of 500 cubic inches. The cylinder configuration is Siamese, with solid metal between bores for added strength and rigidity. No coolant passage cavity exists between the cylinders. Main bearing journals are the smaller 351C size (2.749" diameter) to reduce friction and heat when compared with the production 351W or 460 journals (3.000" diameter). Head bolt locations are designed to fit M-6049-E460, which is the SVO Pro Stock canted valve wedge cylinder head.

Part number M-6010-A94 — Made of 356 T-6 aluminum this 429 SVO engine block features a deck height of 11.700" and overbore capacity of 4.625" to deliver a total displacement of 705 cubic inches. The cylinder configuration is Siamese, with solid metal between bores for added strength and rigidity. No coolant passage cavity exists between the cylinders. Ductile steel sleeves line the cylinders. Head bolt locations are designed to accommodate SVO aluminum hemi heads and M-6049-C460 cylinder heads.

Part number M-6010-A600 — A cast iron 460 SVO block with deck height of 10.322" and overbore capacity of 4.625" to result in a total displacement capacity of 600 cubic inches. Cylinder configuration is Siamese, with solid metal between bores for added strength and rigidity. No coolant passage cavity exists between cylinders. Finished bore measures 4.600" and the block is designed for roller cam bearings.

Crankshaft

Again, the choice must be made between performance building your existing engine, or starting from scratch with all new components. If you're building an existing engine, you'll need to have the crankshaft inspected and measured to see if it's usable for your intended performance application. Otherwise, start looking for a new crank. This is where it is important for you to find an engine builder or a crankshaft grinder you can trust. If there is a local engine shop that builds for local racers, that's probably a good place to start.

Crankshafts are either cast iron or they are forged steel. Forged cranks are preferred for racing applications, but cast iron crankshafts are plenty strong enough for most non-race applications. Before buying a used crank, have it thoroughly cleaned so you can inspect for cracks or other flaws. Use a micrometer to check each journal to determine exact size and condition. Don't necessarily discard a crank just because it will need to be ground to an undersize. Final machining to an undersize, and installing appropriately sized bearings, is fine for street and mild performance applications. Examine for visible cracks along the radiused junction of each journal and throw, because this is the most common location for cracks to develop. After a visual inspection, have the crank Magnafluxed to reveal any possible problems that could not be detected with the naked eye. For street applications, minor flaws may be able to be worked out during grinding, but for pure performance applications, search until you find a flawless crank.

Final preparation should include pressure washing all the oil passages, then using small wire brushes to clean the bores. Deburr the counterweights carefully, just enough to eliminate sharp edges. Chamfer the oil holes slightly — not enough to reduce the load-bearing surface of the journal, but just enough to make it easier for the oil to flow from the holes onto the bearings.

Ford offers factory new crankshafts for all truck applications, both street and performance. Here is a brief description of each of them.

V6

For those who are building a 4.5-liter V6 engine, there are two SVO crankshafts to choose from.

Part number M-6002-A380 — Odd-fire crankshaft made from an AMS 6415 steel forging. This crankshaft is semi-finished and has no oil holes, so some finish work will need to be performed by a reputable machine shop. Minimum rod journal diameter is 2.100" and minimum rod journal width is 1.900" in measurement. Maximum stroke capability is 3.79".

Part number M-6303-E380 — Even-fire crankshaft made from billet steel. Minimum rod journal diameter is 2.100" and minimum rod journal width is 1.900" in measurement. Maximum stroke capability is 3.54".

Small-Block V8

If you want to buy a new small-block crank from Ford SVO, the company offers no less than six finished crankshafts for performance engine building, and one raw forging that can be custom finished to suit the engine builder's specifications. All of the

SVO Crankshafts

Performance Modifying Ford Trucks

Part Number	Application	Material	Notes	Minimum Rod Journal Dia.	Minimum Rod Journal Width	Max. Stroke Capability
M-6301-B351	351 SVO	AMS 6415 steel forging	Raw forging	—	—	4.25"
M6303-A302	302/302 SVO	AMS 6415 steel forging	Finished (stock stroke)	2.123"	1.690"	3.00"
M6303-A340	302/302 SVO	AMS 6415 steel forging	Finished (stroker)	2.123"	1.690"	3.40"
M-6303-A410	351 SVO	AMS 6415 steel forging	Finished (stroker)	2.100"	1.900"	3.90"
M-6303-B351	351 SVO	AMS 6415 steel forging	Finished	2.099"	1.900"	3.50"
M-6303-C351	351 SVO	AMS 6415 steel forging	Finished	2.099"	1.900"	3.45"
M-6303-A454	351 SVO	AMS 6415 steel forging	Finished (stroker)	2.0991"	1.900"	4.25"
M6301-B460	429/460	AMS 6415 steel forging	Raw forging	—	1.900"	4.50"
M6303-B600	429/460	AMS 6415 steel forging	Finished (stroker)	2.200"	2.000"	4.50"

SVO offers this "stroker" crankshaft, part number M-6303-A454 for use in building a high-performance 351 SVO engine. This is an AMS 6415 steel forging with a finished rod journal diameter of 2.0991" and a minimum rod journal width of 1.900". Maximum stroke capability is 4.25". This is a monster crank, that results in a 454-cubic-inch small-block, when used in conjunction with block # M-6010-K351.

small-block SVO finished crankshafts listed below feature high-speed oiling systems, precision ground rod and main journals, and large fillet radii. The 351 cranks have knife-edged counterweights and pin-lightening holes. The journals are polished and nitride hardened. 351 crank rod journals are finished to accept 0.940" wide steel connecting rods. Before installation, all crankshafts should be balanced for piston and rod combinations.

Part number M-6301-B351 — This is the raw forging, made of AMS 6415 steel for 351 SVO application. As an unfinished forging, this crank has no minimum rod journal diameter or width, but the maximum stroke capability is listed as 4.25".

Part number M-6303-A302 — Made from an AMS 6415 steel forging, this finished 302/302 SVO crankshaft features a stock stroke, with maximum stroke capability of 3.00" and minimum of 2.123" rod journal diameter. Minimum rod journal width is 1.690".

Part number M-6303-A340 — Very much like the unit mentioned immediately above, this finished 302/302 SVO crankshaft is made from an AMS 6415 steel forging. Unlike the unit above, it is a stroker crank, with maximum stroke capability of 3.40". Minimum rod journal diameter is 2.123" and the minimum rod journal width is 1.690".

Part number M-6303-B351 — For the 351 SVO engine, this finished crank is made from an AMS 6415 steel forging. It features a minimum rod journal diameter of 2.099" and a minimum rod journal width of 1.900". Maximum stroke capability of this crankshaft is 3.50".

Part number M-6303-C351 — For the 351 SVO engine, this finished crank is made from an AMS 6415 steel forging. It features a minimum rod journal diameter of 2.099" and a minimum rod journal width of 1.900". Maximum stroke capability of this crankshaft is 3.45".

Part number M-6303-A410 — This is the finished mild stroker crank for the 351 SVO engine, with a maximum stroke capability of 3.90". Minimum rod journal diameter is 2.100" and minimum rod journal width is 1.900".

Part number M-6303-A454 — This is the wild finished stroker crank for the 351 SVO engine. Known as the "Monster Crank" when this unit is installed in the M-6010-K351 SVO engine block with a bore measuring 4.125" it will produce a 454 cubic-inch small-block engine! Maximum stroke capability is 4.25" and minimum rod journal diameter is 2.0991". Minimum rod journal width is 1.900".

Big-Block V8

Big-block factory crankshafts from Ford carry the following part numbers and basic descriptions:

Part number M-6301-B460 — This is the raw forging for the 429/460 SVO engines, made of AMS 6415 steel. As an unfinished forging, this crank will require the attention of a qualified machinist. It has no minimum rod journal diameter or width, but the maximum stroke capability is listed as 4.50".

Part number M-6303-B600 — This is the finished stroker crank for the 429/460 SVO engine, with a maximum stroke capability of 4.50". Minimum rod journal diameter is 2.200" and minimum rod journal width is 2.000".

Pistons and Rings

The Ford Motorsports SVO Performance Equipment catalog doesn't list high-performance replacement pistons for the types of applications we are discussing in this book. But the aftermarket is loaded with all different types of pistons to choose from. Deciding in advance what type of driving will be done is very important when choosing pistons. Like many other components, pistons are available for applications ranging from street performance to all-out racing, and prices vary according to the type of piston you choose.

Pistons come in cast aluminum, Hypereutectic (high silicone alloy), and forged aluminum versions. Cast pistons are adequate for most applications, especially for street and non-race off-road use. Cast pistons offer the advantage of good dimensional stability, which prevents skirt expansion during normal operation. This permits a relatively tight tolerance fit, which diminishes cold start engine noise, oil consumption and ring wear. In addition to that, cast pistons are designed to use press-fit wrist pins, eliminating potential problems associated with pin retainer failure. While it is generally agreed that factory stock cast pistons will perform well when the engine speed is kept below 6000

RPM, higher engine speeds cause excessive heat, which can contribute to seizing of the pistons in the cylinders. So, when using cast pistons, care must be taken to prevent high engine speed, high temperature operation, and detonation. These conditions will damage cast aluminum pistons.

One of the new buzz words in the world of engine building is "hypereutectic." As silicone is added to an aluminum alloy, it reaches a point of saturation when all of the silicone is dissolved into the aluminum and none precipitates out. This point of optimum saturation is known as the "eutectic," and occurs when there is a silicone level of 11% to 12%. If the level of silicone in the aluminum is less than 12%, it is known as hypoeutectic (pistons in this category normally have about 9% silicone). Aluminum with a silicone level above 12% is called hypereutectic. As an example, Silv-O-Lite KB Signature Series pistons contain a silicone level of about 16% to 18% so a certain amount of the silicone precipitates out into hard primary silicon particles that act as tiny insulators to keep the heat in the combustion chamber and prevent heat transfer. This allows the piston to run cooler. These pistons also have 15% less thermal expansion than conventional cast aluminum pistons. While they are more expensive than cast pistons, hypereutectic pistons cost less than stepping all the way up to forged. Hypereutectic pistons were developed to withstand the higher levels of stress that are common in high-performance street and some race applications, but they do not claim to be as strong and durable as forged pistons.

If all-out racing is in your truck's future, you may want to consider forged pistons. Due to their inherent strength and durability at high engine speed and when temperatures are hotter than normal, forged pistons are generally chosen for serious racing applications or for other types of competition where the engine will be placed under abnormal levels of stress. But even though forged pistons are tougher than their cast cousins, they can still be subject to problems. In fact, because of the greater density of the forged alloy, dimensional changes caused by heat expansion requires that forged pistons have a greater clearance between the skirt and cylinder wall than would be required of a cast piston.

Piston rings work hard and are subjected to a lot of stress, as they try to do their job of sealing the cylinder to prevent oil from contaminating the combustion chamber, preventing blow-by, and surviving the rigors of combustion heat and friction, and an all around difficult lifestyle.

For low-speed (below 5500 RPM) operation, single moly rings of factory specifications are an excellent choice. Wide factory rings seal the cylinder better than anything else at these speeds. They break in well, seat quickly, and endure non-race conditions in excellent fashion. For off-road racing applications, where grit and grime are likely to get into the engine, chrome rings will deliver more reliable service.

Turbocharged or supercharged engines may benefit from the use of plasma-spray moly rings, because they are more resistant to damage that can be caused by detonation. Detonation being one of the prime concerns with blown engines, these rings should be considered if you are planning on adding a turbocharger or supercharger. Plasma moly rings are made of high-strength ductile iron with a plasma moly facing.

When building an engine, one of the vital considerations is ring gap. The gap must be kept small enough to seal the cylinder well, yet large enough to prevent the ends of the ring from butting and causing internal damage as the engine heats up and components expand. Ring gap must be adjusted for different applications. For moderate performance, the top ring should have a gap of .004" per inch of bore diameter, while the second ring should have a gap measuring .003" per inch of bore diameter. Drag racing and using nitrous oxide will require larger gaps, with the top ring needing .008" per inch of bore diameter and the second ring needing .0065" per inch of bore diameter. Supercharged engines generally get

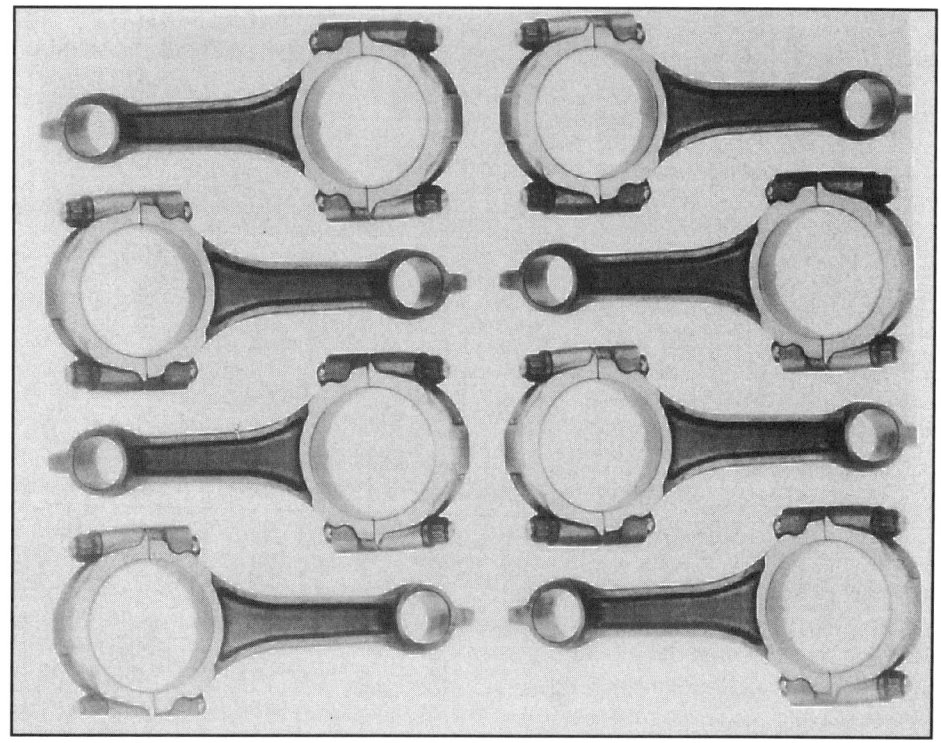

Sold in complete engine sets, Ford SVO connecting rods for 5.0-liter engines are machined to fit journal diameters of 2.1232" and are made of forged SAE 4340 steeling. Center-to-center length is 5.090" and feature 3/8" diameter ARP Wave Loc rod bolts.

along well with .006" per inch of bore diameter for the top ring and .005" per inch for the second ring. To discover the actual feeler gauge measurement of the gap, multiply these figures times the bore diameter. For example, if you are building a moderate-performance engine with a 4.00" bore, the top ring gap should run between .016" and .18" while the second ring gap is .012" to .014".

Connecting Rods and Bearings

Making sure the piston and crankshaft remain in touch with each other is the job of the connecting rod. Factory rods can do the job for most high-performance engine build-ups that would be used in truck applications. There are numerous aftermarket companies that manufacture high-performance rods, and in fact they are too numerous to mention, so we will restrict our coverage in this volume to the factory units. The Ford Motorsports SVO Performance Equipment catalog lists only three special sets of forged connecting rods, and they are for the 302 CID engine with 2.1232" journal diameter.

Small-Block V8

Part number M-6200-A50 — Heavy-duty forged SAE 4340 steel connecting rod with stock center-to-center length of 5.090" for use with SVO crankshaft number M-6303-A302 or with stock crankshaft and piston. Rod and cap feature beefy construction in high-stress areas, and use heavier 3/8" diameter ARP Wave Lock rod bolts. This rod uses a press-fit piston pin.

Part number M-6200-B50 — Heavy-duty forged SAE 4340 steel connecting rod with stock center-to-center length of 5.090" for use with SVO crankshaft number M-6303-A302 or with stock crankshaft and piston. Rod and cap feature beefy construction in high-stress areas, and use heavier 3/8" diameter ARP Wave Lock rod bolts. This rod is bushed for 0.912" diameter full floating piston pin.

Part number M-6200-C50 — The "stroker" rod. It measure 5.315" long and is bushed for 0.912" diameter piston pins. This rod can be used in conjunction with the M-6303-A340 stroker crankshaft to build a 355 cubic inch 5.0-liter engine.

Heads

An engine is really nothing more than a big air pump, taking air in through the intake system, processing it in the middle, then expelling it through the exhaust system. Central to this whole process are the heads. They play a major role in controlling intake air/fuel mixture flow to the combustion chambers, and they control exhaust flow. The way the heads are designed, manufactured and machined is vitally important to performance, because it is the configuration of the heads, in conjunction with camshaft and valvetrain, that permits the intake and exhaust systems to function properly, delivering the air/fuel mixture to the combustion chamber, and then removing exhaust gasses when the combustion process is completed.

Keep in mind that if you are building an existing engine, you may be able to have a cylinder head shop tune up your heads to deliver the kind of performance improvement you are looking for. On the other hand, if you are building from scratch, or you want to swap your heads for something a bit more exotic, the Ford Motorsports SVO Performance Equipment catalog will be a good place to start your search for the ideal cylinder heads. Ford offers several cylinder head options, both aluminum and cast iron, so you can probably find exactly what you need right from the factory. Following are factory offerings.

Small-Block V8

Part number M-6049-L302 — This is the GT-40 "High Flow" cast iron bare cylinder head for all 302 and 351 street and strip applications. Street legal per EO# D-308. The GT-40 heads are designed as direct bolt-on replacements for late-model 5.0-liter cylinder heads, and accept bolt-on rocker arms. Machined for 1.84" intake and 1.54" exhaust valves. Fitted with exhaust valve seat inserts to prevent recession. Also fits all other Windsor type blocks. Piston to valve clearance should be checked when using this head with flat topped pistons without valve relief or when using non-production camshafts. Use Motorcraft head bolt kit M-6065-B289

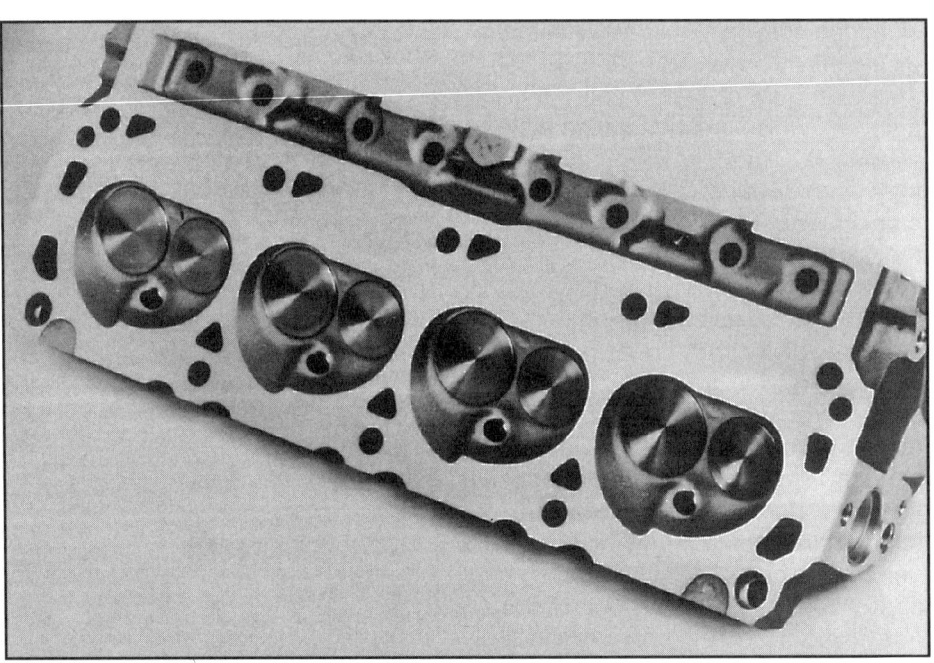

Here is the SVO GT-40 "Turbo Swirl" aluminum complete cylinder head assembly for 289/302/351 Windsor style engines. Claimed to be a simple bolt-on 40-horsepower improvement over stock heads.

SVO Performance Heads for Small-Block V8

Part Number	Description	Material	Combustion Chamber Vol. (cc)	Valve Diameter	Notes
M-6049-C3	NASCAR heads by Robert Yates Racing	Aluminum	40	I: 2.10 E: 1.60	Designed for Winston Cup and other maximum competition applications.
M-6049-C3L	NASCAR heads by Robert Yates Racing	Aluminum	67	I: 2.10 E: 1.60	Designed for Winston Cup and other maximum competition applications.
M-6049-C33	NASCAR heads by Robert Yates Racing	Aluminum	48	I: 2.10 E: 1.60	Designed for Winston Cup and other maximum competition applications.
M-6049-C34	NASCAR heads by Robert Yates Racing	Aluminum	48	I: 2.10 E: 1.60	Designed for Winston Cup and other maximum competition applications.
M-6049-N351	Bare head. Fits 351W engines	Cast Iron	64	I: 2.02 E: 1.60	State of the art cylinder heads for Sportsman Racing applications.
M-6049-R351	Complete assembly, fits 351W engines	Cast Iron	64	I: 2.02 E: 1.60	State of the art cylinder heads for Sportsman Racing applications.
M-6049-L302	GT-40 High Flow bare head, fits 289/302/351W	Cast Iron	65.5	I: 1.84 E: 1.54	Street legal, great choice for street/strip performance. Pistons must be notched.
M-6049-L303	GT-40 High Flow complete assembly, fits 289/302/351W	Cast Iron	65.5	I: 1.84 E: 1.54	Street legal, great choice for street/strip performance. Pistons must be notched.
M-6049-Y302	GT-40 Turbo Swirl bare head, fits 289/302/351W	Aluminum	64	I: 1.95 E: 1.54	40 HP over stock 5.0-liter heads. 25-lb. lighter than cast iron production heads.
M-6049-Y303	GT-40 Turbo Swirl complete assembly, fits 289/302/351W	Aluminum	64	I: 1.95 E: 1.54	40 HP over stock 5.0-liter heads. 25-lb. lighter than cast iron production heads.

when installing heads on blocks with 7/16" diameter threads.

Part number M-6049-L303 — This is the GT-40 "High Flow" cast iron complete cylinder head assembly for all 302 and 351 street and strip applications. Street legal per EO# D-308. The GT-40 heads are designed as direct bolt-on replacements for late-model 5.0-liter cylinder heads, and includes M-6090-L302 valvetrain kit. Machined for 1.84" intake and 1.54" exhaust valves. Fitted with exhaust valve seat inserts to prevent recession. Also fits all other Windsor type blocks. Piston to valve clearance should be checked when using this head with flat topped pistons without valve relief or when using non-production camshafts. Use Motorcraft head bolt kit M-6065-B289 when installing heads on blocks with 7/16" diameter threads.

Part number M-6049-Y302 — GT-40 "Turbo Swirl" aluminum bare cylinder head for 289/302/351 Windsor style engines. Claimed to be a simple bolt-on 40-horsepower improvement over stock heads. "Turbo Swirl" combustion chamber provides increased efficiency and power. Combustion chamber volume is 64cc. Machined for 1.94" diameter intake valves and 1.54" exhaust valves. Each head weighs 25 pounds less than cast iron GT-40 heads.

Part number M-6049-Y303 — GT-40 "Turbo Swirl" aluminum complete cylinder head assembly for 289/302/351 Windsor style engines. Includes M-6090-X302 valvetrain kit, featuring stainless steel valves. Claimed to be a simple bolt-on 40-horsepower improvement over stock heads. "Turbo Swirl" combustion chamber provides increased efficiency and power. Combustion chamber volume is 64cc. Machined for 1.94" diameter intake valves and 1.54" exhaust valves. Each head weighs 25 pounds less than cast iron GT-40 heads.

Part number M-6049-C3 — SVO "High Port" aluminum cylinder head for small-block applications. This is a NASCAR Robert Yates Racing head with high compression and 40 cc

SVO Performance Heads for Big-Block V8

Part Number	Description	Material	Combustion Chamber Vol. (cc)	Valve Diameter	Notes
M-6049-C460	Standard Bolt Pattern	Aluminum	65	I: 2.450 E: 1.900	Designed for serious competition applications.
M-6049-D460	18-Bolt Pattern	Aluminum	65	I: 2.450 E: 1.900	Designed for serious competition applications.
M-6049-E460	18-Bolt Pattern	Aluminum	n/a	I: 2.450 E: 1.880	Pro Stock head, wedge style combustion chamber, canted valves.
M-6049-A429	Standard Bolt Pattern	Aluminum	72	I: 2.250 E: 1.750	Replacement for production CJ and SCJ cast iron heads.
M-6049-B429	Standard Bolt Pattern	Aluminum	72	I: 2.250 E: 1.750	Replacement for production CJ and SCJ cast iron heads.

chamber volume. Machined for 2.100" intake valve diameter and 1.600" exhaust valve diameter. All ports are fully machined, and no hand finishing is required. Intake port volume is 210 cc, and exhaust port volume is 119 cc. Premium valve seat inserts are compatible with titanium valves. Water passages between combustion chambers. These heads are designed for Winston Cup and other maximum competition applications.

Part number M-6049-C3L — SVO "High Port" aluminum cylinder head for small-block applications. This is a NASCAR Robert Yates Racing head with low compression and 67 cc chamber volume. Machined for 2.100" intake valve diameter and 1.600" exhaust valve diameter. All ports are fully machined, and no hand finishing is required. Intake port volume is 210 cc, and exhaust port volume is 119 cc. Premium valve seat inserts are compatible with titanium valves. Water passages between combustion chambers. These heads are designed for Winston Cup and other maximum competition applications.

Part number M-6049-C33 — SVO "High Port" aluminum cylinder head for small-block applications. This is a NASCAR Robert Yates Racing head with low compression and 48 cc chamber volume. Machined for 2.100" intake valve diameter and 1.600" exhaust valve diameter. All ports are fully machined, and no hand finishing is required.

Intake port volume is 228 cc, and exhaust port volume is 131 cc. Premium valve seat inserts are compatible with titanium valves. Water passages between combustion chambers. These heads are designed for Winston Cup and other maximum competition applications.

This photo shows the GT-40 "High Flow" cast iron bare cylinder head for all 302 and 351 street and strip applications. Street legal, the GT-40 heads are designed as direct bolt-on replacements for late-model 5.0-liter cylinder heads, and accept bolt-on rocker arms. Machined for 1.84" intake and 1.54" exhaust valves. Fitted with exhaust valve seat inserts to prevent recession. Also fits all other Windsor type blocks.

Part number M-6049-C34 — SVO "High Port" aluminum cylinder head for small-block applications. This is a NASCAR Robert Yates Racing head with low compression and 48 cc chamber volume. Machined for 2.100" intake valve diameter and 1.600" exhaust valve diameter. All ports are fully machined, and no hand finishing is required. Intake port volume is 221 cc, and exhaust port volume is 131 cc. Premium valve seat inserts are compatible with titanium valves. Water passages between combustion chambers. These heads are designed for Winston Cup and other maximum competition applications.

Part number M6049-N351 — This is the bare version of the "Sportsman" cast iron racing head, recommended for all 351W short track engines. Features large intake ports with volume of 195 cc, and exhaust valve port volume of 67 cc. Combustion chamber volume is 64 cc. Machined for intake valve diameter of 2.02" and 1.60" diameter exhaust valves. Uses stud mount rocker arms, and is compatible with stock and aftermarket 302/351W intake manifolds. Must use head bolt kit M-6065-B289 to install on 302 block.

Part number M6049-R351 — This is the complete head assembly version of the "Sportsman" cast iron racing head, and it is identical to the bare cylinder head version mentioned immediately above, except for the fact that it comes equipped with all of the required valvetrain components.

Big-Block V8

Part number M-6049-C460 — If your game is drag racing, this is the Ford 460 Pro Stock Wedge-style aluminum cylinder head designed for professional and serious sportsman competition. This particular head is the bare version, and it features raised intake and exhaust ports as well as a 67 cc wedge style combustion chamber. Includes bronze valve guides and premium valve seat inserts that are compatible with titanium valves. Recommended bore size is 4.600" and recommended valve sizes are 2.450" on the intake side and 1.900" on the exhaust side. Standard head bolt pattern requires 10 bolts.

Part number M-6049-D460 — If your game is drag racing, this is the Ford 460 Pro Stock Wedge-style aluminum cylinder head designed for professional and serious sportsman competition. This is the complete cylinder head assembly version, and it features raised intake and exhaust ports as well as a 67 cc wedge style combustion chamber. Includes bronze valve guides and premium valve seat inserts that are compatible with titanium valves. Recommended bore size is 4.600" and recommended valve sizes are 2.450" on the intake side and 1.900" on the exhaust side. Requires 18 bolts, for usage on block M-6010-C460.

Part number M-6049-E460 — This is the SVO Pro Stock cylinder head that features wedge style combustion chamber, canted valves and high-flow ports. Machined for 2.450" diameter intake and 1.880" diameter exhaust valves. Employs an 18-bolt head bolt pattern and bolts directly on block M6010-A500. Other blocks will require some modification to accept this head. Requires rocker shaft system.

Part number M-6049-A429 — For "Cobra Jet" enthusiasts, this is the aluminum bare cylinder head that is claimed by Ford to increase horsepower by 100 HP when used in conjunction with intake manifold M-9424-G429 and SVO camshaft M-6250-A443. This is the lightweight aluminum replacement for production CJ and SCJ cast iron heads, and it bolts on production blocks. Accepts production-type valves, springs, retainers and other valvetrain components, as well as production-type intake and exhaust manifolds. Combustion chamber volume is 72 cc.

Part number M-6049-B429 — For "Cobra Jet" enthusiasts, this is the aluminum complete cylinder head assembly that comes equipped with all the necessary valvetrain components already installed. Claimed by Ford to increase horsepower by 100 HP when used in conjunction with intake manifold M-9424-G429 and SVO camshaft M-6250-A443. This is the lightweight aluminum replacement for production CJ and SCJ cast iron heads, and it bolts on production blocks. Accepts production-type intake and exhaust manifolds. Combustion chamber volume is 72 cubic centimeters.

Camshaft and Lifters

The job of the camshaft is to open and close valves a specified amount for a precise duration at

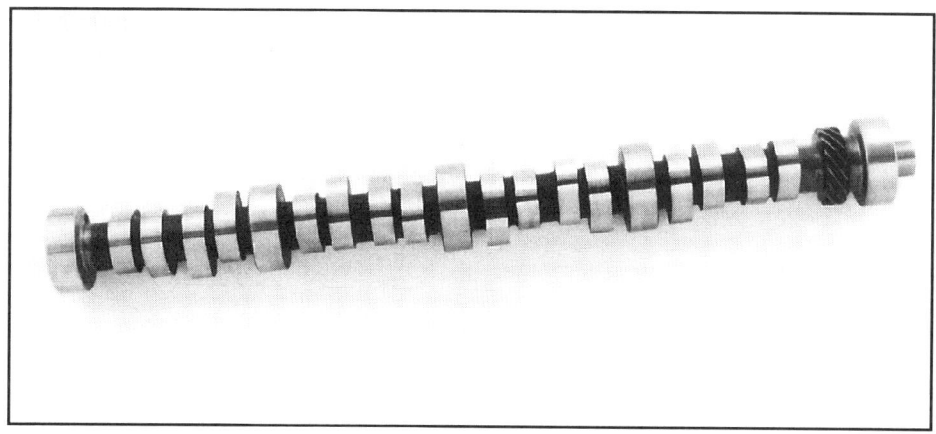

The Ford Motorsports SVO Performance Equipment catalog lists many camshafts for both small-block and big-block performance applications. Pictured above is part number M-6250-B303 which is designed for use in 1985 to '96 5-liter engines with roller tappets. This particular camshaft delivers good performance at the low end and great performance at higher engine speed levels above 4000 RPM.

SVO Performance Camshafts for Small-Block V8

Part Number	Engine	Description	Peak RPM	Duration	Valve Lift	Notes
M-6250-E303	1985-'96 302 w/roller cam	Hydraulic roller tappet	Torque: 2500 BHP: 5500	I: 282 E: 282	I: 0.498 E: 0.498	Excellent low and mid range power. Great with supercharger.
M-6250-F303	1985-'96 302 w/roller cam	Hydraulic roller tappet	Torque: 2800 BHP: 6000	I: 288 E: 288	I: 0.512 E: 0512	More mid range and top-end power. Great for supercharger.
M-6250-B303	1985-'96 302 w/roller cam	Hydraulic roller tappet	Torque: 3300 BHP: 5100	I: 284 E: 284	I: 0.480 E: 0.480	Good low-end, great top-end power above 4000 RPM.
M-6250-X303	1985-'96 302 w/roller cam	Hydraulic roller tappet	Torque: 3500 BHP: 6000	I: 286 E: 286	I: 0.542 E: 0.542	Ultra high-perf cam. Makes big torque and HP up to 6500 RPM.
M-6250-A	1985-'96 302 w/roller cam	Hydraulic roller tappet	Torque: N/A BHP: N/A	I: N/A E: N/A	I: N/A E: N/A	Cam core for those who want to grind their own profiles.
M-6250-A311	289/302	Hydraulic flat tappet	Torque: 3500 BHP: 4750	I: 280 E: 290	I: 0.448 E: 0.472	High torque below 4000 RPM. Good for towing and street.
M-6250-A312	289/302	Hydraulic flat tappet	Torque: 3500 BHP: 5000	I: 290 E: 300	I: 0.472 E: 0.496	Good all around performance cam.
M-6250-A313	289/302	Mechanical flat tappet	Torque: 3500 BHP: 5000	I: 282 E: 292	I: 0.512 E: 0.536	Requires enlarged valve clearance notches in piston.
M-6250-A314	289/302	Hydraulic flat tappet	Torque: 3500 BHP: 5250	I: 290 E: 300	I: 0.496 E: 0.520	Great HP increase. Requires piston valve clearance notches.
M-6250-A315	289/302	Hydraulic flat tappet	Torque: 4000 BHP: 6250	I: 292 E: 292	I: 0.534 E: 0.534	Substantial HP increase at high RPM. Requires piston valve clearance notches.
M-6250-D	302/351W/351SVO	Mechanical flat tappet	Torque: N/A BHP: N/A	I: N/A E: N/A	I: N/A E: N/A	Cam core for those who want to grind their own profiles.
M-6250-E	302/351W/351SVO	Mechanical flat tappet	Torque: N/A BHP: N/A	I: N/A E: N/A	I: N/A E: N/A	Cam core for those who want to grind their own profiles.
M-6250-A331	351W	Hydraulic flat tappet	Torque: 3000 BHP: 4000	I: 280 E: 290	I: 0.448 E: 0.472	High torque below 4000 RPM. Good for towing and street.
M-6250-A332	351W	Hydraulic flat tappet	Torque: 3000 BHP: 4500	I: 290 E: 300	I: 0.472 E: 0.496	Increased torque and HP at all RPM. Good all around cam.
M-6250-A333	351W	Mechanical flat tappet	Torque: 3500 BHP: 5000	I: 282 E: 292	I: 0.512 E: 0.536	Great HP increase. Requires piston valve clearance notches.
M-6250-A334	351W	Hydraulic flat tappet	Torque: 3500 BHP: 4750	I: 300 E: 310	I: 0.520 E: 0.544	Substantial HP increase at high RPM. Requires piston valve clearance notches.
M-6250-A335	351W	Hydraulic flat tappet	Torque: 3500 BHP: 5250	I: 290 E: 300	I: 0.491 E: 0.509	Increased torque and HP at all RPM. Good all around cam.
M-6250-A351	351W	Hydraulic flat tappet	Torque: 4500 BHP: 5750	I: 296 E: 306	I: 0.520 E: 0.538	May require piston modification for adequate clearance.
M-6250-B351	351W	Hydraulic flat tappet	Torque: N/A BHP: N/A	I: 268 E: 276	I: 0.448 E: 0.464	Recommended for EFI engines.
M-6250-A341	351C/351M/400	Hydraulic flat tappet	Torque: N/A BHP: N/A	I: 282 E: 292	I: 0.510 E: 0.536	Good all around performer.
M-6250-A342	351C/351M/400	Mechanical flat tappet	Torque: N/A BHP: N/A	I: 282 E: 292	I: 0.580 E: 0.606	Requires mechanical tappets & adjustable valve train.

SVO Performance Camshafts for Big-Block V8

Part Number	Engine	Description	Peak RPM	Duration	Valve Lift	Notes
M-6250-A411	390/427/428	Hydraulic flat tappet	Torque: N/A BHP: N/A	I: 282 E: 292	I: 0.493 E: 0.519	Good all around performance cam.
M-6250-A442	429/460 Wedge	Hydraulic flat tappet	Torque: 3000 BHP: 4500	I: 280 E: 290	I: 0.510 E: 0536	HP/torque increase throughout RPM range. Some head work required.
M-6250-A443	429/460 Wedge	Hydraulic flat tappet	Torque: 3000 BHP: 5000	I: 300 E: 310	I: 0.562 E: 0.588	Substantial HP increase at high RPM. Some machine work required on heads.
M-6250-A460	429/460 Wedge	Hydraulic flat tappet	Torque: 3250 BHP: 4750	I: 288 E: 292	I: 0.493 E: 0.502	Good all around performance cam, increased HP/torque.
M-6250-C460	429/460 Wedge	Hydraulic flat tappet	Torque: 4750 BHP: 6000	I: 310 E: 320	I: 0.588 E: 0.614	Excellent cam for improved torque and horsepower.

exactly the right time, to allow the passage of intake and exhaust gasses into and out of the combustion chamber. Each lobe of the camshaft lifts one valve, either on the intake or the exhaust side of the combustion chamber. Depending upon performance requirements, camshafts are designed with a variety of lift and duration characteristics. We have the same situation with camshafts as we faced with connecting rods, and in fact many other Ford engine components, in that the aftermarket is so active in this field that we cannot even begin to cover all that is available. For that reason, we will restrict our specific coverage to pieces available through the Ford Motorsports SVO Performance Equipment catalog. But be aware that there is a whole world of high-performance camshafts and associated hardware out there.

There are so many part numbers in this component category that it is best to refer you to the accompanying charts, which list all of the pertinent data relating to both small-block and big-block camshafts.

Valve Springs

At low-speed operation, stock valve springs may be fine. But if the engine is going to be pressed into high-speed service, heavy-duty valve springs will be necessary to help prevent valve float. However, for street use, heavy-duty valve springs may be overkill. Unless you are running the engine in an RPM range that requires the heavier springs, standard-duty

The GT-40 valve train kits, available through the Ford Motorsports SVO Performance Equipment catalog, include stainless steel valves, springs, retainers, valve keepers and a valve seal kit. Here, under one part number (M-6090-L302), are all the pieces necessary to assemble a pair of GT-40 cast iron cylinder heads. A separate part number (M-6090-X302) contains the same parts except for different diameter intake valves, for application in aluminum GT-40 cylinder heads.

Performance Engines **25**

SVO Valve Springs for Big-Block Cylinder Heads

Cylinder Head	Camshaft	Recommended Valve Spring	Installed Height
GT-40 Type M-6049-L302/L303	M-6250-B303, -E303, -F303, -X303	M-6513-A50	1.820"
429-460 Production Type and M-6049-A429 "CJ"	M-6250-A441	Production	1.810-1.820"
	M-6250-A460	Production	1.810-1.820"
	M-6250-A442	M-6513-A351	1.850"
	M-6250-A443	M-6513-D221	1.900"

springs are the way to go, because heavy springs may cause accelerated valve seat wear.

Again, we would like to refer you to the accompanying charts, which list all of the pertinent data relating to both small-block and big-block valve springs that are available through the Ford Motorsports SVO Performance Equipment catalog.

Complete Engine Assemblies

Rather than building an engine from scratch, you may want to consider ordering a high-performance engine assembly from SVO. You can choose from short-blocks, long-blocks and complete engine assemblies from the Ford Motorsports SVO Performance Equipment catalog. Taking this approach, you can shortcut the work necessary to get your truck up and running, and these engines are assembled using all the best new components at either the Ford Windsor or Cleveland engine plants.

Part number M-6007-C460 — The Cobra Jet SVO big-block complete engine assembly. Just add carburetor, headers, wiring and accessory drives and this engine is race ready. Rated at 560 horsepower at 6000 RPM, and 535 lb. ft. of torque at 4750 RPM. Forged aluminum pistons with a compression ratio of 11.0:1. Cobra Jet aluminum cylinder heads, Victor Jr. intake manifold, SVO valve

SVO Performance Valve Springs for Small-Block Cylinder Heads

Part Number	Application	Type	I.D.	O.D.	Minimum Loads – New Springs	
					Closed	Open
M-6513-A50	289/302/351W with GT40 heads	Single	1.006"	1.500"	110 lbs. @ 1.820"	240 lbs. @ 1.400"
M-6513-B221	289/302/351W	Single	0.981"	1.465"	85 lbs. @ 1.690"	260 lbs. @ 1.090"
M-6513-D221	351C/351M/400	Dual	0.735"	1.545"	130 lbs. @ 1.900"	450 lbs. @ 1.200"
M-6513-C302	289/302/351W	Single	1.040"	1.440"	95 lbs. @ 1.703"	260 lbs. @ 1.200"
M-6513-A341	302BOSS and 351C/351M/400	Single	1.065"	1.501"	90 lbs. @ 1.820"	255 lbs. @ 1.320"
M-6513-A351	289/302/351W SVO 351 H.O.	Dual	0.800"	1.460"	135 lbs. @ 1.850"	394 lbs. @ 1.175"

train, SVO valve covers, SVO crankshaft damper, Ford Duraspark distributor, oil pump and water pump all included.

Part number M-6007-A351 — The 351 CID H.O. SVO complete engine assembly. Air cleaner, carburetor, wiring and headers are not included, but otherwise this engine is ready to run. Rated at 385 horsepower at 5750 RPM, and 377 lb. ft. of torque at 4500 RPM. Includes Windsor high-flow aluminum cylinder heads with SVO premium stainless steel valves, SVO flat tappet camshaft, SVO forged aluminum roller rocker arms and dual valve springs, Victor Jr. high rise single plane aluminum intake manifold, SVO "tall" aluminum valve covers, production oil pump and heavy duty chrome moly drive shaft, SVO steel billet flywheel, SVO crankshaft damper, and Ford OEM 351W electronic distributor.

Part number M-6007-B351 — The cast iron head 351 GT-40 SVO engine long block. To complete this engine, the engine builder needs to add an induction system (either carburetor or fuel injection), distributor and ignition module, spark plug wires, headers and accessory drives. This powerplant is rated at 346 horsepower at 5750 RPM, and 364 lb. ft. of torque at 4250 RPM. Compression ratio is 9.0:1. Features SVO GT-40 high-flow cast iron cylinder heads, SVO hydraulic flat tappet camshaft, standard rocker arms, SVO "tall" aluminum valve covers, oil pump and oil pan, flywheel and crankshaft damper. Recommended intake manifold is a high rise, dual plane, aluminum unit.

Part number M-6007-A50 — The cast iron head version of the 5.0-liter GT-40 SVO engine long block. It has been dyno tested at 285 horsepower with a 780 CFM Holley 4V carburetor and shorty headers. Features 9.0:1 compression ratio, SVO GT-40 high-flow cast iron cylinder heads, GT-40 valve train and SVO roller camshaft. Builder needs to add induction system, distributor and ignition module, spark plug wires, headers and accessory drives. Bolts directly into F-Series trucks with manual transmission. This engine is street

Pictured here is the short-block for building a 5.8-liter 351W "Lightning" engine. The completed engine is rated at 310 horsepower, with installation of Motorsport induction, a set of headers, GT-40 heads, and 65mm throttle body. This short-block features a 2-bolt main 351W block, crankshaft, connecting rods, hypereutectic pistons, 8.8:1 compression ratio, plasma moly-filled steel top ring, roller timing chain and timing gears.

Pictured above is part number M-6007-A50, the cast iron head version of the 5.0-liter GT-40 SVO engine long block. This engine has been dyno tested at 285 horsepower with a 780 CFM Holley 4-barrel carburetor and shorty headers.

Performance Engines

The quick way to add performance is by installing a complete SVO 5.0-liter engine assembly. This one is part number M-6007-D50.

legal with installation of stock camshaft and other emission-related components.

Part number M-6007-B50 — The aluminum head version of the 5.0-liter GT-40 SVO engine long block. It has been dyno tested at 320 horsepower with a Motorsport induction kit, headers and 65mm throttle body. Features 9.0:1 compression ratio, SVO GT-40 aluminum cylinder heads with "turbo-swirl" combustion chambers and 1.94" diameter intake valves and 1.54" diameter exhaust valves, GT-40 valve train and SVO roller camshaft. Builder needs to add induction system, distributor and ignition module, spark plug wires, headers and accessory drives. Bolts directly into F-Series trucks with manual transmission. This engine is street legal with installation of stock camshaft and other emission-related components.

Part number M-6007-D50 — Here's a great way to add performance on a limited budget. This is the 240-horsepower 5.0-liter V8 that features 9.0:1 compression, a high-torque camshaft, and 60mm throttle body fuel injection. Comes complete with stainless steel headers, and is street legal when used with other emission related equipment.

Part number M-6009-B50 — The short-block for building a 5.0-liter 302 "Cobra" engine. Rated at 285 horsepower with installation of Motorsport induction, headers, GT-40 heads, and 65mm throttle body. This short-block features a 2-bolt main 302 block, crankshaft, connecting rods, hypereutectic pistons, 9.0:1 compression ratio, high torque roller camshaft, and silent timing chain and gears.

Part number M-6009-B58 — The short-block for building a 5.8-liter 351W "Lightning" engine. Rated at 310 horsepower with installation of Motorsport induction, headers, GT-40 heads, and 65mm throttle body. This short-block features a 2-bolt main 351W block, crankshaft, connecting rods, hypereutectic pistons, 8.8:1 compression ratio, plasma moly-filled steel top ring, roller timing chain and gears.

Part number M-6009-C460 — The 460 H.O. SVO engine short-block assembly. This engine is capable of more than 500 horsepower and 500 lb. ft. of torque when assembled with aluminum Cobra Jet cylinder heads and intake manifold. Compression ratio with Cobra Jet heads is 11.5:1. Assembly features aluminum pistons, heavy duty forged steel connecting rods, nodular iron crankshaft, SVO hydraulic flat tappet camshaft, roller timing chain, and is externally balanced.

Part number M-6011-B600 — The short-block offered by SVO for building a 600 cubic-inch monster motor. The block casting is bored and honed to 4.600" diameter cylinders and is completely machined. The crankshaft has a 4.5" stroke and is balanced. High silicone forged racing pistons with mini-domes provide 14.5:1 compression ratio, when used in conjunction with M-6049-C460 cylinder heads. Forged aluminum connecting rods are supplied. Piston rings feature a top compression ring of 1/16" width with plasma moly spray chrome over ductile iron. Main bearings, rod bearings and rear main seal complete the assembly.

Building A 351 SVO Tunnel-Port Engine

Back in the high-performance era of the sixties, one of the legendary muscle engines was the Ford 427 tunnel-port. This was considered by many automotive enthusiasts to be the ultimate wedge-head engine.

Even though original versions of these engines are rare today, the technology is still valid. And the best part is that you can build a modern tunnel-port engine by shopping for all the right components through the Ford Motorsports SVO Performance equipment catalog. Granted, you're not going to end up with a 427 tunnel-port. But building a 351 tunnel-port engine will give you a very strong small-block.

If we compare a conventional engine with a tunnel-port engine, we can identify some of the reasons why

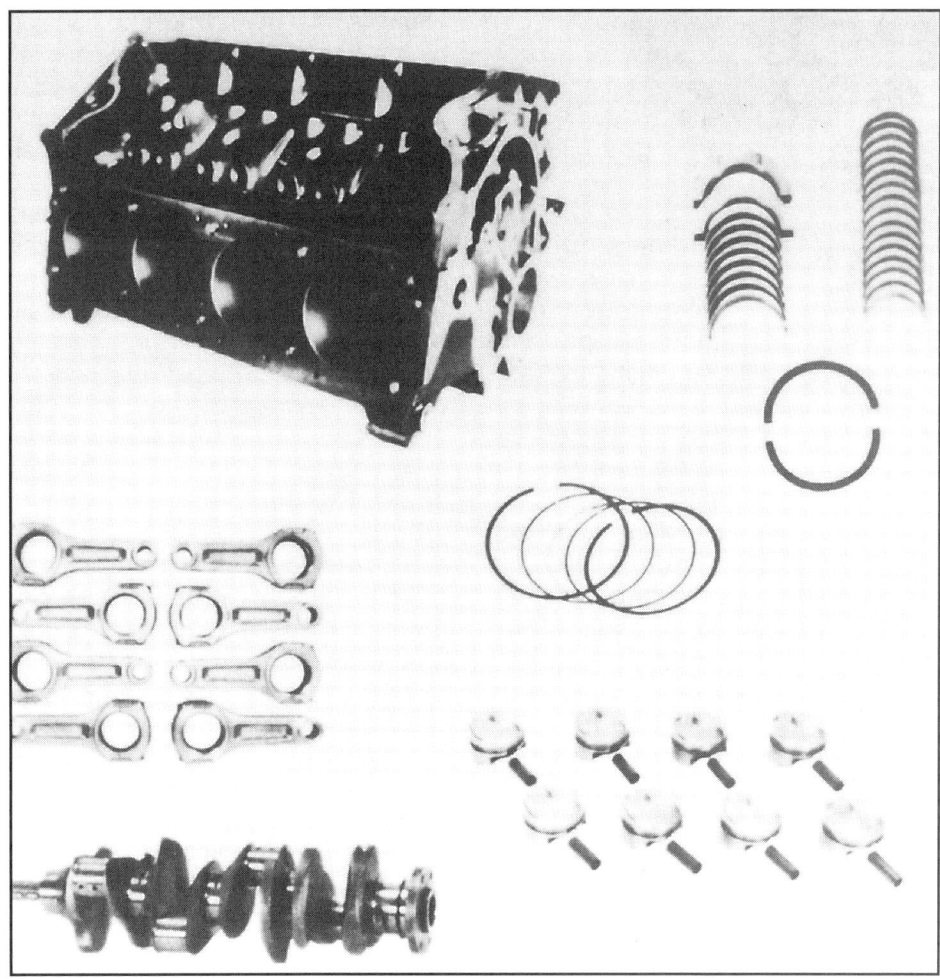

Imagine building a massive 600-cubic-inch engine out of a big-block Ford. Well, it can be done by using short-block part number M-6011-B600, pictured above. With an overbore capacity of 4.625 inches, and a deck height of 10.322 inches, this cast iron block features Siamese cylinders for greater block rigidity and strength. There is solid metal and no water passages between bores. If it's a monster engine you're after, this may be a good place to start.

the tunnel-port design is so effective. Conventional pushrod engines are designed in such a manner that the intake passages curve around the pushrods. This results in airflow restriction that limits top-end horsepower. The usual method for improving airflow in a conventional engine is to port and polish the intake passages. This helps, but cannot entirely overcome the restrictions.

Tunnel-port design has the intake passages routed almost directly from the bottom of the carburetor venturis into the cylinder head, resulting in optimum airflow. The pushrods of the 427 tunnel-port engine were encased in tubes that were pressed into the intake manifold ports.

The 351 tunnel-port design is slightly different from the 427 engine. In the 351 version, the pushrods operate through cast aluminum vanes that are shaped like airfoils. These vanes are polished and inserted into each intake ports of the cylinder head, but they are removable.

To build a 351 SVO tunnel-port engine, you will need to begin with cylinder block with the **part number M-6010-T351**. Camshaft **number M6250-T351** and cylinder heads **number M-6049-T351**, with head bolt kit **number M-6065-T351** are also required. Next comes intake manifold with **part number M-9424-T351**, and the intake manifold gasket **number M-9439-T351**. And finally there are the valve covers **number M-6582-T351**.

This collection of components, properly assembled, will result in a very special high-performance engine. Unique design characteristics of the Ford Motorsports SVO tunnel-port engine requires that only matched components be used. To build the engine properly, do not try to substitute other components.

The intake manifold is a single-plane design with very short, equal-length runners. The tunnel-port cylinder heads feature intake ports that are shaped and spaced for optimum airflow to the intake valves.

Performance Engine Cooling Systems

Horsepower is created at a cost, and part of that cost can be measured in heat generation. Combustion is a very hot process, ranging in temperature from 2,000 degrees to 3,000 degrees F. Some of this heat escapes through the exhaust system, but much of it is absorbed by the engine block, heads and intake hardware. As heat is absorbed by the engine, the metal components expand, and if heat is not dissipated, the engine can seize.

To remove heat from the engine, a cooling system has been designed in which coolant is propelled by a water pump and is routed through tunnels in the block and heads where it absorbs heat. This hot coolant is eventually routed through a radiator, which acts as a heat exchanger to dissipate heat into the air. After the coolant has been through the radiator and has lost some of its heat, it circles back through the engine again to absorb more heat which it will then dissipate through the radiator in a continuing cycle.

Obviously, it is very important to pay special attention to cooling the engine. There are a couple of ways to accomplish this task. One approach to improving engine cooling is to increase the size of the radiator. But secondary considerations should include such tactics as improving airflow through the engine compartment, reducing air-flow restrictions to the radiator, installing supplementary fans to move air through the radiator,

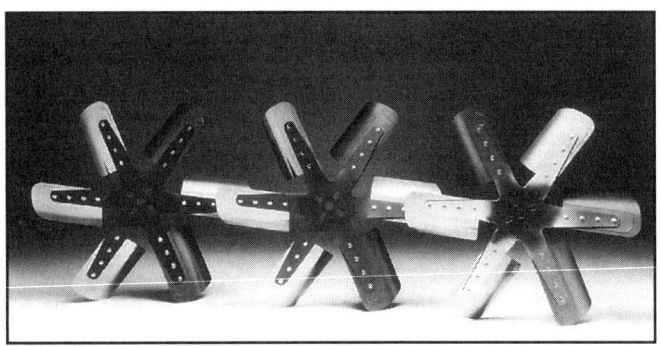

Flattened fan blades create less drag on the engine, when operating at high RPM. This is the concept behind the Flex-a-lite 1300 series stainless steel fan blades, which are used in performance applications.

Increased air-flow across any heat exchanger improves dissipation of heat. Perma-Cool offers this Combination Coil and Electric Fan Assembly, which serves as a heat exchanger and increases air-flow at the same time.

Perma-Cool's engine oil cooler kit comes with all the hoses and hardware necessary to install the unit in front of the vehicle's radiator. In that position, air that passes through the radiator will help cool the engine oil.

swapping to an entirely different type of primary fan, and the addition of an engine oil cooler.

Even if the engine's primary cooling system is working perfectly, there are parts of the engine that are not affected by coolant. The crankshaft, main bearings, rod bearings, camshaft and cam bearings, pistons and rings, timing gears and other internal components are all cooled by the engine oil, rather than by the coolant. It is estimated that fully 20 percent of the engine's heat output must be handled by the engine oil. This is a significant amount of heat. And in stock vehicles all this heat is simply absorbed by the oil, and there is no provision to dissipate it.

On a hot day, when the engine is under stress, oil temperature can reach more than 300 degrees F. And unlike coolant that enjoys the benefit of a radiator and fan, and has the added ability to dispel heat quickly because it is a thin liquid, oil holds onto its heat and cools slowly. When temperatures rise to those levels, the oil's ability to provide an adequate lubricating barrier against friction diminishes. Ideally, engine oil temperature in the oil pan should be kept to no more than the 250 to 270 degree F. range.

Performance drivers know the value of installing an engine oil cooler, to prevent the oil's lubricating ability from breaking down under the stress of high temperature. These oil coolers look and act like miniature radiators that are installed in a posi-

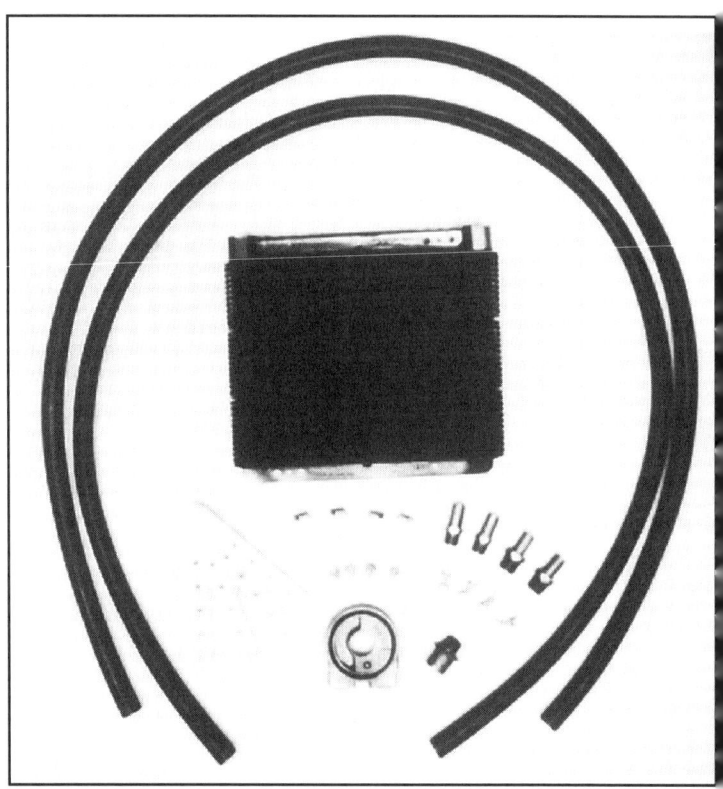

The SVO engine oil cooler kit, part number M-6642-S101 employs a patented "stack plate" design for improved cooling efficiency over "fin and tube" coolers. This 8"x11"x1.5" unit has a heat rejection capacity of 20,500 BTU's per hour.

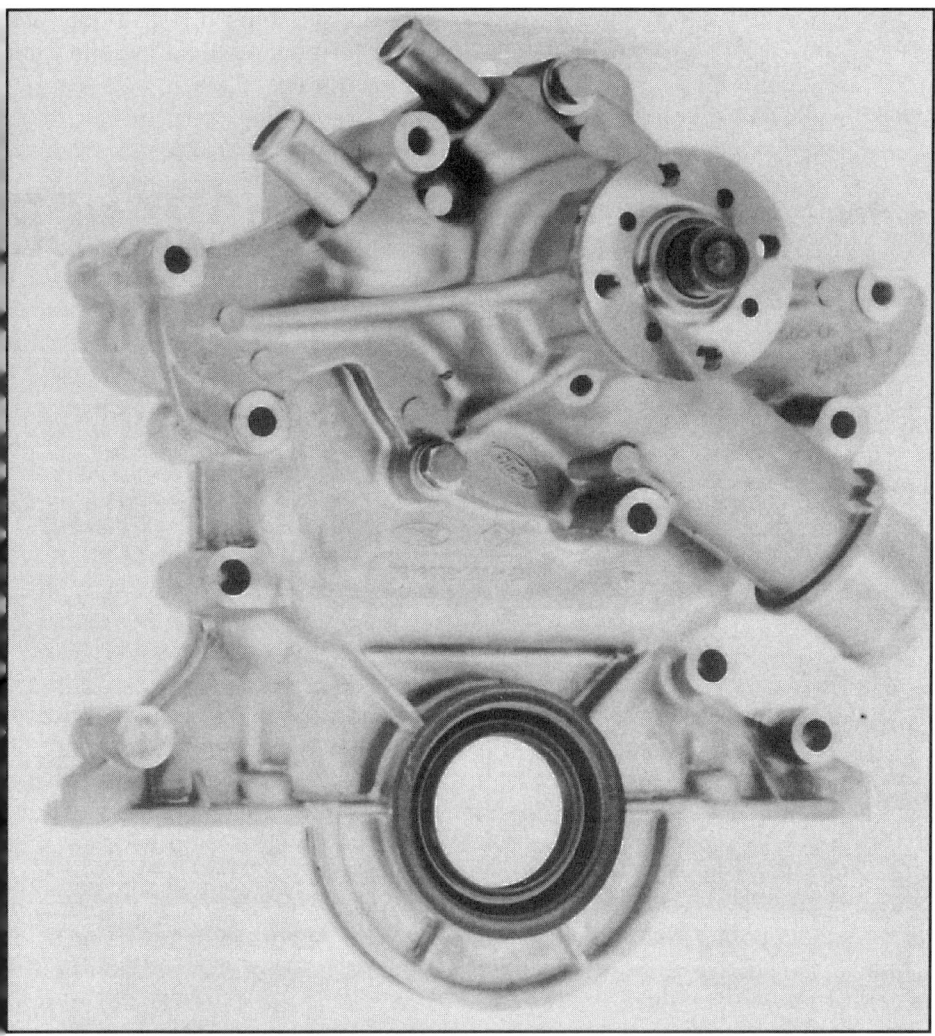

The Short Serpentine Belt Water Pump Kit (part number M-8501-A50) fits 289/302/351W engines. The kit includes a special timing chain cover with short water pump and gaskets. Pump is approximately 1-3/4" shorter than old-style pumps. Must electric fuel pump, and requires special pulleys.

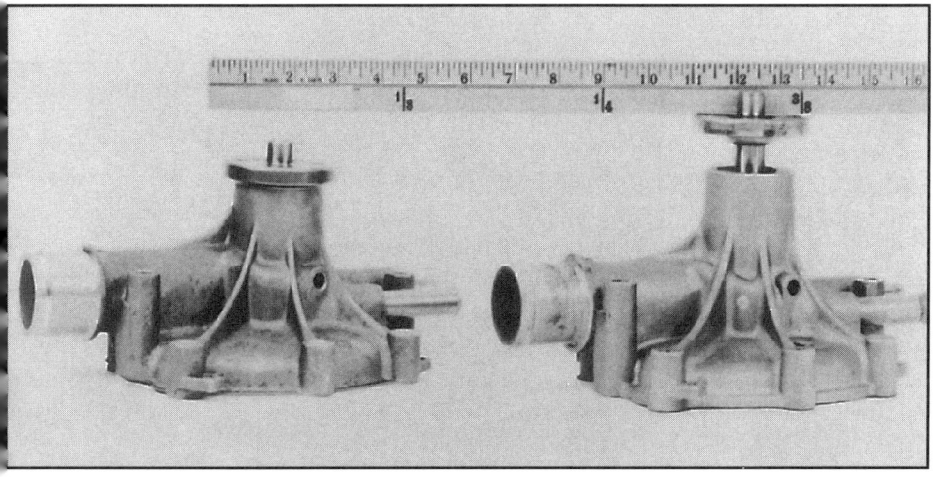

The Shorty V-Belt Water Pump (part number M-8501-E351), shown at the left in this photograph, fits 289/302/351W engines and features a driver's-side radiator hose inlet. The shorty pump provides approximately 1-1/2" of space at the front of the engine, allowing for more fan to radiator clearance. This pump meets all OEM specifications for water flow.

tion to receive fresh air across the cooling fins, and yet be protected from damage.

High-volume water pumps are available to help move coolant through a performance engine steadily and at the proper speed for optimum engine cooling.

Whenever an engine is rebuilt, whether for high-performance purposes or just for the street, the old water pump is one of those components that needs to be discarded and replaced with a new unit.

Through the Ford Motorsports SVO Performance Equipment catalog, you can order water pumps for a small-block. Both of the available units are pictured at left, along with pertinent specifications.

Many aftermarket companies offer water pumps as part of their product line. Edelbrock, for example, carries a line of aluminum water pumps under their Victor Series. According to the company, Edelbrock has designed these "super cooling" aluminum water pumps to provide maximum flow, maximuym pressure and equal distribution to both sides of the block to within 1%. They are available inboth long and short styles, and the pumps flow in only one direction, for optimum efficiency. The castings feature computer-designed internal passages and a CNC-machined cast iron impeller. Clearances are to aircraft industry tolerances,and the Victor Series water pumps have been accepted by NASCAR racers in divisions ranging from street stock to Winston Cup.

For Ford truck applications, the Victor Series offers several part numbers. For each of the part numbers listed here, there is another number that indicates the pump is polished. **Part number 8840** is for 5.0-liter engines from 1986 to '93 that use a serpentine accessory drive belt. It measures 5-3/4" from block surface to hub. **Number 8845** is the polished unit.

Part number 8843 fits 1970 to '78 302 engines and 1970 to '87 351W engines. The polished version carries **number 8848**. These water pumps have a left-hand inlet and a back plate.

Performance Engines **31**

To bring all the cylinders into dimensional perfection, boring and honing are performed. Notice that a torque plate has been installed on this block prior to boring. This is to simulate actual operating stresses when the engine will have a cylinder head in place.

hub, and features a heavy-duty 3/4" ball/roller bearing. The polished unit carries **number 8876**.

PERFORMANCE ENGINE BUILDING TECHNIQUES

Boring & Honing

Align boring is a special procedure that is not related to boring of the cylinders. Rather, align boring is a process that is used to straighten and align the main bearing saddles. This should be done on blocks that may have suffered dimensional shifting or warping. Whether or not your block requires align boring or align honing can be determined by simply installing a properly clearanced set of main bearings into the saddles, then carefully placing a crankshaft on the bearings. Give the crankshaft a spin and if it rotates easily there is no need for going through the align boring or honing process.

For 1970 to '79 351C and 351M/400 engines, there is **part number 8844**, and the polished counterpart is **number 8849**. Both of these units have a left-hand inlet with no back plate.

Big-block For engines ranging from 1970 to '92 are covered by **part number 8866**, which measures 5-1/2" from the block surface to the

Having a proper valve grind done is vital to good performance. A 3-angle cut is best, with angles of 30 degrees, 45 degrees, and 60 degrees being standard.

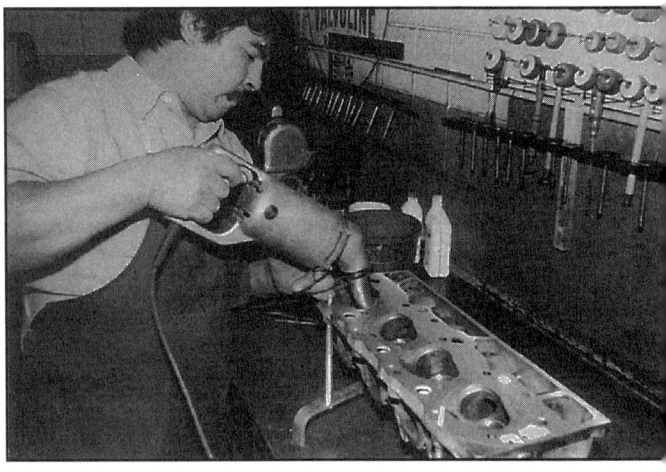

A shop that does head work can grind the valves and also prepare the valve seats to match the angles that are being cut on the valves.

However, under special circumstances, such as when installing specialty 4-bolt main bearing caps or when using bearing spacers to install a small-journal crank in a block that was made for large-journal crankshafts, align boring will be necessary.

Boring and honing of the cylinders is another story. Cylinders must be absolutely perfect in every dimension. They must be true and they must be round if they are to work well with pistons and rings to provide a proper seal. In order to ensure that the cylinders are machined in a manner that will simulate actual operating stresses, torque plates are typically bolted in place of cylinder heads and torqued the specified amount. The best procedure involves installation of a head gasket between the block and torque plate. Then the boring machine can prepare each cylinder with the boring bar referenced directly off the centerline of the crankshaft.

Honing should be done by machine, with Sunnen, CK-10 or similar power honing machines being the preferred by most machinists. Talk to

Air flow through the heads can be improved by the process of porting. This is done by using a small high-speed grinding tool to smooth and contour the air passages to eliminate sharp corners and other obstructions that may cause turbulence. Porting ranges from mild to wild, and for street applications only a light porting job is needed. Care must be taken to avoid removing too much material or creating flat spots or sharp angles, as this will hurt performance.

the operator of the machine shop to let him know what kind of rings you will be installing. Cylinders should be finished by using a 400 to 500 grit hone and plenty of fresh honing oil. If you aren't going to assemble the engine right away, make sure an ample coating of oil is left on the cylinder walls after the machining process is completed, to prevent rust from getting a start.

Decking

Decking is a machining process that removes material from the surfaces of the block where the cylinder heads will be installed. When the job is done properly, it results in deck surfaces that are exactly perpendicular to the centerlines of the cylinders, as well as being parallel to the centerline of the crankshaft. Naturally, this process controls the exact measurement from the crankshaft centerline to the deck, and thus controls the distance from the top of the piston to the cylinder head. The result of all this is that compression in each cylin-

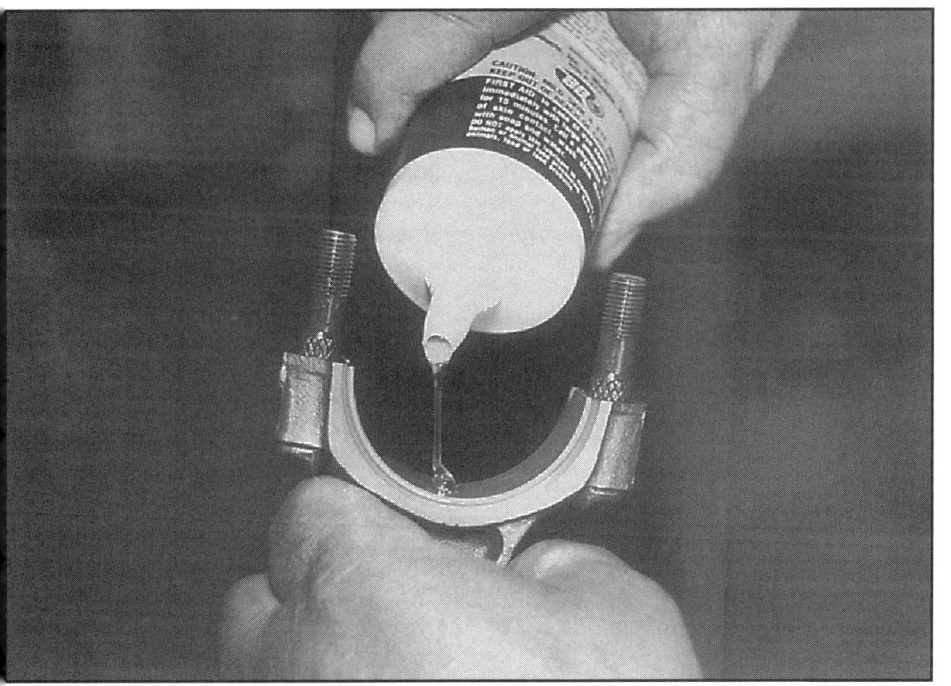

Before installing the piston and rod assemblies in the cylinders, apply a liberal amount of assembly lube on the rod bearing surfaces. Also, place rubber covers over the connecting rod studs before slipping the piston and rod assembly into the cylinders. This will protect the cylinder walls from possible damage that can occur as a result of contact with the studs during installation. Small matters such as this can prevent serious and costly damage.

Performance Engines **33**

Connecting rods should be balanced to help the engine run smooth and enjoy a long life. Balancing the rods begins by carefully weighing each rod in the set to discover the lightest rod. Using a highly sensitive scale, the rods are first weighed and marked with their weight. Then the bottom lobe portions of the heavier rods are carefully ground and reweighed until they are brought into very close balance with the lightest rod.

der can be precisely equalized. It goes without saying that having equal compression in each cylinder helps to optimize engine performance. By choosing from among a variety of head gasket thicknesses, final piston-to-cylinder head distances and compression ratios can be controlled.

If you are beginning with a used block, check deck heights in relation to piston tops to determine if it will be necessary to perform the decking process. If things are tolerably close, and you are building more for the street than for all-out racing, you may be able to avoid the expense involved in decking. In some cases where decking is performed, it may be necessary to also do some machining of the pistons to maintain proper clearances.

Porting

Even the best set of performance cylinder heads can benefit from a good porting job. Porting is the process of smoothing and contouring the inside of the port passages to eliminate obstructions to air flow. Depending upon your intended application, you may be able to do a bit of the porting work yourself by taking a high-speed grinder and a variety of stones, and gently working over the ports. Matching the port openings to the shape of the gasket is a good place to start. You may also be able to smooth the floor contour where it flows toward the combustion chamber. The object is to provide the optimum passage for air flow. That means smooth passageways and nicely radiused corners. Care must be taken not to remove too much material, nor to reduce radiuses to flattened angles, because this will disrupt air flow and decrease performance.

For street applications, mild porting that you can do yourself will improve performance, but caution and restraint must be used. Overzealous use of the grinder may result in a head that has worse air flow characteristics than stock. For racing applications, the best advice is to take the heads to a reputable cylinder head shop and have the work professionally done.

Balancing

When components are moving at several thousand cycles per minute, it is critical that everything be as closely balanced as possible. Like an out-of-balance tire that becomes more of a problem the faster it travels, the faster an out-of-balance engine runs, the more it tries to tear itself apart. So, not only is it important that the engine be balanced from the standpoint of optimum performance, but also from the standpoint of safety and longevity. A properly balanced engine will survive longer than one that is lumpy. Connecting rods, bearings, piston pins and crankshaft are all subjected to brutal punishment when an engine is operating at high RPM and is out of balance.

It is possible to buy a pre-balanced engine building kit, with crankshaft and piston assemblies already balanced. But you may prefer to have a local engine builder do the balancing for you. Be aware that bathroom scales are not quite good enough for balancing an engine, so if your local engine shop doesn't have equipment to do the job right, you will be better off to either haul your engine components to a good builder or buy a balanced kit from one of the suppliers who offer them.

Since you won't be doing this at home, we won't go into great detail about the balancing process, other than to let you know what is involved. Balancing an engine entails bringing piston assemblies into as close a weight relationship with each other as possible. It also involves spinning the crankshaft on a dynamic balancer to locate heavy spots, which are then removed by one machining process or another. It is best not to balance the crankshaft until after you have done a pre-assembly fitting of all the components to make sure that everything works well together. Then balance the crankshaft.

Even precision-made pistons will vary slightly in weight, right from the factory. So a new set of pistons should be weighed to determine which one is lightest. Then, all the rest of the pistons need to be machined to bring them down to the precise weight of the lightest one. That will balance the pistons. Next come the rods. Again, the procedure is to weigh them all to discover the lightest one, then machine the rest until they all match.

Chamfering the crankshaft oil holes will help oil flow across the bearing surfaces more easily. Only a light touch with a high-speed grinder is needed to remove the proper amount of material along the edges of the oil holes. Care must be taken during this process to ensure that the chamfering doesn't get too radical.

When the piston assemblies are put together, they are again checked to make sure that the process of installing the piston pins and rings didn't throw things back out of balance. Final machining work, if any is necessary, can be done to the rods to restore perfect balance.

Balancing should also be done to the flexplate, or flywheel and clutch pressure plate (whichever is applicable), because these spinning components also play a part in smoothness and longevity of an engine.

Blueprinting

Blueprinting is a process by which all tolerances and clearances are brought as close to perfect as possible. It involves serious detail work, checking dimensions to minute degrees, making sure there are no areas within the engine where things are too tight or too loose.

Blueprinting is a broad category,

Before installing the rings on the pistons, check gap clearance by pushing the rings down into the cylinder and using a feeler gauge. If the gap is too tight, a little material can be removed with a file.

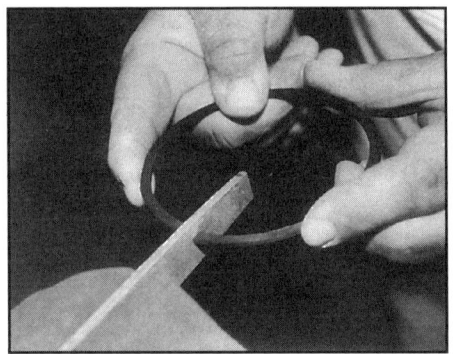

After determining that a ring is too tight in the cylinder, it can be adjusted by taking a few strokes on a fine file. Clamp the file in a vise, then very gently pass the ring gap over the file to remove a small amount of material.

involving the verification that all components fit precisely. High-performance engines are not those engines that are built "tight". In fact, performance engines should spin easily, creating as little internal resistance-related heat and friction as possible, because heat and friction cause drag on an engine and are performance killers.

When you have an engine blueprinted, or if you do the job yourself, the tools involved will include feeler gauges, micrometers, calipers, torque wrenches, and Plastigage. The process involves putting things together and tightening them to the specified torque, checking to see that the clearances are within specified tolerances, then taking them apart again and making adjustments where necessary.

Plastigage is a product that starts out looking like a piece of thread and ends up looking like a piece of ribbon. A short piece of Plastigage is placed between bearings and journals, and when the caps are torqued, the Plastigage flattens. By removing the cap and bearing, and measuring the width of the flattened Plastigage, an engine builder can determine if clearances between bearings and journals

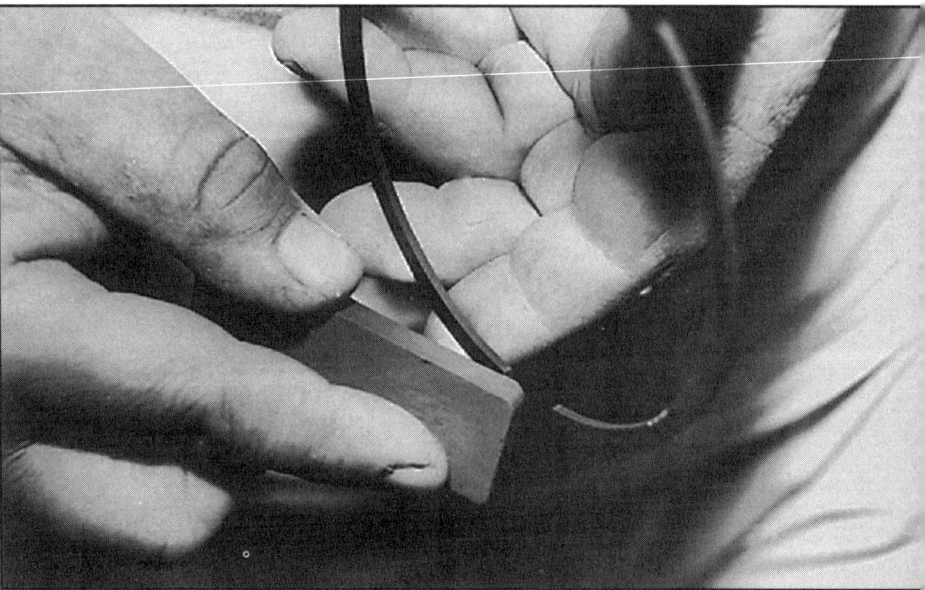

Making adjustments to the ring gap by using a file can result in tiny burrs, so the next step is to use a fine stone to deburr the edges of the ring in the vicinity of the gap. Do this before trying to fit the ring in the cylinder again to check for proper clearance, because even small burrs can score the cylinder.

are correct — neither too loose nor too tight. If the Plastigage doesn't widen enough, there is too much space between bearing and journal. This would indicate that some work needs to be done on the bearing ends to allow the two halves of a bearing to close more tightly on the journal. If the Plastigage is flattened so much that it becomes too wide, the indication is that the bearings are too tight on the journal.

Blueprinting is time consuming and expensive, but worth it if you want to know for certain that all the components will be happy living inside your block. When an engine has been balanced and blueprinted, it will spin easily, start quickly, and run contentedly. It will perform at its best and deliver maximum efficiency. And that's all we can ask of a performance engine.

Naturally, there are many other high-performance engine building procedures that can be performed on the various components of an engine as the powerplant is prepared for a life on the field of competition. But for the purposes and scope of this book, the processes and techniques we have outlined here will suffice.

Volumes of books have been written about nothing other than building performance engines, and space limitations in this volume require that we recommend that you expand your reading in those directions if you need more information about building a high-performance Ford engine.

There is very little about working on a performance vehicle that is more gratifying than building an engine. The building process is a time to go slow and careful, inspecting and cleaning every component. The builder develops an intimate relationship with the engine, as each piece is perfected prior to installation.

Perhaps the only thing that beats the fun of building the engine is the feeling you get when it is fired up for the first time. It's about as close to automotive heaven as you can get.

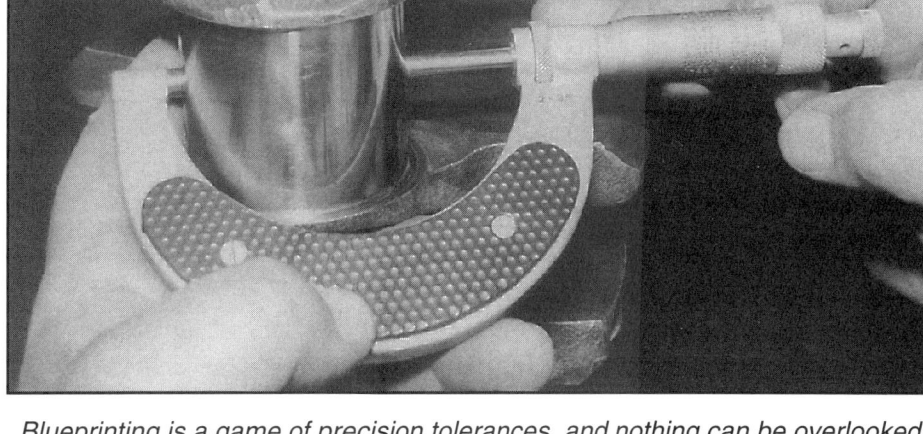

Blueprinting is a game of precision tolerances, and nothing can be overlooked in the pursuit of an engine that fits together with near perfection. Even though you may buy a high quality crankshaft from an aftermarket supplier, it is important to check journal dimensions with a micrometer to ensure that all journal-to-bearing clearances will be within acceptable parameters. If there are unacceptable variations, the crankshaft needs to be taken to a machine shop where it can be brought into specifications.

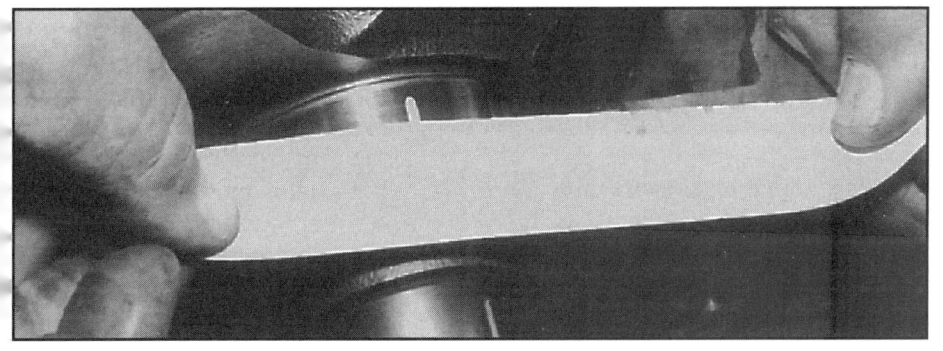

Using Plastigage is a two-stage process that is illustrated by these two photos. In the photo above, a short strand of Plastigage has been positioned on the crankshaft journal. The next step is to place the bearing and cap over the journal and tighten the cap bolts to the factory specified torque. This places pressure on the Plastigage, flattening it out. The photo below shows how to check for proper bearing-to-journal clearance. Remove the cap and bearing, then measure the width of the smashed Plastigage, using a special measuring tape that is supplied with the Plastigage. If the width is too narrow, not enough pressure was placed on the Plastigage, so there is too much slop between the bearing and journal. This indicates that the bearings and cap need to be machined slightly to permit a tighter fit. If the Plastigage is wider than it should be, the indication is that the bearing is fitting too tightly against the journal. To remedy this problem, the crankshaft can be machined slightly to reduce the diameter of the offending journal.

Performance Engines **37**

Performance Modifying Ford Trucks

Induction System

Whether your truck engine will be running with natural aspiration or some kind of forced induction system (turbocharger or supercharger), it will be necessary to make some choices about the type of intake manifold to be used, and whether to deliver fuel via carburetion or an electronic fuel injection system. This is a subject that has many options and many aftermarket companies ready to sell you their products. Ultimately the choices you make will depend upon the desired performance level of the engine, as well as the intended application. What works great on the street may not be appropriate for the strip, and something entirely different may be needed for off-road driving.

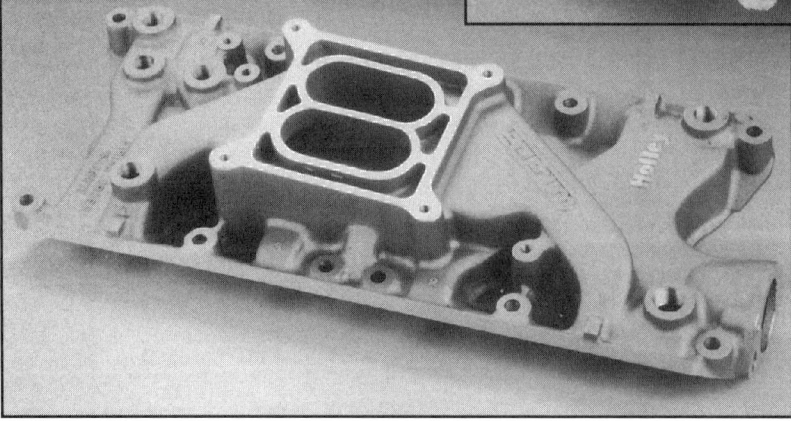

This is where the owner needs to really get serious about just what type of performance demands and driving conditions will be most common for the truck.

Intake Manifolds and Carburetors

Intake manifolds are manufactured in a wide variety of configurations, to meet a diversity of special performance needs. Most factory units are of dual-plane design, in which the manifold air chamber (plenum) is divided down the middle by a partition that separates the manifold into two separate air chambers — one that runs to the left bank of the engine, and the other runs to the right bank. According to some, this is the ideal street manifold configuration for a couple of reasons. One reason is that the dual-plane design eliminates pulsations resulting form exhaust reversion that can occur in a single plane design. The other reason is because of the relatively smaller ai chamber, when compared with single-plane manifolds. As a result of the smaller air chamber, the carburetor feels a stronger induction impulse, which permits the use of carburetors that can flow a greater cubic feet per minute (CFM) of air/fuel mixture. This delivers good street performance and efficiency, and the use of a larger carburetor helps overcome the slightly restrictive characteristics of the dual-plane manifold at high engine speed.

One of the drawbacks to dual-

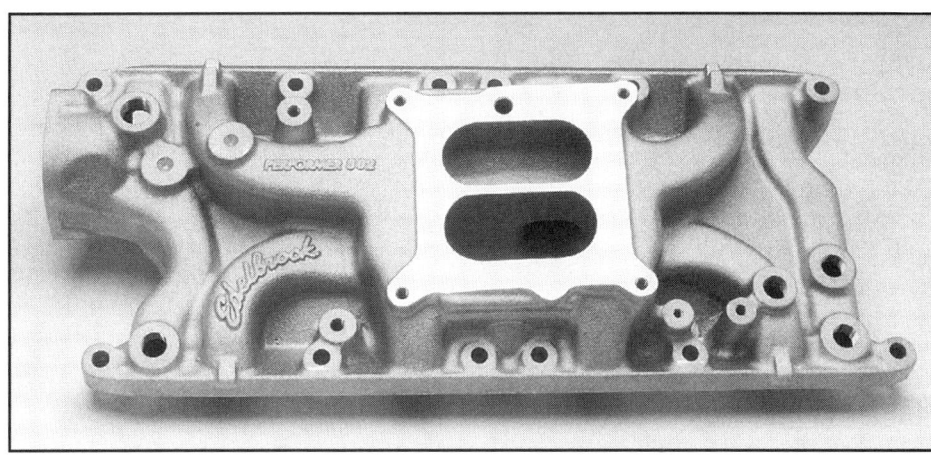

Edelbrock Performer 302 intake manifold is of dual-plane design. From this angle, it's easy to see that the air chamber, or plenum, is divided down the middle. This separates the incoming air/fuel mixture so half feeds the left bank of cylinders and half feeds the right bank. This separation also prevents exhaust reversion pulses from one side of the engine from affecting the intake characteristics on the opposite side.

Edelbrock's Performer RPM 351-W manifold, pictured above, is designed for use on 351 Windsor Ford V8 engines dating from 1969 through 1991. This manifold works with Edelbrock Street Heads #6025, OEM 12- or 16-bolt, AR/Ford aluminum M-6049-J302, Ford GT-40 cast iron M-6049-L302, Dart cast iron TFS/Street Heat aluminum or equivalent.

a single-plane intake manifold should be restricted to carburetors of lower CFM rating because the larger air chamber absorbs the induction pulse. A small carburetor will generally respond better to a weak induction pulse than would a large carburetor.

plane design is that it generally incorporates intake runners of varying lengths. As the air/fuel mixture races through the runners enroute to the combustion chambers, fuel-dropout becomes a problem in the longer runners. The higher the engine speed, the greater this problem becomes. At very high engine speed, the ideal intake manifold would have runners of equal length. This is one reason a dual-plane manifold is more suited to low and moderate speed operation, rather than high-speed operation. So, for street trucks, a dual-plane manifold may be the best choice.

But when it comes to high engine speed operation, nothing will compare with a single plane intake manifold. Designed with intake runners of equal length, there is less problem with fuel-dropout. On the other hand,

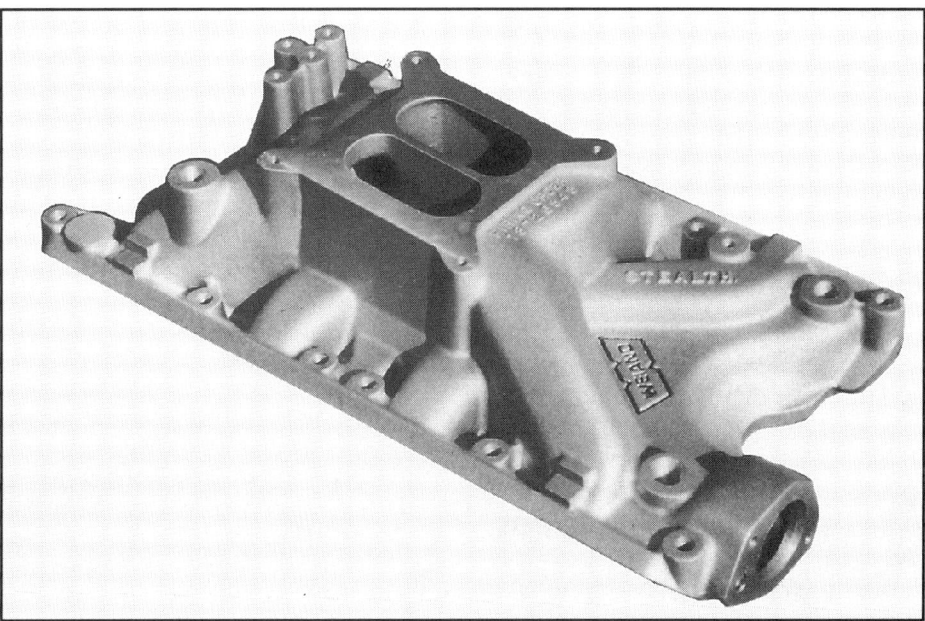

Weiand's Stealth 351W manifold is for use with 600-750 CFM vacuum secondary or double pumper carburetors in street applications, or with 750-850 CFM double pumpers in performance applications.

A smaller carburetor will maintain a higher air/fuel velocity than a large carburetor would, which offsets the lower velocity provided by single-plane manifolds at low engine speed. And the nearly straight runners deliver a large volume of air/fuel mixture at high engine speed.

Due to the open plenum design, exhaust reversion pulses can affect the intake process on the opposite side of the engine. Common theory is that a large air chamber helps dissipate the reversion pulses. So there may be a benefit to enlarging the air chamber by installing a tall spacer between the carburetor and the intake manifold, but this is only true for single-plane manifolds used with big engines and high RPM operation.

Big, dual-quad tunnel ram intake manifolds are designed for very high-performance applications, not for the street. They look great on a street truck, but you have to decide if you're building a truck just to impress the curbside crowd, or are you building with specific performance requirements in mind. However, there is a place for tunnel ram intake manifolds and dual-quad carburetion. If your truck is being built for truck pulls, or other full-on performance applications that will require maximum induction capability, this is the way to go. For those who simply cannot resist the temptation of installing a tunnel ram and dual-quads on a street truck, it is possible to tinker them into moderately good drivability on the street, but it will take some effort to dial in the system so it will work at low to partial throttle.

Most street trucks that are not fuel injected should probably be running a dual-plane manifold and a single moderately-sized four-barrel carburetor, because this is the setup that will deliver decent street performance and efficiency. If a single-plane manifold is what you want, make every effort to keep carburetor size to a minimum. Remember, a small carburetor will respond better to a weak induction impulse created by an open plenum, and a large carburetor will require a stronger induction impulse created by a divided plenum.

Now, here's a look at factory

For serious high-performance applications, where maximum induction effort is required, a dual-quad tunnel ram intake manifold is the ticket. This one is Weiand's Pro Hi-Ram manifold for use on big-block Ford V8 engines. A pair of Holley 4500 Series Dominator carburetors are specified for best performance.

intake manifolds available for the Ford small-block V8 and big-block V8 engines through the Ford Motorsports Special Vehicle Operations (SVO) Performance Equipment catalog.

Small-Block V8

Part number M-9424-A321 — A dual-plane aluminum intake manifold designed for use on 289-cid and 302 cid small-block V8 engines equipped with cylinder heads that feature inline valves. 8.206 deck height. This manifold is for engines that will live within the 1500 to 6000 RPM range.

Part number M-9424-A331 — This single-plane aluminum manifold is for the SVO 351 engine block that will be fitted up with cylinder heads with canted valves. 9.200 deck height. This model will not fit the 351 C cast iron cylinder heads.

Part number M-9424-A51 — GT-40 tubular upper EFI unit for the SVO 302 and 351W engine block.

Part number M-9424-D50 — Cast EFI "Cobra" upper unit for use with the GT-40 lower intake manifold on the SVO 289, 302 and 351W engine block.

Part number M-9424-D302 — Single-plane "Victor Jr." aluminum intake manifold for use on 289-cid and 302-cid small-block V8 engines that are equipped with inline valve cylinder heads. 8.206 deck height. Intended for performance operation between 3500 and 8000 RPM.

Part number M-9424-E302 — Aluminum dual-plane "Performer RPM" intake manifold for use on 289-cid and 302-cid small-block V8 engines that are equipped with inline valve cylinder heads. 8.206 deck height. Intended for performance operation between 1500 and 6500 RPM.

Part number M-9424-V351 — Aluminum single-plane "Victor Jr." intake manifold for use on 351-cid small-block V8 engines that are equipped with inline valve cylinder heads. 9.500 deck height. Intended for performance operation between 3500 and 7500 RPM.

Part number M-9424-Z351 — Aluminum dual-plane "Performer RPM" intake manifold for use on 351-cid small-block V8 engines that are equipped with inline valve cylinder heads. 9.500 deck height. Intended for performance operation between 1500 and 6500 RPM.

Part number M-9461-A50 — The lower GT-40 EFI intake manifold for the SVO 302 engine block that will be fitted up with inline valve cylinder heads.

Part number M-9461-A58 — The lower GT-40 EFI intake manifold for the SVO 351 engine block that will be fitted up with inline valve cylinder heads.

Part number M-9424-A351 — Single-plane aluminum intake manifold for use on 351-cid small-block V8 engines that are equipped with Yates NASCAR cylinder heads. 9.200 deck height. Flange cut for Yates C3L head.

Part number M-9425-A351 — Single-plane aluminum intake manifold for use on 351-cid small-block V8 engines that are equipped with Yates NASCAR cylinder heads. Flange cut for Yates C3L head. Differs from M-9424-A351 in deck height of 9.500.

Part number M-9424-B302 — Single-plane aluminum manifold for use on SVO 302-cid small-block V8 engines that are equipped with canted valve cylinder heads. 8.200 deck height.

Part number M-9424-E351 — Single-plane aluminum intake manifold for use on SVO 351-cid small-block V8 engines that are equipped with Yates NASCAR cylinder heads. 9.200 deck height. Flange cut for Yates C3L head.

Part number M-9425-E351 — Single-plane aluminum intake manifold for use on 351-cid small-block V8 engines that are equipped with Yates NASCAR cylinder heads. Flange cut for Yates C3L head. Differs from M-9424-E351 in deck height of 9.500.

Part number M-9424-W302 — Single-plane aluminum intake manifold for use on SVO 302-cid small-block V8 engines that are equipped with Yates NASCAR cylinder heads. 8.200 deck height.

Part number M-9424-W351 — Single-plane aluminum intake manifold for use on SVO 351-cid small-block V8 engines that are equipped with Yates NASCAR cylinder heads. 9.200 deck height.

Part number M-9425-W351 — Aluminum single-plane intake manifold for use on SVO 351-cid small-block V8 engines that are equipped with Yates NASCAR cylinder heads. Differs from M-9424-W351 in deck height of 9.500.

Typical of the popular Model 4160 Holley carburetor is this 780-CFM unit that is designed for use on engines dating back to the early 1970's. Ideal for performance small-block engines, this carb features an automatic electric choke, Ford automatic transmission kickdown and vacuum secondaries.

Big-Block V8

Part number M-9424-C460 — Aluminum single-plane, single four-barrel manifold for use on SVO 460 engines with pros stock cylinder heads. Deck height 10.322.

Part number M-9424-G429 — Aluminum single-plane "Victor Jr." manifold for use on SVO 429 and 460 big-block V8 engines with production and M-6049-A429/-B429 cylinder heads. Deck height 10.322.

Part number M-9424-H429 — Aluminum single-plane manifold for use on SVO 429 and 460 big-block V8 engines with production and M-

Holley's famous 750-CFM "double pumper" (part number 0-3310) is popular among performance enthusiasts, because it delivers a lot of air/fuel mixture when the engine needs it. Featuring power valve blow-out protection and vacuum secondaries, this carburetor is controlled by a manual choke.

Swapping metering rods in an Edelbrock carburetor is a simple process that doesn't require disassembly or removal of the carb. A selection of metering rods, jets and springs comes with the carburetor, so the owner can modify performance.

6049-A429/-B429 cylinder heads. Dominator Flange. Deck height 10.322.

Carburetors

Let's take a look at some of the performance aftermarket carburetors that are available. We can't cover all of them in this book, but at least this will give you an indication of what's available and some of the considerations you should give to carburetor choice.

When selecting carburetor and intake manifold combinations, the primary concern should be to match the induction system to the engine requirements. Over-carbureting is a typical mistake among those who are seeking improved performance, and a carburetor that is too large will hurt performance far more than will a carburetor that is too small. If the carburetor is too large, the metering circuits will not receive an effective signal, and both performance and economy will suffer — low-end acceleration will virtually disappear, and even mid-range performance may be reduced. On the other hand, if the carburetor is too small, the driver will be able to feel performance fall off as engine RPM overcomes the carburetor's ability to deliver an adequate supply of air/fuel mixture. The engine will still run fine, but top-end performance will fall off.

Regardless of engine displacement, factory production manifolds, and aftermarket low-speed manifolds work best with carburetors that are kept to a minimal size. In no case, should a carburetor in excess of 750 CFM be installed for street use, and many engines will respond even better to a carb in the range of 600 CFM.

For true racing conditions in lightweight vehicles with low gears, it's hard to beat a carburetor like the Holley double-pumper. But for good all around street performance, you are better off sticking with a modest-sized carburetor that has vacuum secondaries.

Edelbrock offers a full line of Performer Series square-bore carburetors that are appropriate for installation on just about any domestic truck, because the linkage can be adapted to fit Ford, Chevy, or Chrysler vehicles. Designed to bolt directly to square-bore manifolds, these carbs will also bolt up to spread-bore manifolds if an adapter is used.

One of the notable features of Edelbrock carburetors is the ease with which the metering rods can be changed. It's a modification that can be done without even removing the carburetor or performing any disassembly. Also, there are no power valves to blow or plastic parts to break, and there are no gaskets below the fuel level.

Part number 1404 is a 500-CFM model that is especially recommended for use with small-block Ford applications in which a dual-quad set-up is installed on a tunnel ram manifold. It comes with an assortment of metering jets, rods and springs, and electric choke can be added.

Part number 1406 is a 600-CFM unit that features lean calibration from the factory, for maximum fuel economy. It comes with electric choke as a stock item, and features an assortment of metering jets, rods and springs so you can modify performance to suit your needs.

Part number 1411 is a 750-CFM carburetor that is best when used on a big-block Ford. It features electric choke, both timed and full vacuum ports for ignition advance, and a selection of metering jets, rods and

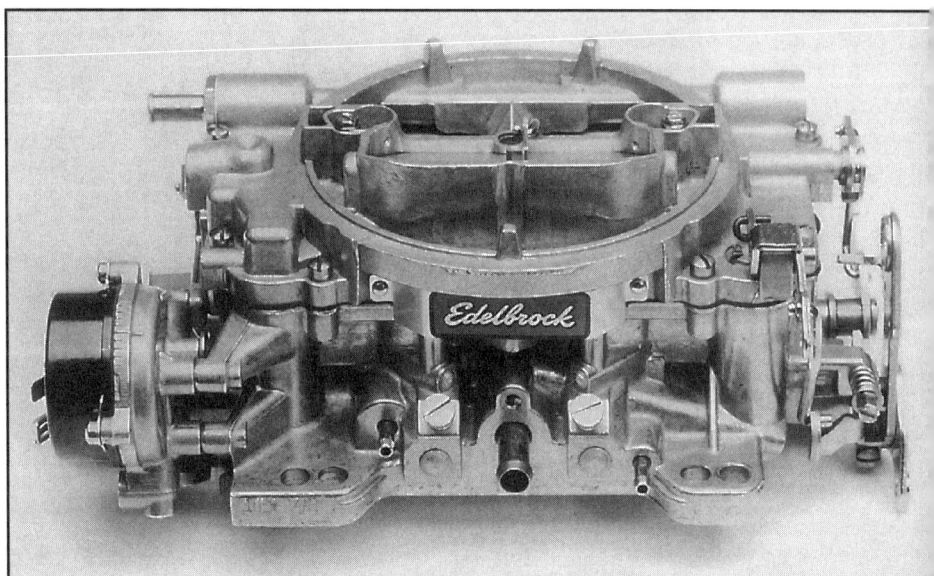

Edelbrock recommends this 600-CFM carburetor (part number 1406) for most Performer intake manifold applications. It is equipped with an electric choke, and is calibrated to run lean, for maximum fuel economy. Comes with an assortment of metering rods, springs, and jets.

springs for personalized adjustment.

Holley is another legendary name in the aftermarket carburetor industry, and Holley carburetor features that are standard on their street legal carbs include all emission provisions, vacuum and mechanical secondaries, square-bore bolt patterns, and engineering that is designed to improve performance. All street legal carbs intended for application on Ford trucks powered by V8 engines of a vintage ranging from 1968 through 1987 are rated at 600-CFM in the square-flange design. The list of part numbers is too long for us to display here. To get the full low-down on all the Holley street legal carburetors, your best move is to obtain the Holley catalog and study the various offerings.

Under the 50-states legal category is a sweet little Model 4160 Street Performance four-barrel carburetor that is rated at 450-CFM. **Part number 0-4548** is intended for use on 1961 - 1967 Ford V8 engines. It features a hot air automatic choke, automatic transmission kickdown and vacuum secondaries.

Stepping up a bit to another 50-states legal carburetor is the Model 4160 Street Performance unit that flows 600 CFM. **Part number 0-4452** is designed for use on 1968 - 1970 Ford big-block engines. It features hot air choke, automatic transmission kickdown and vacuum secondaries.

Part number 0-80457 is a 50-state street legal 600-CFM four-barrel that features Ford automatic transmission kickdown, electric choke, power valve blow-out protection and vacuum secondaries. It's intended for use on small-block engines, and can be combined with Holley's street Performance dual-plane intake manifold **part number 300-39** to build a performance intake system.

In addition to the street legal line of carburetors, Holley also offers a full line of high-performance, show and competition units that are not approved for 50-state street applications. These range from 600-CFM all the way up to 1150-CFM double-pumper Pro-Series carburetors, so there's got to be something in there to satisfy every need that is not associated with emission control applications.

Fuel Injection

Computerized fuel delivery is the essence of fuel injection systems. The concept is that if you can deliver just the right amount of fuel to the combustion chambers, the engine will perform at its optimum level. And, if the system happens to be operator adjustable, the driver can modify fuel delivery on demand as conditions change. Factory fuel injection systems are not operator adjustable, but some aftermarket systems allow a certain amount of adjustment.

Two types of fuel injection systems are available — Throttle Body injection (TBI), and Tuned Port Injection (TPI). Throttle body units

---

Performance Modifying Ford Trucks

Carburetor Tune-Up

Keeping a carburetor running at its optimum level is not particularly difficult, nor mysterious. Regardless of the carburetor brand or model, some tune-up procedures are standard. Of course, specifications for various brands and models will be different than for others, so you need to closely follow manufacturer recommendations regarding specifications.

If the PCV valve is stuck, you'll never get the engine to run properly, so if there is any doubt as to the condition of the PCV valve, install a new one. They're inexpensive, but a bad one can cost a lot in terms of performance.

Because you want to begin tuning the carburetor while the engine is cold, the day before working on the carburetor, set the ignition timing. Only after the timing is correct can you properly tune up the carburetor.

Ensure that there are no vacuum leaks. Inspect all vacuum lines and fittings to verify that no leaks exist. Also, check the intake manifold bolts and carburetor bolts to make sure none are loose and causing a vacuum leak at these points.

Adjust fast idle by using a hand-held tachometer. Fully depress the throttle and then release, then start the engine. Before the engine has a chance to warm up and begin opening the choke, adjust the fast idle setting to the proper RPM. As the engine warms up, the choke should begin to open. A quick tap of the throttle should allow the choke valve to open slightly. When the engine is warm, the valve should be fully open.

When the engine has completely warmed up, set the hot idle speed, again using the hand-held tachometer.

For best performance, set the idle mixture adjustment until maximum vacuum is created. Use a vacuum gauge to test manifold vacuum. A rich mixture, poor compression, or retarded ignition timing will cause low manifold vacuum. When the hot idle mixture is set correctly, manifold vacuum should read high and steady — assuming that the ignition timing is set correctly and there is good compression in the engine.

Test the accelerator pump. Inadequate pump discharge can cause the engine to stumble on acceleration. At high elevation, a longer pump arm setting is advisable.

Failed components in the emission control system can cause performance problems. If you have installed a new PCV valve, properly timed the ignition system, and tuned up the carburetor, but still have serious performance problems, suspect emission control components such as the EGR valve, or perhaps an overly restrictive exhaust system.

Holley Pro-Jection is available in both 2-barrel and 4-barrel versions, and is fairly easy to install. Along with the throttle body unit, an electric fuel pump and inline fuel filter is required for each gas tank. Harness hook-up is simple plug-in design, and the control module is driver adjustable.

resemble carburetors, in that the fuel is delivered through a central unit by the injectors, and then the air fuel mixture is routed to the combustion chambers by the normal method through the intake manifold. In a sense, throttle body injection suffers from some of the same maladies that prevent carburetors from being ideal. You're still working with a less-than-perfect delivery system because of the path the air/fuel mixture must take through the intake manifold. But at least a throttle body injector is controllable by computer, so theoretically it should be more efficient.

Tuned port injection (TPI), on the other hand, delivers a measured amount of fuel directly into each individual combustion chamber at the precise moment it is needed. There is no air/fuel mixture, as such, because the air is delivered "dry" through the induction system, while the fuel is delivered separately to each cylinder by an individual injector that is located near the cylinder head ports.

All electronic fuel injection systems require high-pressure fuel pumps and adequate fuel return lines. These systems are also more sensitive than carburetors to contamination, so it is necessary to pay special attention to the fuel filters.

Ford offers several components for upgrading an EFI system, through their Motorsports SVO Performance Equipment catalog. Ford Motorsports offers two EFI lower and upper intake manifolds for a variety of engine modifications. These include converting either a 302-cid V8 or a 351-cid V8 engine from carburetor to fuel injection. Or you can upgrade a standard 302-cid V8 EFI engine to the higher "Cobra" performance level or to the even higher "GT-40" performance level.

Two kits — Cobra and GT-40 — are available for the popular 302-cid V8, and the kits include gaskets necessary for the installation. Both SVO lower manifolds feature staggered ports for improved airflow over the inline ports of products systems. Adding a high-flow throttle-body to one of these Ford Motorsports manifold combinations will significantly increase airflow and horsepower.

In addition to the intake manifolds for EFI, Ford Motorsports also offers their EEC-IV EFI RPM Extender which is an electronic module that allows you to achieve full power potential from a fuel injected small block. With the twist of a screwdriver you can set the RPM limit anywhere from 6,500 RPM to 13,000 RPM, and you can also set the wide open throttle air-fuel ratio in a range from 10.25:1 to 14.0:1. Ford Motorsports says all this can be accomplished without adversely affecting emissions or driveability during normal driving.

Part of the Motorsports EFI offerings include harnesses, injectors sensors and other essential components that can assist the knowledgeable do-it-yourselfer to assemble an

Stock Ford truck throttle bodies can be replaced with units like these from BBK that are claimed to increase performance by 8 to 12 horsepower. These are direct bolt-on pieces that require no modification, and they are EPA legal in all 50 states. Available for 1987 through 1996 302, 351 and 460 truck engines.

EFI system.

The aftermarket offers several throttle body or tuned-port systems that can be installed at home or by your favorite speed shop mechanic, to convert a carbureted engine to a fuel injected one. One of the popular aftermarket Throttle Body electronic fuel injection systems was developed by Holley, and goes by the name of Pro-Jection. Several models, both 2-barrel and 4-barrel, have been designed as retro-fit units to replace carburetors on non-computerized V8 engines. These units are not legal for sale or use in California on any pollution controlled motor vehicle.

Holley part number 502-1 — This 2-barrel, 670-CFM analog unit is the lowest cost complete fuel injection system package Holley makes available. It is a complete stand-alone system with dual 80-lb./hour injectors, designed to retro-fit carbureted, non-computerized V8 engines, and includes all components necessary for installation on a spread bore intake manifold. Manifold not included as part of package.

Holley part number 502-2 — This 2-barrel, 670-CFM analog unit is the lowest cost complete fuel injection system package Holley makes available. It is a complete stand-alone system with dual 80-lb./hour injectors, designed to retro-fit carbureted, non-computerized V8 engines, and includes all components necessary for installation on a square flange intake manifold. Manifold not included with package.

Holley part number 504-2 — This 4-barrel, 700-CFM analog unit is a complete stand-alone system that features four 65-lb./hour injectors, designed to retro-fit carbureted, non-computerized V8 engines in the 150-horsepower to 350-horsepower range. Package includes all components necessary for installation on the manifold of your choice. Manifold not included with package.

Holley part number 504-12 — This 4-barrel, 700-CFM digital unit with microprocessor based engine management is a complete stand-alone system that features four 65-lb./hour injectors, designed to retro-fit carbureted, non-computerized V8 engines, and includes rev limiter and all other components necessary for installation on the manifold of your choice. Manifold not included with package.

Holley part number 504-22 — The ultimate engine management system for applications ranging in horsepower from 150-hp to 300-hp. This 700-CFM, four-barrel competition digital system features microprocessor based engine management to analyze many engine factors in a matter of milli-seconds. A true speed density system which measures engine load. An IBM compatible PC is required for initial start-up and fine tuning of this system.

Holley part number 504-1 — This 4-barrel, 900-CFM analog unit is a complete stand-alone system that features four 80-lb./hour injectors, designed to retro-fit carbureted, non-computerized V8 engines in the 300-horsepower to 500-horsepower range. Package includes all components necessary for installation on the manifold of your choice. Manifold not included with package.

Holley part number 504-11 — This 4-barrel, 900-CFM digital unit with microprocessor based engine management is a complete stand-alone system that features four 80-lb./hour injectors, designed to retro-fit carbureted, non-computerized V8 engines in the 300-horsepower to 500-horsepower range. Package includes a rev limiter and all other components necessary for installation on the manifold of your choice. Manifold not included with package.

Holley part number 504-21 — The ultimate engine management system for applications ranging in horsepower from 300-hp to 500-hp.

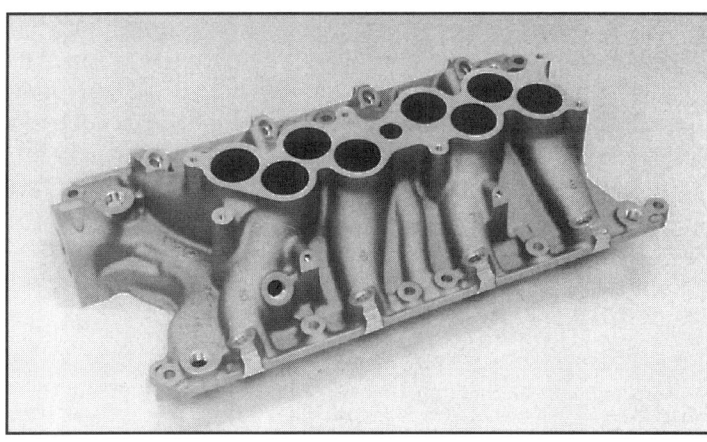

*Ford's EFI lower manifold for the 5.8-liter engine is **part number M-9461-A58** is designed to work in conjunction with the upper manifold section pictured below, to add more punch to 5.8-liter engines or to convert 351W engines to fuel injection. Requires the use of production 5.0-liter EFI fuel rail and 5.0-liter sensors and wiring harness.*

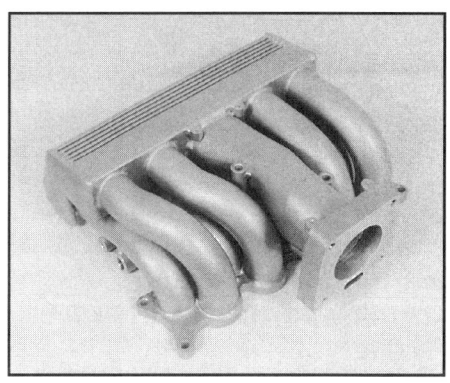

*This is the upper manifold section, **part number M-9524-A51** that is used in the 5.0-liter of 5.8-liter Ford EFI system. Features generous 1.65" diameter runners and 2.75" throttle opening to promote free breathing and a big increase in horsepower, according to the folks at SVO.*

This 900-CFM, four-barrel competition digital system features microprocessor based engine management to analyze many engine factors in a matter of milli-seconds. A true speed density system which measures engine load. An IBM compatible PC is required for initial start-up and fine tuning of this system.

Fuel Pumps

A vital component in the whole process of induction and fuel delivery is the fuel pump. Depending upon how far upscale you decide to go in the induction department, it may be

Induction System **45**

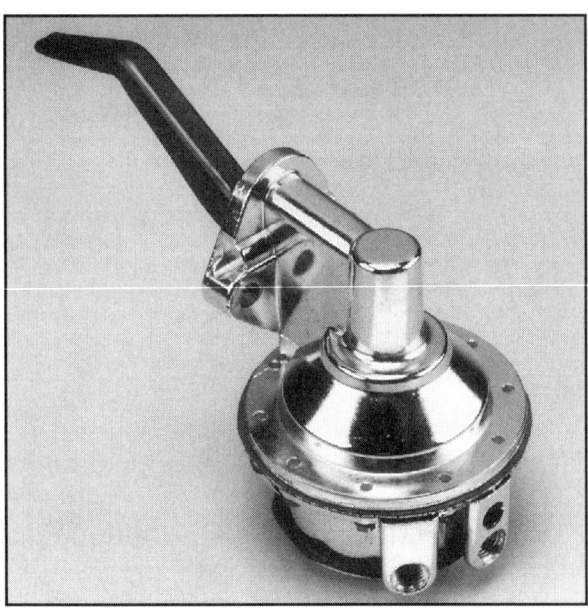

Holley mechanical fuel pump #12-833 is designed for installation on big-block Ford engines, and boasts a flow rate of 80 gallons per hour at 7.5 psi shutoff pressure. An adjustable housing permits rotation of the fuel inlet and outlet fittings, which comes in handy when space is at a premium.

If you need an electric fuel pump, this one from Holley (part number 12-801) free-flows 97 gallons per hour, and flows 67 gallons per hour at 5 psi. Not recommended for use with fuel injection systems.

necessary to upgrade the fuel pump, in order to be able to keep pace with the increased demand for fuel. An engine, operating at wide open throttle requires approximately half a pound of gasoline every hour per horsepower. If you're running a 300-horsepower engine at wide open throttle, it will require 150 pounds of fuel per hour. Gasoline weighs approximately 6 pounds per gallon, so under those conditions approximately 25 gallons per hour would be consumed.

In the Ford Motorsports SVO Performance Equipment catalog, the following mechanical fuel pumps are listed:

Part number M-9350-C302 — This is the standard-duty mechanical fuel pump with a 6 psi rating. Intended for use on small-block Ford V8 engines from 221-cid through 351-cid.

Part number M-9350-D302 — This is the heavy-duty high-output race version of the mechanical fuel pump that is used for NASCAR and TransAm competition. It has a 7.5 psi rating, and is intended for use on small-block Ford V8 engines from 221-cid through 351-cid.

Part number M-9350-B390 — This is the standard-duty mechanical fuel pump with a 6 psi rating. Intended for use on Ford V8 engines from 352-cid through 428-cid.

Part number M-9350-C111 — This is the heavy-duty electric race fuel pump with a 7 psi, 100 gallon-per-hour rating. Features include noise dampening device, and a positive displacement rotary vane design for non-pulsing fuel delivery.

Naturally, Holley, Edelbrock, Bosch, and several other aftermarket manufacturers carry their own line of fuel pumps that are designed to satisfy the thirst of their carburetors or fuel injection systems.

Edelbrock offers their Victor Series Racing fuel pump for small-block applications, but it is not legal for use on pollution controlled vehicles. **Part number 1715** is for the Ford small-block V8, 289 to 351 Windsor. This pump is designed for applications that demand a high volume of fuel delivery, and is rated at 130 gallons per hour, and 10 to 13 psi. It can be used with both gasoline and alcohol fuels.

Edelbrock's Performer Series Street fuel pump does not carry the restriction regarding pollution controlled vehicles, and has a flow capacity of 110 gallons per hour and a fuel pressure of 6 psi. This pump is designed for street applications, and is for gasoline or mixed fuels only. **Part number 1725** is the small-block pump for 289 to 351 Windsor engines, and **part number 1726** is for the 429 to 460 V8.

Holley Street Performance mechanical fuel pumps are not legal

Edelbrock's Victor Series Racing fuel pump, part number 1715, is for the Ford small-block V8, 289 to 351 Windsor. This pump is designed for applications that demand a high volume of fuel delivery, and is rated at 130 gallons per hour, and 10 to 13 psi. It can be used with both gasoline and alcohol fuels.

for sale or use in California on any pollution controlled vehicles. Flow rate is up to 80 gallons per hour at 7.5 psi shutoff pressure. An adjustable lower housing permits 360-degree rotation of fuel inlet and outlet fittings. **Part number 12-832** is for 1955 to 1970 Ford 292-cid, 352-cid, 390-cid, 406-cid, 427-cid and 428-cid V8 applications. **Part number 12-833** is for 221-cid, 260-cid, 289-cid, 302-cid, and 351W engines. **Part number 12-854** is for 1970 through 1975 351C, 351M, and 400-cid V8 engines. And **part number 12-860** is for 429-cid, and 460-cid V8 engines.

Holley also has an electric fuel pump (**part number 12-801**) that free flows 97 gallons per hour and flows 67 gallons per hour at 5 psi. Pressure is pre-set at 7 psi. Use of a safety shut-off switch (#12-810) is strongly recommended, and the pump is not recommended for use with fuel injection systems.

Holley's Competition fuel pump line includes an electric unit (**part number 12-802**) that free flows 110 gallons per hour, and moves 90 gallons per hour at 9 psi. The pump is pre-set at 14 psi. Use of a safety shut-off switch (#12-810) is strongly recommended, and the pump is not recommended for use with fuel injection systems.

Competition Mechanical fuel pumps free flow 110 gallons per hour and have shutoff pressure of from 6.5 psi to 8 psi. **Part number 12-289** is for 289-cid, 302-cid, and 351W V8 applications, while **part number 12-460** is for 429-cid and 460-cid big-block applications. None of these units are legal for use in California on pollution controlled vehicles.

Holley's Pro-Series fuel pumps free flow 130 gallons per hour and are pre-set at 7.5 to 9 psi shutoff pressure. **Part number 12-289-2** is for use on small-block V8 applications, and **part number 12-460-2** is for big-block engines. In this series, there are two electric pumps, **part number 12-705** is rated at 160 gallons per hour free flow, and is pre-set at 15 psi, and **part number 12-706** is rated to free flow 250 gallons per hour and is pre-set at 15 psi. This last pump is not intended for continuous use. None of the fuel pumps in the Pro-Series are legal for use on pollution controlled vehicles in California.

Whether you decide on single or multiple carburetion, or electronic fuel injection, will depend to a great degree upon engine size and the internal components that were chosen. Naturally, the other part of the decision-making formula is the type of driving that will be done.

But no matter which way you go, a properly designed induction system will deliver the right amount of air/fuel mixture at the right time and in all the right places, resulting in optimum performance.

As with all other aspects of building a performance truck, it isn't as simple as just bolting the biggest carburetor on the tallest manifold, and feeding the system with the most powerful pump. It is much more complex than that. And it is well worth the effort to make sure this part of the performance package is designed and set up properly.

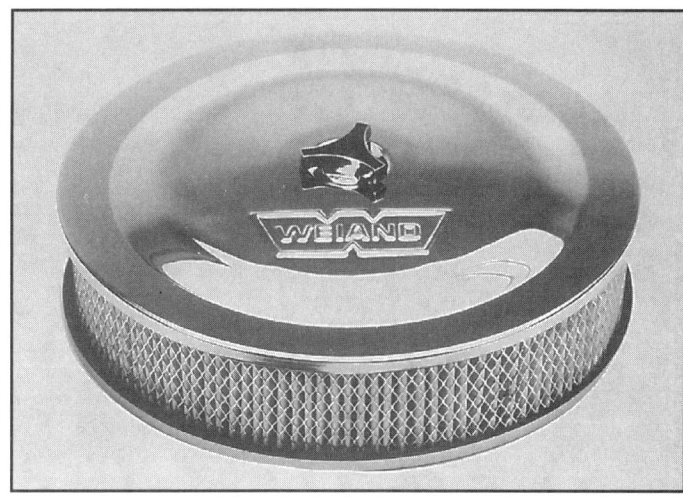

A standard paper element air filter is good enough for many street applications. They are inexpensive and readily available at every discount department store. For a custom touch, there are aftermarket air filter housings that brighten up the underhood area, such as this chrome unit from Weiand.

The unique pleated design of these filters indicate that they are oiled gauze air filters from K&N, a product that is highly favored among off-roaders. The B&M filter housing that holds these K&N filters is beautiful and distinctive, a nice addition to the engine compartment of any truck.

Performance Modifying Ford Trucks

Turbocharging vs. Supercharging

There are only so many ways to make an engine produce more horsepower and torque. You can either make the engine bigger, or you can make it pump more air/fuel mixture. Stepping away from the "bigger engine" question for a moment, let's take a look at methods for pumping more air/fuel mixture through the engine. An engine is basically just a big air pump. Air comes in, goes through the engine, and goes out the tailpipe. In order to keep the engine turning, the air is mixed with a specific amount of fuel, and that mixture is burned in the combustion chamber. When combustion takes place at just the right time, the piston is forced down in the cylinder, and during it's downward travel the connecting rod turns the crankshaft. When the piston comes back up, exhaust gasses (spent air/fuel mixture) are expelled. So, the engine is just a big air pump that makes functional use of the air while it's inside.

On its own, the engine has to suck air in. That's called natural aspiration. The engine simply inhales as a result of vacuum pressure created by the downward movement of pistons inside cylinders during the intake cycle. Restricting an engine's ability to inhale reduces efficiency and power production. The harder the engine has to work to get air in, the less power you end up with. The easier you make it for the engine to have an abundant supply of air, the more power the engine can produce.

It follows that if you can figure out how to force more air/fuel mixture through the system, you can get more work out of the engine. Up to a point, this works, but there are limits to how far you can go with forced induction before you run up against barriers imposed by the physical constraints of the engine. The two methods commonly used to force more air into an engine are turbocharging and supercharging. Under a broad umbrella, both of these systems can be referred to as blowers, and both

48   Performance Modifying Ford Trucks

methods can be referred to as blowing the engine.

The act of forcing more air through the intake results in "boost" to the air charge. Boost is nothing more than the amount of increased air-charge pressure that is created by a blower. Boost is measured in pounds per square inch (psi), and in a broad general statement would be that the more boost you have, the more horsepower you can make.

Naturally, there are limits to the amount of boost you can use while still keeping the engine alive. One of the most important concerns related to boost is the engine's initial compression ratio. For street performance applications, in which the truck will be running on 92 octane pump gas, the initial compression ratio should be about 8.5:1 and the boost pressure should remain at or below 7 psi. If you're interested in running a blower that makes between 7 and 9 psi of boost pressure, the engine's initial compression ratio should be limited to about 8.0:1.

It is possible to have a blown engine that is very streetable, and yet will produce enormous amounts of horsepower increase. Generally speaking, you can figure on about a 7% increase in horsepower production for every pound of boost pressure created by the blower. Using that calculation, a blower that produces 7 psi of boost pressure will increase power by nearly 50%. And still, the truck would be very streetable, if everything is done right.

Both turbocharging and supercharging have their strong supporters and equally vocal critics. This is because there are significant differences between turbocharging and supercharging, and there are performance enthusiasts on both sides of the issue who believe that their chosen method is superior to the other.

Turbocharging

Popular on diesel engines used in pickup trucks, motorhomes, and 18-wheelers, as well as on small gasoline engines used in compact cars, turbochargers have proven themselves to be very effective at increasing horsepower and torque. Some diesel mechanics and operators believe that a diesel engine isn't complete unless it has a turbocharger on it, and the increase in performance seems to prove their point. In before-and-after turbo tests of diesel-powered trucks, I have come to believe that no diesel engine should be without a turbocharger. Not only does turbocharging increase power dramatically over a naturally aspirated engine, but the black smoke problem tends to disappear as well.

Gasoline engines, however, are another story. While small gas engines, such as those used compact cars, commonly benefit from factory turbocharging, big V8 gas engines have not been prime candidates for turbocharging. Why is this the case? Although turbochargers can be perfectly suited to V8 engines, as was proven by Gale Banks and his twin turbo Firebird that ran at the Bonneville Salt Flats a few years ago, typically, owners of trucks with V8 engines tend to think in terms of supercharging, rather than turbocharging for a couple of reasons. One undeniable reason is that superchargers are more visible at the drag races, bolted atop fire-breathing V8 engines, so performance-oriented truck owners naturally tend to think of a supercharger as belonging on a V8 engine. Other reasons for shunning turbochargers include concern about excessive heat and a distaste for turbo lag.

Turbos are driven by extremely hot exhaust gasses. A turbine is positioned in the flow of exhaust, and the pressure of that flow spins the turbine. A shaft connects the turbine to an impeller that serves as an air compressor to force additional air into the intake system. This approach is seen by some as strong evidence that turbochargers are superior to superchargers. The claim being that because the turbine is being turned by exhaust gasses which are a natural byproduct of operating the engine, running a turbo is essentially "free" horsepower. However, nothing at the lunch counter is entirely free. The turbine causes a certain amount of exhaust backpressure, which diminishes optimum performance. Yes, you get more than you pay, but the part about "free" horsepower doesn't ring entirely true. Another problem arises from heat transfer from the turbine, through the connecting shaft to the impeller, and from there into the intake system. Rather than allowing the exhaust system to rid the engine and engine compartment of heat, a turbocharger recycles some of the heat through the intake system. The combination of heat and backpres-

B&M kits come complete with all the necessary components and hardware for a clean installation.

sure are problems that turbocharger manufacturers have sought to overcome for years. And they have succeeded, to a point, by using various turbine designs to reduce backpressure, and intercoolers to remove some of the excess heat. Aftermarket manufacturers have also come up with special heat shielding materials that can be used to protect adjacent engine components.

The heat issue becomes important when you realize that the turbine and impeller are extremely hot and can be spinning at 20,000 RPM when you pull into your driveway and shut the engine down. But just because the engine stops running and oil stops flowing, that doesn't mean the turbine stops spinning. Actually, it takes some time for the turbine and impeller to come to rest, and during that spin-down time, there is no oil being delivered to the turbocharger bearing surfaces. What oil is there quickly cooks. One mechanic I know described it as, "the oil turns to coal." As might be expected, this is not good for the engine oil (which is used to lubricate the turbocharger) nor for the turbo bearings. For this reason, owners of turbocharged vehicles are instructed to let the engine idle-down for several minutes after running before turning it off, to give the turbo a chance to slow down and cool off under the influence of a continuous fresh flow of oil. Frequent engine oil and filter changes are also recommended, as well as use of synthetic oil specified for use in turbocharged engines. Another approach to the oil problem is installation of an electrical after-oiler that continues to pump oil through the engine after the ignition has been shut off. There are a few of these on the market.

Turbo lag is perhaps the most commonly perceived drawback. In order for the turbocharger to function, it depends upon a strong flow of exhaust gasses to turn the turbine. But until the engine is up and running at a fairly high RPM, there isn't enough flow in the exhaust system to activate the turbo. You don't enjoy the benefits of a turbocharger off idle, so there is a lag time between tromping the accelerator and feeling the

Performance Modifying Ford Trucks

B&M Superchargers For Small-Block Ford Engines

BLOWER PART #	UPPER PULLEY PART #	ENGINE SIZE	BOOST PRESSURE
90675	90721	289 CID	4-5 PSI
90675	90638	302 CID	4-5 PSI
90675	90638	289 CID	6-7 PSI
90675	90537	302 CID	6-7 PSI
90675	90537	289 CID	8-9 PSI
90675	90536	302 CID	8-9 PSI
90675	90536	289 CID	10-11 PSI
90675	90538	302 CID	10-11 PSI

To adapt 351 engines, use belt number 91071 and optional kit.

With the hood shut, one would never know this engine had a B&M blower installed, because the unit tucks neatly below the air filter housing.

turbocharger come to life. This is known as turbo lag.

Engineering a turbocharger for use on any engine is critical. Overboost, and you can ruin the engine. Ideally, a vehicle on which a turbocharger is to be installed will undergo a comprehensive approach to this performance upgrade, incorporating the right camshaft profile, waste gate management and exhaust system design to interface with the intended boost pressure, and utilizing high technology electronic ignition system and fuel management components to make sure everything happens at the right time and in the right amount.

Supercharging

On the other side of the street, there is supercharging, which has been popular and highly visible on performance vehicles at the drag races for decades. Superchargers are essentially belt-driven air compressors, so from the moment the engine starts to run, the supercharger comes to life. A supercharged vehicle can jump straight up and run from the get-go, without having to wait for the engine to produce enough of something else (like exhaust flow) to make it work. With some superchargers, simply swapping among a variety of drive pulleys allows the owner to customize the blower configuration to produce maximum boost pressure at low RPM or high RPM levels to match the type of driving most often done.

Because superchargers are in no way related to hot exhaust gasses, they deliver basically "room temperature" air to the intake. Except for relatively minor air temperature increase caused by compression, whatever the air temperature is outside, that will be the air temperature inside. Air density is directly affected by heat. The cooler the air, the more dense it is. And dense air makes more horsepower than thin air. So, keeping the intake air cool is important to performance gain.

Of course, there is no free lunch. Superchargers are driven by a belt that derives its power from the crank-

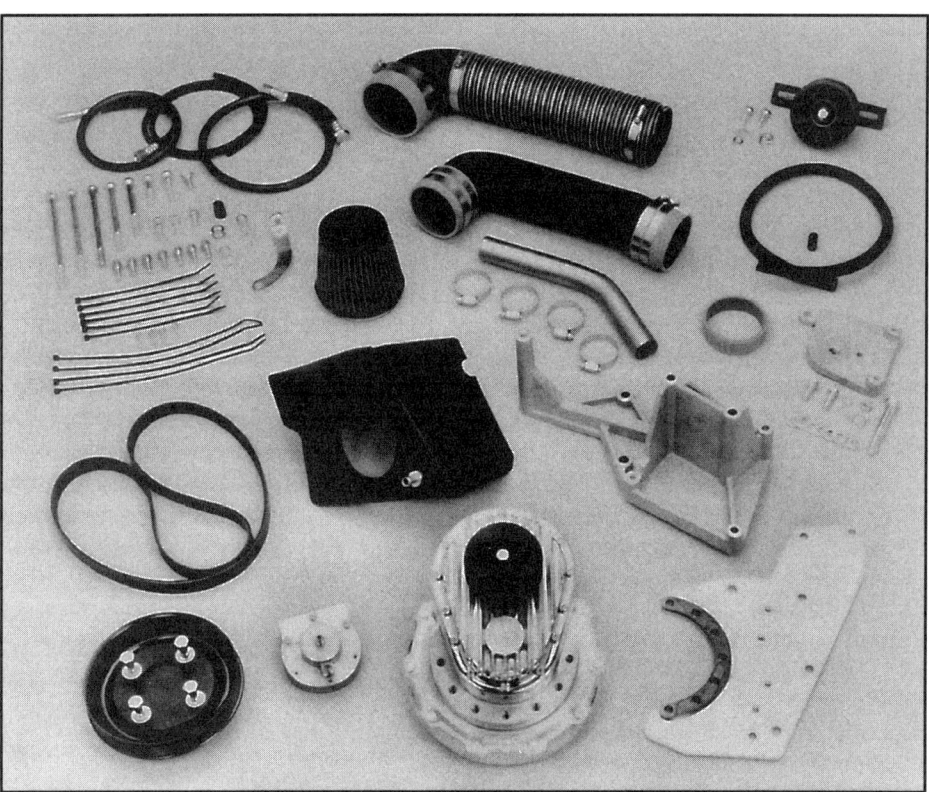

Direct from the Ford Motorsports SVO factory is this 6-psi supercharger that is designed for installation on 1987 through 1995 Ford truck small-block V8 engines. Ford advertises up to a 35% increase in horsepower over production engines. The unit features an internal belt drive that operates very quietly. No lubrication is necessary, and the kit is a simple bolt-on.

shaft. This means that some horsepower and torque are borrowed from the engine to turn the blower. Undeniably, you get more than you pay, but critics of supercharging point to this as a cost that must be paid in order to enjoy the benefits of the blower. Proponents of supercharging just call this an investment that delivers an exceptionally high return.

Available through the Ford Motorsports SVO Performance Equipment catalog is a factory centrifugal supercharger kit that is designed especially for installation on small-block Ford truck engines. Both of the kits listed here feature the quiet operation of an internal belt drive system, aerospace ceramic bearings that require no lubrication, simple bolt-on installation, and a claimed 35 percent increase in power over non-supercharged production engines. Ford says that after installation, daily drivability is unaffected and the truck will operate as smoothly and reliably as it did before installation. Because there is no need to plumb the supercharger to the engine's oil system, installation is vastly simplified, and there is no heat transfer to the engine oil. this results in cooler supercharger temperatures, greater power production and longer life. The unit has an impeller with curved-tip blades, which Ford says produces more power than a straight blade impeller. Everything is included for installation, so there is nothing else to buy, with the exception of a 110 liter/hr electric fuel pump that is recommended. The SVO supercharger fits cleanly beneath the hood without the need for modifications, and perhaps best of all, this supercharger is street legal in all 50 states.

Part number M-6066-T50 is designed for use on 1987 and later 5.0-liter and 5.8-liter Ford truck and full-size Bronco applications, and offers 6 psi of boost pressure.

Part number M-6066-T51 is for 1993 and later 5.8-liter Lightning applications and produces 6 psi of boost pressure.

A Roots-type supercharger has the familiar blower housing that you're used to seeing as the crowning feature on top-fuel dragster engines. Inside the housing are rotors that capture and compress the air, then force it into the engine, creating boost pressure.

Of course, some of these units are overkill for everyday truck use, but there are Roots-type blowers available for street, strip and off-road use. Companies like B&M manufacture Roots-type blowers for many Ford light truck applications. And in defence of the Roots-type blowers, B&M has this to say: "It would be a mistake to compare Roots vs. centrifugal boost figures when determining the engine's anticipated horsepower and torque output. Eight pounds of boost from a B&M Roots-type blower is equal performance-wise to 12 lbs. of boost from a centrifugal blower. Additionally, a Roots blower has a very flat and wide torque curve. Unlike a centrifugal unit which produces power only at higher rpm's (above 3000), the B&M Roots units begin producing additional horsepower and torque at 1500 RPM."

We will focus our discussion on the 50-state legal superchargers that are most appropriate for moderately high-performance street, strip and off-road use. Boost pressure is the major deciding factor that separates a streetable blower from a pure race unit.

Boost pressure is a function of three factors: engine size, blower size, and the speed the blower is driven in relation to engine RPM. A big blower will develop more boost pressure than a small blower, if they are both installed on the same size engine and both engines are turning the same RPM. Blower pulley size controls how fast the blower will turn at any given engine RPM, so boost pressure produced by a particular blower can be increased or decreased by selecting different pulley sizes. This allows a blower to be optimized for various engine sizes and applications.

B&M offers their 144 Street Legal Powercharger for small-block Ford truck engines, delivering peak performance for engine displacements up to a maximum of 351 cid. Legal in all 50 states, this package features a unique offset input shaft that clears the front-mounted distributor. Blower displacement per revolution is 144 cid, and the boost pressure can be altered by swapping pulleys to supply pressures ranging from approximately 4 psi to 11 psi.

Another type of supercharger is centrifugal in design. Paxton has long been known for their centrifugal superchargers, and they offer two models, one designed mainly for street use, and the other for racing. The SN 93 (non-race) version of the Paxton puts out between 8 to 10 psi of boost. This blower can be installed on a stock engine, as long as the engine is in reasonably good condition. Paxton offers kits that are essentially bolt-on units, requiring no modifications to the engine for installation. They are emissions legal in all 50 states, compatible with stock camshaft profiles, stock engine components, and stock transmissions.

Paxton also offers their VR-4 supercharger, which is a race version. It pumps out higher boost pressures (12 to 17 psi), and does require significant engine modification to withstand the higher boost pressures. Both the SN 93 and VR-4 superchargers are internally-lubricated

Performance Modifying Ford Trucks

Paxton Superchargers For Ford Trucks

YEAR	APPLICATION	PAXTON PART #'s SN 93	VR-4
1987-'93	302 with EFI	1001904	1001904-1
1987-'93	351 with EFI	1001901	1001901-1
1988-'93	351 Lightning	1001903	1001903-1
1994-'95	351 Lightning	1001905	1001905-1
1988-'95	460 with EFI	1102000	1102000-1

Legal in all 50 states, Paxton superchargers are designed to fit neatly in the engine compartment, requiring no modifications to the truck body. Available in VR-4 (race) and SN 93 (street) models, both are internally lubricated with automatic transmission fluid. Model SN 93 is intended for installation on basically stock engines.

(using a quart of type F automatic transmission fluid for lubrication), and are designed to fit compactly under the hood with no body modification necessary to make room for the blower and a scoop. These units are quiet and virtually invisible to outside observers, so they don't announce that the vehicle is blown. So, if you're looking for that "blown truck" appearance, the Paxton won't deliver. But if you're looking for blown truck performance without the obvious dragstrip appearance, the Paxton will do the job.

Vortech Engineering, Inc. has developed a line of centrifugal superchargers for use on full-size Ford trucks with V8 engines. According to the company, these units are easy to install, requiring no modification to the stock engine, and they are street legal in all 50 states. Advertising torque and horsepower gains of between 35% and 45%, the Vortech system includes not only the blower but, among other features, a supplementary fuel injection computer system that enables the truck to take complete advantage of the increased output of the supercharger.

Building a Blown Engine

You might think that building a blown engine will entail a lot of exotic, high-performance stuff, but that's just not necessarily true. Everything depends upon what the engine will be used for. If you're building for the dragstrip, and you anticipate 8,000 RPM engine speeds, yes, you'll need to be thinking about exotic high-performance stuff. But if you're building an engine to be used mainly on the street, or for some friendly Saturday night stoplight drags, or for towing, or for off-road fun, you might already have the engine you need. A factory stock engine can work perfectly with a blower. But let's go over some basics.

Internal Components: If you're willing to live below 5000 RPM, you can get away with stock cast pistons and a stock camshaft. However, if you want to see just how high you can peg the tachometer needle, you should consider fully blueprinting the engine to get the tolerances right, balancing the crankshaft and piston assemblies, and swapping to forged pistons. To produce maximum horsepower at very high RPM, a more radical camshaft profile will also be necessary. It all depends upon what kind of driving is intended.

Performance Modifying Ford Trucks

Vortech Superchargers For Ford Trucks

YEAR	VEHICLE DESCRIPTION	VORTECH PART #'s
1987-'94	F-Series Pickups with 460-cid (satin)	4FB218-040
1987-'94	F-Series Pickups with 460-cid (polish)	4FB218-048
1987-'94	F-Series Pickups with 302-cid (satin)	4FE218-070
1987-'94	F-Series Pickups with 302-cid (polish)	4FE218-078
1987-'94	F-Series Pickups with 351-cid (satin)	4FC218-030
1987-'94	F-Series Pickups with 351-cid (polish)	4FC218-038

Vortech Engineering, Inc. has developed a number of different centrifugal superchargers that can be used in a variety of applications, including Ford truck V8 engines.

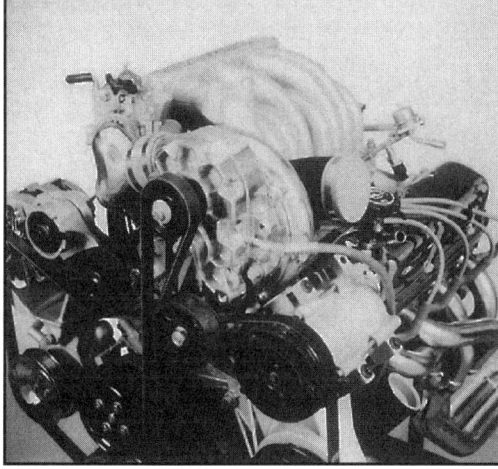

With a Vortech supercharger kit, this is what the final installation looks like on a Ford truck powered by a small-block V8 engine. This unit fits either the 302 or 351 V8 engine. Component design is such that there are no modifications necessary to the stock engine, and the entire unit fits nicely beneath the stock hood.

When it comes to the valve train, you need to consider that the internal combustion chamber temperatures are higher in a blown engine than they are in a naturally aspirated engine. To properly cool the valves, a 3-angle "street-type" valve grind is best. If porting work is to be done,

Turbocharging vs. Supercharging **53**

Vortech offers superchargers for both the small-block and big-block Ford engines. Here is one of their 460 Ford units, showing the compact design that will fit nicely beneath a truck hood without body modifications.

concentrate most of the effort on the exhaust ports. The blower can overcome minor deficiencies on the intake side, but opening up the exhaust side is very beneficial from a performance standpoint. If valve springs are replaced, install factory heavy duty springs, but if a new camshaft is installed, follow recommendations of the cam manufacturer.

Compression Ratio: In all cases, when an engine is blown — whether turbocharged or supercharged — the compression ratio is artificially increased. If the vehicle is to be streetable and easy to drive, the engine should not have high-compression to begin with. The higher the blower boost pressure, the lower the engine's original compression ratio should be. For streetable blown trucks, the optimum compression ratio is about 8.5:1.

Fuel: Part of the problem with a high compression ratio is trying to keep the engine from detonating during combustion. The higher the compression, the higher the fuel octane rating needs to be. Because compression ratios are effectively raised by boost pressure (see effective compression ratio chart), use gasoline with the highest possible octane rating, to help prevent engine-damaging detonation. The recommendation is to use a minimum of 92 octane or higher premium unleaded gasoline.

Fuel Delivery: One of the characteristics of a blown engine is that it wants more fuel and more air to work with. After all, that's the whole function of a blower, to deliver more fuel/air mixture to the engine. That being the case, it is necessary to ensure that there is adequate fuel delivery, beginning with the fuel pump and going right on through the carburetor. Generally, if you won't be operating the engine above 4000 RPM, you can stick with the factory original carburetor. But if you intend to run the engine at speeds higher than 4000 RPM, a larger carburetor may be necessary. If the fuel delivery system is inadequate, the air/fuel mixture may be too lean, which causes excessive heat and detonation in the combustion cycle, resulting in engine damage. But an oversupply of fuel may cause puddling and backfire. So, balance the system to make sure there is plenty of fuel available, but not so much that it overwhelms the system.

Ignition System: Most late-model factory electronic ignition systems will work well with a supercharger, but it may still be necessary to do some tweaking. One way to combat detonation is to retard the ignition timing. In some cases, it is necessary to install and use an ignition timing retardation system so you can dial back the spark advance, when necessary, to prevent detonation.

Cooling System: It is imperative that the engine cooling system perform well. If engine overheating occurs, detonation will follow, resulting in engine damage. If necessary, install a larger radiator, and make sure the fan and shroud are in good condition. A high-volume water pump will also help keep the coolant moving at a faster rate through the system.

Engine oil coolers also play a big part in keeping engine temperatures

Effective Compression Ratio

STATIC COMPRESSION RATIO	SUPERCHARGER BOOST PRESSURE					
	2 lbs.	4 lbs.	6 lbs.	8 lbs.	10 lbs.	12 lbs.
7.0:1	8.0	8.9	9.9	10.8	11.8	12.7
7.5:1	8.5	9.5	10.6	11.6	12.6	13.6
8.0:1	9.1	10.2	11.3	12.4	13.4	14.5
8.5:1	9.7	10.8	12.0	13.1	14.3	15.4
9.0:1	10.2	11.4	12.7	13.9	15.1	16.3
9.5:1	10.8	12.1	13.4	14.7	16.0	17.3

Supercharged or turbocharged engines need to have the ignition timing advance carefully controlled, to avoid detonation. The unit at left is the Boost Timing Master, MSD part number 5462, which retards timing as boost pressure increases, automatically protecting against detonation.

MSD part number 8680 (below) is an adjustable timing control module that permits the driver to dial in the desired ignition timing advance from the driver's seat, to prevent damage to the engine's internal components as a result of detonation.

under control. These units are easily installed in similar fashion to transmission coolers, are relatively inexpensive, and are good insurance against engine overheating.

Exhaust System: In order to take full advantage of a blower, the exhaust system must be as free-flowing as possible. It does no good to force more air/fuel mixture into the engine if the system can't get rid of the exhaust fast enough. For optimum performance, use large tube headers and low-restriction mufflers and catalytic converters.

Upgrading from natural aspiration

to a blower can add lots of horsepower and torque to your truck engine. But study the products carefully, and make sure you understand completely what the ramifications will be insofar as preliminary drivetrain preparation, maintenance, warranty, and performance expectations are concerned. Then make your choice.

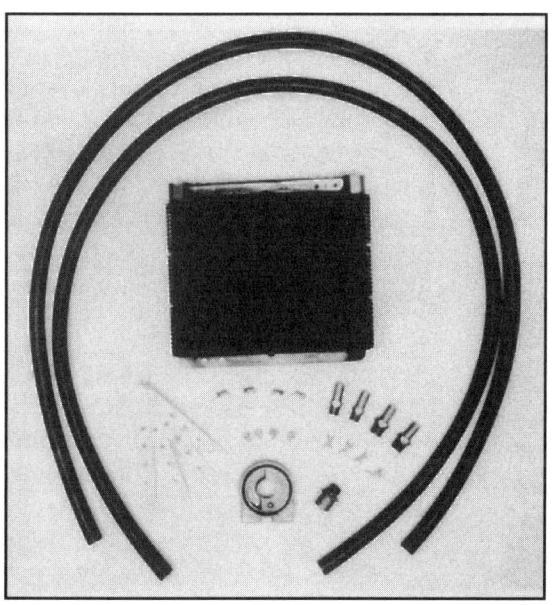

An engine oil cooler, like this unit from Ford SVO, will help keep engine temperatures under control. This is especially important for a blown engine.

Nitrous Oxide

If you've ever been to the dentist to have some painful work done, you may have already experienced "happy gas." Nitrous oxide of a medical quality is used as an anesthetic to make the patient oblivious to the jackhammer work going on in his mouth. Nitrous oxide also has another reputation as a "happy gas," but for very different reasons. When introduced in the induction system of a performance engine, nitrous oxide is instant horsepower. And it just naturally makes the driver happy.

Nitrous oxide (N2O) is two-parts nitrogen and one-part oxygen. Until ready for use, it resides in a high-pressure blue metal tank, which by itself is enough to raise eyebrows among those who know what the pretty blue bottle indicates. If you want people to know you're driving a performance truck, just having the blue bottle visible says a lot. If you want to surprise people, hide the bottle and let them find out the hard way.

This is horsepower on tap, ready when you need (or want) it, but not until. Nitrous oxide is not something

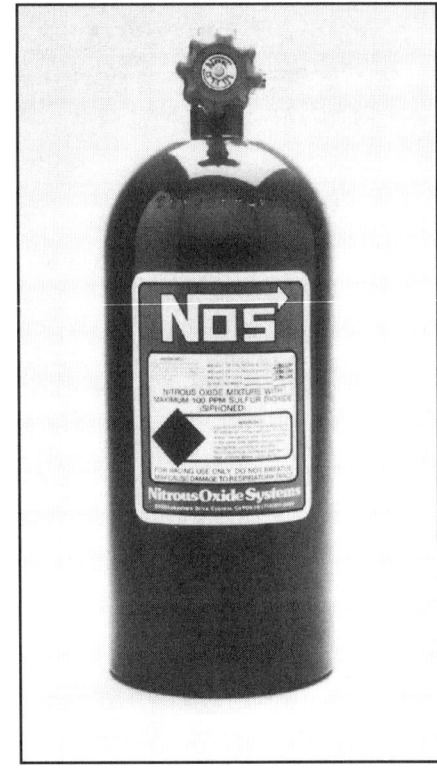

that is used all the time. The valve on the top of the bottle may be turned on all the time, but unless you press the hot button from your position in the driver's seat, the N2O stays in the bottle. It is only under wide-open throttle conditions that you want to use the nitrous, and then only in a short burst. Just long enough to put the other guy in the weeds.

There is justifiable concern about the potency of nitrous oxide, and how it can damage engine components. It's true that if the engine is not in top condition, and if the nitrous system calibration is maladjusted, and if the driver is a lunatic, nitrous oxide may spell the end of that engine. But, on the other hand, if the driver knows how to use the system properly, and if the engine is strong and the nitrous system well calibrated, there should be nothing but happiness.

Understanding how nitrous oxide works will help eliminate some of the potential problems. Under pressure, N2O is a liquid until it is released from its pressurized state by being injected into the induction system, whereupon it becomes a gas. As it changes from liquid to gas, nitrous oxide expands and chills to a minus 127 degrees F. Both the expansion and the cooling effect has an impact on what happens inside the combus-

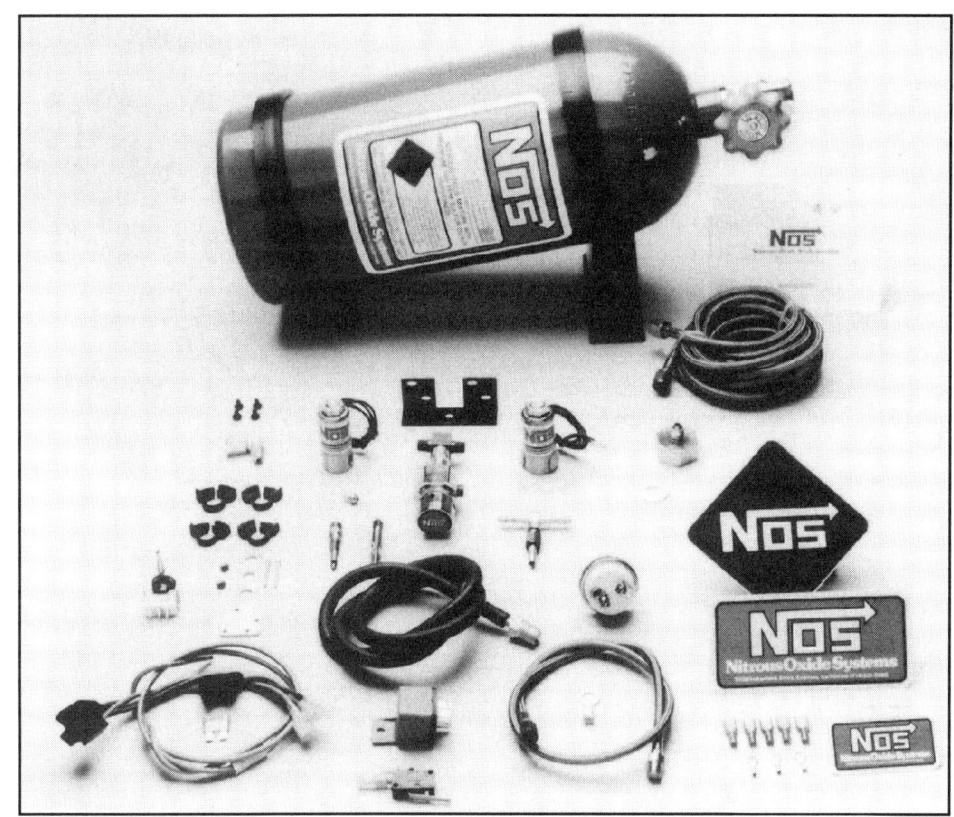

Nitrous Oxide Systems, Inc. can provide individual components or complete kits with everything included for a clean and easy installation. The famous blue bottle rests in a cradle that maintains the proper angle for optimum N2O delivery.

tion chamber. Cooler air is denser air, so the cooling (approximately 65 to 75 degrees F.) of the intake charge temperature increases the density of the atmosphere in the combustion chamber. This is kind of like a mini-boost of combustion chamber pressure. For every 10 degrees F. that the intake charge is cooled, 1% increase in horsepower can be expected. So, if you're running a 300-horsepower engine, and you succeed in reducing the intake charge temperature by 70 degrees F., the increase in performance would be approximately 21 horsepower.

But that's not all. As nitrous oxide reaches a temperature of 572 degrees F. during the compression stroke, the N2O molecule breaks down and releases extra oxygen. Additional oxygen in the combustion chamber allows the burning of additional fuel, creating more energy. Naturally, the injection of just the right amount of nitrous oxide at just the right time is the key to enjoying a boost in performance.

Nitrous Oxide Systems, Inc. is a leader in the manufacture of N2O injection systems and individual components for all kinds of applications, ranging from stock V6 engines to full-blown big-block professional competition engines. So, if what you have under the hood falls between those two extremes, you are a candidate for nitrous oxide injection.

The NOS Powershot is called the low-buck high-performance option, and is designed for use with carbureted V6 and V8 applications that are looking for horsepower increases in the 90 hp to 125 hp range. The Super Powershot kit is referred to by NOS as the adjustable high-performance option, because it includes a set of jets that permit adjusting the power output from 100 hp to 175 hp over and above what the engine already develops. The information on this system claims the jet change takes only seconds.

Then there's the Cheater System, designed for use with carbureted V8 engines that are in search of between 150 hp and 250 hp gain, again by using replaceable jets. For all of these systems, part numbers vary according to carburetor size and brand.

And then there's the NOS kit designed for use with factory fuel injected engines. Power increases with this kit range from 40 hp to 150 hp, depending upon applications and the replaceable jets.

Another system is available for those who really feel the need to get there in a hurry. The Pro Shot Fogger system is used by professional drag racers. The heart of this kit are the fogger nozzles that inject the fuel-laden "fog" of nitrous oxide directly into the combustion chamber. This is the most effective system, and is owner-adjustable to boost horsepower by 150 to 500 hp. Naturally, this system is intended for use on highly modified engines that are being pressed into duty for maximum acceleration effort. This is not the kit to install if you just want a quick ride to the grocery store.

There are some important accessories that can be installed to make the nitrous system easier to use. For example, if you want the system to become active automatically any time you reach a specified RPM, there is **part number 15879**, a NOS RPM switch which will accomplish just that between 2,000 RPM and 9,000 RPM. And, if you want to be able to open or shut the valve to the nitrous bottle without having to physically turn the valve, you can get the remote bottle valve (**part number 16058**), which will allow you to control the valve by using a dashboard-mounted switch. Another important accessory is the fuel pressure gauge, because the best performance is available when nitrous oxide pressure is in the 700 to 900 psi range.

Nitrous oxide can be injected into any size 2-cycle or 4-cycle engine, and will even work with fuels other than gasoline. The determining factor in the question of whether or not an engine can benefit from nitrous oxide injection is the strength of the engine components and their ability to withstand the increased energy and heat production.

Heat becomes a factor because the burning of additional fuel, which is allowed by the presence of additional oxygen released from the N2O molecule during combustion, can easily double the amount of energy released in a cylinder during the combustion cycle. The natural by-product of this additional energy is extra heat. So, although there is a lowering of the intake charge temperature, once combustion takes place a lot of extra heat is created.

This heat can be an enemy, a friend, or totally neutral. If heat production is not carefully controlled by proper calibration of the N2O injection system, internal engine damage can result. However, if the heat doesn't get out of control, no problems should arise from the use of nitrous oxide. In fact, if the engine is turbocharged, the extra heat can be captured and utilized by the exhaust system to help spool up the turbo more quickly, somewhat reducing turbo lag.

According to Nitrous Oxide Systems, Inc. most stock engines can take immediate advantage of an N2O injection system, without the need for expensive and extensive modifications. The key is that the engine must be in good condition to begin with, so it can endure the 25 to 140 horsepower gain resulting from using the system. High-compression engines are likely to be more sensitive to the injection of nitrous oxide. As the compression ratio increases, the engine becomes less tolerant of high levels of N2O in the air/fuel mixture. However, with careful attention to fuel quality (high octane is recommended) and proper tuning of the ignition timing, the nitrous system can be made to work very well.

One of the conditions created by injecting N2O into an engine is that the combustion temperatures and pressures are increased. This can lead to detonation, and engine component damage can result. For that reason, an adjustable ignition timing control module is recommended for use with nitrous systems. MSD offers several timing control devices, including the Adjustable Timing Control (**part number 8680**), which allows the driver to control ignition timing by way of a dash-mounted knob to compensate for altitude changes, fuel octane, and heavy loads. Timing can be advanced or retarded to prevent engine ping and to optimize performance and fuel economy.

Installation of an aftermarket PROM for the vehicle's computerized fuel and ignition management system is not recommended, because "performance" PROMs tend to use more aggressive ignition timing as a way of increasing performance, and when nitrous oxide is used, the ignition timing should actually be retarded to prevent detonation. How much retard to dial in is something that will have to be determined by road testing the engine and using the nitrous system. Beginning at the recommended total advance, the vehicle is driven, then the spark plugs are checked for signs of detonation, and the timing retarded in 2-degree increments until detonation no longer occurs.

In some applications, colder spark plugs may be used in conjunction with nitrous oxide, because the temperature of the electrode and ground strap will increase by 300 to 400 degrees F. when using N2O. Stepping down the spark plug temperature scale by two levels cooler than the factory specification is a good place to start. Then check the plugs after running with the nitrous system active, and determine if a change to another temperature range is needed.

So, there you have the basics. But before we leave this subject, perhaps we should talk about how to actually use the system.

If the system is calibrated properly, activating the system any time the engine is running faster than 2,500 RPM at wide-open throttle is safe. You can hold down the button as long as you want, if the engine and cooling system can stand the strain. But it's a good idea to keep an eye on engine temperature and not push things to the limit.

Keep in mind, also, that a 10-pound nitrous bottle will only last a little over a minute and a half total

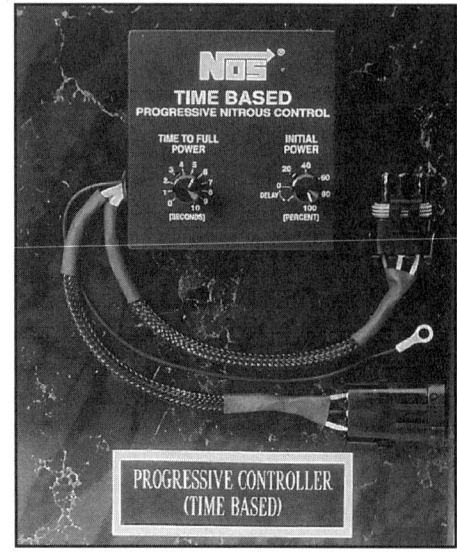

This time-based progressive controller from NOS allows the driver to select how quickly the nitrous system becomes active, and how active it will be. Driver-adjustable knobs control the progressive injection of N2O from 0 - 100%, and also control the time to full power from 0 - 10 seconds. This allows the driver to select the power level best suited to traction conditions, and also how quickly to ramp up to full power.

operating time when feeding a moderate V8 engine. A truly high-performance big-block can suck a bottle dry in a single run down the quarter mile! So, go easy with the happy gas button.

As with anything else, common sense should be employed when installing and using a nitrous oxide system. Don't go overboard. Bigger isn't necessarily better. Calibration of the system to the engine is vital, and then using the system with a certain amount of self discipline will help the engine live a long and happy life in the fast lane.

Performance Modifying Ford Trucks

Exhaust System

High-performance exhaust systems can make a lot of difference in engine efficiency. Because an engine is essentially just a big air pump, the exhaust system is an excellent place to begin looking for performance improvement. Borla makes long-lasting stainless steel systems, like the one pictured here, that feature free-flowing components.

A variety of approaches can be taken in the quest to increase a truck's performance. Some are more expensive than others. Some work better than others. But one good place to concentrate on performance improvement is in the exhaust system. Typically, modification of a stock exhaust system is a very effective yet relatively inexpensive area to achieve performance gains.

Although they are getting better in recent years, most factory stock exhaust systems are not designed to provide optimum performance. To the contrary, most factory systems are performance killers. This is due to the fact that stock systems are designed with one thing in mind — a budget approach to noise reduction. Unfortunately, a direct side-effect of low-cost noise reduction efforts is performance reduction.

Worse yet is the fact that stock exhaust systems can actually promote conditions that are potentially damaging to the engine. This may sound like a harsh indictment of Detroit, but evidence of its truth can be found in muffler shops all across America in the form of warped or cracked manifolds, exploded mufflers, dead catalytic converters, and distorted pipes. If you look to the engine shops, you'll hear stories about overheating engines and see further evidence in the form of cracked heads. Much of the blame for this can be laid at the feet of poor exhaust system design.

If you are in the process of building a performance engine and you don't upgrade the exhaust system at the same time, you will only increase the potential for problems. By upgrading the exhaust system, not only will

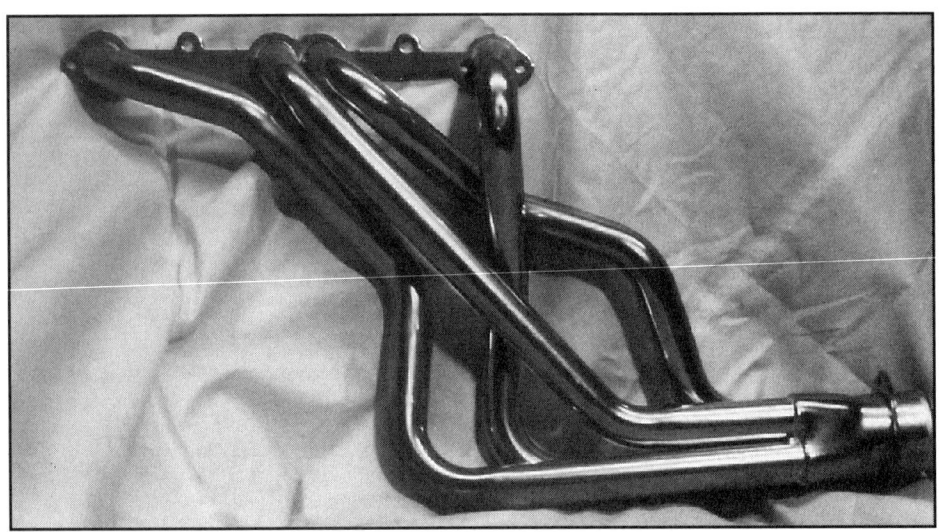

Exhaust headers provide individual exhaust tubes for each cylinder, and in a tuned header, each tube is engineered to be of equal length. This is intended to deliver the exhaust impulse from each cylinder to the collector at the bottom of the header in equal intervals. As the exhaust impulse exits the tube and enters the large collector chamber, it expands and provides a "scavenging" effect to help pull exhaust gasses from the other tubes. The tuned header pictured here is from Speed-O-Motive.

you enjoy increased performance, but one of the side benefits of these modifications is that your truck will probably live longer.

An engine is essentially an air pump. Air is drawn in through the intake system, it makes torque by means of the combustion process, then it is pumped out through the exhaust system. Restrictions to this flow of air result in the build-up of excessive heat and backpressure in the system, both of which reduce performance.

The major role of a properly designed exhaust system is to route the spent combustion gasses away from the combustion chamber and remove heat from the engine. From a performance standpoint, noise control is a secondary consideration. If nobody else lived on the planet, or if you could always drive where nobody cares about noise, you could do away with most of the exhaust system altogether. However, in real world applications, noise control is very important. So, the challenge is to design an exhaust system that presents the least amount of backpressure, disposes of the heat and fumes in the most efficient manner possible, and is reasonably quiet at the same time.

The majority of exhaust system problems are directly related to heat — the few exceptions being vibration, physical abuse, and simple rot caused by corrosion. Excessive backpressure is the primary cause of heat build-up in an exhaust system. The factory designs an exhaust system with high backpressure because restricting exhaust flow is the cheapest and easiest way to make the engine run smoothly and quietly. An example of how this is done is the typical factory muffler with a 2-1/2" inlet that is immediately reduced to a tube with a diameter of 2" or less inside the muffler. Of course, you would never know about this tube diameter reduction unless you cut a muffler apart to see what actually happens inside. A reduction like this creates heat — enough to actually melt the inside of a muffler when the system is under heavy load.

I have seen mufflers that still looked new on the outside, but have ballooned up until the seams burst. These are typical cases of overheated mufflers that have suffered internal meltdown, and become so choked that they eventually split open to relieve the pressure. Fortunately, exploding mufflers are the exception rather than the rule. Unfortunately, there are many other very common problems related to inadequate exhaust systems.

Noted performance exhaust guru Jerry Jardine showed me his collection of mufflers that he cut open to expose exactly what happens inside. Stock mufflers are commonly made with reductions of internal pipe diameter that severely restrict exhaust

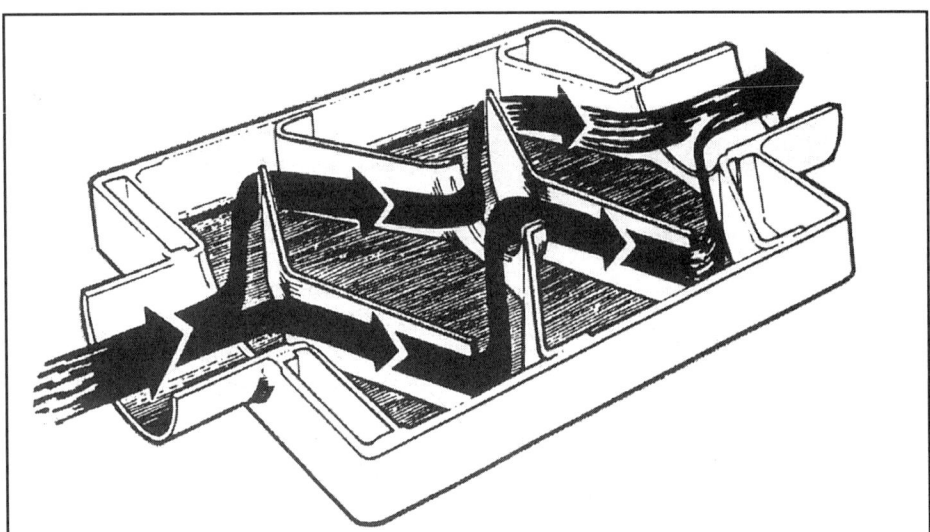

A free-flowing muffler is essential to an efficient exhaust system. One of the major problems with factory exhaust systems is that, in an effort to reduce noise, the mufflers are overly restrictive, thereby reducing performance. Installation of a more open system will allow the engine to breath more easily. Flowmaster manufactures mufflers that are noted for their free-flowing design. This illustration shows how the internal baffles are wedge shaped to control exhaust flow and noise, yet permit a high level of performance.

flow. Some manufacturers actually close off the tubes inside the muffler so there can be no flow of exhaust, except through small perforations in the walls of those internal tubes. As might be expected, this results in a quiet muffler, but it also creates tremendous backpressure. The bottom line is an over-heated and performance-killing piece of equipment. Mufflers like these cause many other exhaust system problems.

If the muffler or other exhaust components are excessively restrictive, heat will back up toward the engine rather than being channeled away as it should be. One of the expensive problems caused by excessive heat in the exhaust system is damage to the exhaust manifolds and the heads. The common manifestation of excessive heat build-up is that cast iron exhaust manifolds warp or crack. When an exhaust manifold warps, it can break the bolts that hold the manifold to the head. When this happens, the manifold will begin to act as a lever, being secured tightly in some places and loose in others. As the engine passes through normal cycles of heating and cooling, this unequal pressure and leverage can crack the cylinder head.

Solutions

The good news is that all of the problems mentioned above can be prevented by opening up the exhaust system all the way through, including through the muffler. Don't be fooled by the size or number of the inlet and outlet pipes on the muffler. It isn't what's on the outside of the muffler that counts — it's what's inside. Even though the exterior may look big and have large inlet and outlet pipes, the interior may be severely restricted.

For optimum performance and maximum life expectancy, the exhaust system needs to be upgraded as a whole, rather than just replacing a few individual parts. It makes little sense, for example, to install headers while retaining the same old restrictive muffler — or to install a great muffler while keeping the old, restrictive exhaust pipes. When you upgrade the system in search of per-

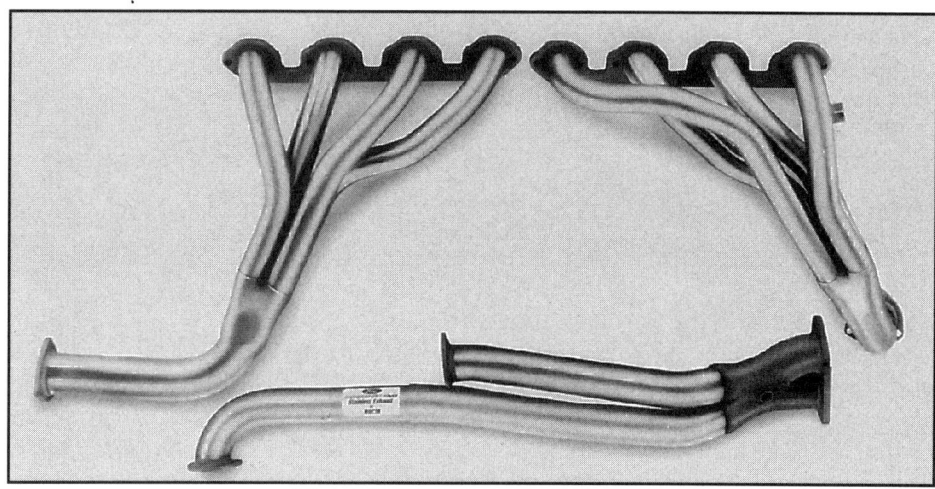

This T-304 stainless steel header system from Borla is designed for use on Ford F-Series trucks with 460-CID engines and 4-speed automatic transmissions from 1987 through 1995 model years. Because the system is designed so exhaust from both banks of the engine ultimately join in a single collector, this is not as efficient as a dual-exhaust system.

formance, do the whole job, all the way from the manifolds to the tailpipes.

Headers

One of the first things a person tends to think about when considering an upgrade to the exhaust system is a set of headers. They look neat. And with all those individual tubes, they must work better, right? The answer to that question is that it all depends upon the application. Odd

Edelbrock RPM Series mufflers feature the internal Tru-Flo core which utilizes equal length runners made from 409 perforated stainless steel. A special high-temperature ceramic material is packed between the inner and outer case and inner core. Exhaust flows through the runners without restriction, and the ceramic packing material quiets the exhaust note. The heavy-duty race muffler is designed especially for competition and heavy-duty applications. They feature a stainless steel wool wrap around the ceramic packing material for additional sound absorption.

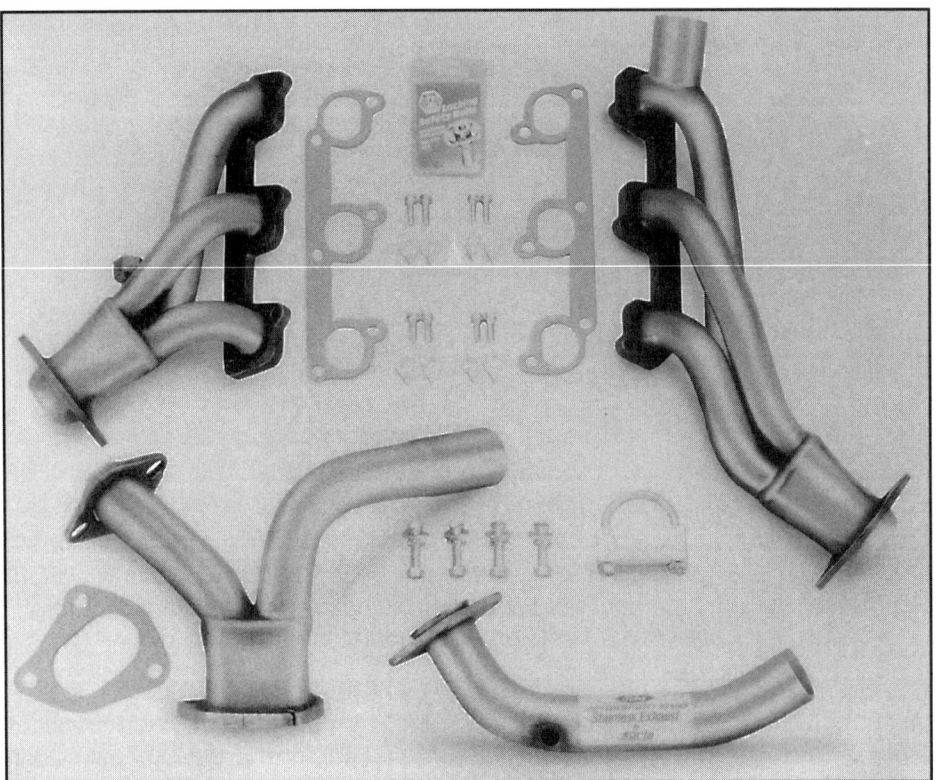

Borla's #17030 header system with EGR for Ford Explorer or Ranger with the 4.0-liter engine. Notice the smooth mandrel bends, which reduce exhaust flow restriction. Emission legal in all 50 states, Borla systems are made of aircraft quality T-304 stainless steel to resist corrosion.

as it may sound, for many applications, stock cast iron exhaust manifolds are just fine.

Headers are mandatory on true race engines that live above 5000 RPM. But think about it for a minute, how often does a street truck hit those heady RPM levels? And how important is it in the life of a street truck to be able to shave 3/10 of a second off the zero-to-sixty time? Now, if you intend to take that street truck to the drags, 3/10 of a second may be important, but if the truck will only be used for street performance, stock manifolds will do the job.

However, Detroit never made cast iron manifolds that look as nice as a set of chromed headers. And in the realm of hot street trucks, appearance ranks as high in importance as speed or elapsed time.

But to discover where the performance gains come from, let's take a look at how headers and stock manifolds function. Factory cast iron manifolds are designed so that exhaust gasses from all adjacent cylinders are routed into a single chamber immediately as they exit the combustion chamber. It's like people pouring out of four different elevators into a single hallway leading to a single door out of the building. It gets crowded, and there's a lot of jostling and people can't move very fast. The same applies to exhaust. As the manifold becomes crowded with gasses from all the cylinders trying to escape at once, turbulence and backpressure build up. This leads to greater heat in the engine, and less efficient breathing. All of which results in reduced performance.

At low engine speed, this is less a problem than at high engine speed, which is why headers are not so critical for street trucks as they are for high-performance race applications.

Headers, with their individual tubes, allow the exhaust gasses from each cylinder to have an unrestricted path away from the engine. This improves the engine's ability to breathe by reducing backpressure, turbulence and heat. If the headers are "tuned," the length of each tube is carefully designed to correlate with the lengths of the others. Because only one exhaust pulse is in the header system at a time, as that impulse reaches the collector it can create what is known as a "scavenging" effect. This is when one exhaust impulse actually creates a bit of a vacuum pressure in the other tubes, which helps draw out the exhaust impulse coming from adjacent cylinders. Rather than having backpressure, you end up with just the reverse, which improves performance.

The questions naturally arise — are large-diameter header tubes better than small-diameter tubes? Are long tubes better than short tubes? Answers to both of these questions are: yes and no. As in everything else related to building a high-performance engine, it all depends upon your particular application.

Let's discuss tube diameter first. As each exhaust impulse leaves the combustion chamber and enters the primary tube, a small-diameter tube will flow less volume, but the exhaust will flow faster. Until the engine reaches the RPM where exhaust volume is so great that larger diameter tubes are required, the small tube will scavenge better than a large tube.

If your engine will live mostly in the 1500 to 3500 RPM range, you want 1-1/2" to 1-5/8" tubes for a small-block, and 1-3/4" to 1-7/8" tubes for a big block. Even with a blower, nitrous oxide, and other radical modifications, small tube headers will probably be more than adequate. Small-tube headers don't begin to fade out in horsepower and torque until you exceed about 5500 RPM, so unless your intent is to do most of your driving at full throttle, you won't need to go to larger-diameter tubes.

The question of long-tube (tuned) vs. shorty style headers is, again, a question of application. Shorty headers are a great step up from stock manifolds, and they are fairly affordable. They won't deliver as much power as tuned headers, but the difficulty of designing a tuned header that will fit under the hood and around all the other stuff cluttering the engine compartment increases the price of tuned headers.

The trade-off may or may not be worth it. For all-out racing applications, the increased cost may be justified to gain the slight edge in performance. For street trucks, the extra cost of custom fitted headers would almost certainly is not be justifiable.

Pipes, Mufflers & Stuff

Installing headers alone is not enough. To realize optimum performance gains, it is necessary to take a holistic approach to the entire exhaust system.

Replace damaged pipes, or those with restrictions, making sure the new pipes are routed with as few bends as possible. Some exhaust pipes are intentionally dented or crushed to provide additional clearance where they run adjacent to the frame or over an axle. This deformity causes exhaust flow turbulence and restriction, which is a performance killer and increases heat retention in the system. Mandrel bends reduce turbulence and backpressure, so find a shop that can mandrel bend the pipes.

Popular these days are Cat Back systems, which consist of everything needed to replace all the components from the catalytic converter on back. Typically, these packages include a muffler with one inlet and dual outlets, to mimic dual exhaust. However, if you're looking for a true dual exhaust system, you will have to look elsewhere.

A complete dual exhaust system will deliver the best performance. This will eliminate the restriction created by a "Y" pipe at the junction of the left and right banks of a stock exhaust system. A trick used by truck manufacturers to make owners think they have dual exhaust is to run the exhaust pipes from both sides of the engine into a single catalytic converter and then into a single muffler that has two outlets. At the tailpipe, it may look like a dual exhaust system, but it isn't. A true dual exhaust system will have two of everything — head pipes, mufflers, catalytic converters, exhaust pipes and tail pipes.

To optimize a dual exhaust system, have a crossover pipe installed ahead of the muffler. This will equalize the pressure between the left and right sides, quiet the exhaust and tend to smooth out the engine. The crossover pipe should be of the same diameter as the head pipe, and, if you can arrange it with the installer, made of thicker wall tubing than that used in the rest of the system.

For maximum life expectancy, use components that are made of stainless steel. Of course, you don't want to use badly designed or poorly constructed components, even if they are made of stainless steel. Exhaust flow should be the first priority, followed closely by the choice of components that are made to last the longest. I would prefer to have a well-engineered muffler made of regular old steel, that a poorly designed one made of stainless.

Make sure the shop doing the installation uses flexible or slip-joint type hangers, to prevent component damage when the pipes heat up and expand. The worst thing is to use a piece of steel strap or angle iron welded to the frame and to the pipe as a hanger or bracket, because no movement will be permitted during expansion, and this can result in serious damage to the system.

Performance Improvement

So, how much performance improvement can you expect from upgrading your exhaust system? It all depends upon what you had to begin with and what you decide to end up with. But if you're moving up from a factory exhaust system, you can expect some performance gains. Extra horsepower is freed up as the engine breathes more easily.

This additional power can be used for more enthusiastic driving, or it may be translated into fuel economy — but not both. Generally, when people notice that the engine is performing better they use that power to go faster or to get away from the stoplight more quickly. When you use the extra power, you don't also get to enjoy better fuel economy at the same time. Let's not get greedy!

But regardless of how you define performance improvement, whether it's increased fuel economy, more towing power, higher top-end, or quicker off the line performance, switching to a free-flowing system will pay off in every respect. You and your truck will both be happier.

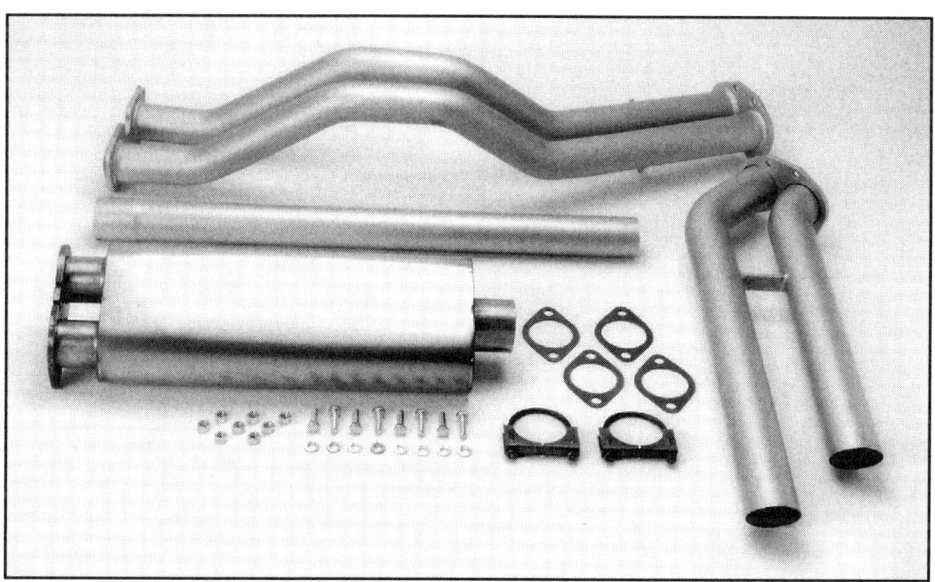

Edelbrock's RPM Series Cat Back exhaust system is a simple bolt-on replacement for all of the factory stock exhaust system components from the catalytic converter on back. The system includes an RPM Series muffler, pipes, and all the hardware necessary for the complete installation. Tubing is aluminized 16-gauge mild steel that is mandrel bent to reduce restriction to exhaust flow. This system is emissions legal in all 50 states.

Performance Modifying Ford Trucks

Ignition System

The purpose of the ignition system is to set fire to the entire charge of air/fuel mixture in the combustion chamber at exactly the right moment. The importance of accomplishing this task precisely is that if the entire charge of mixture is not ignited at exactly the right time, both power and economy suffer. Unburned fuel goes out the exhaust pipe and performance potential is lost.

There have been many factory and aftermarket "solutions" to the problem of trying to make sure all the air/fuel mixture gets ignited properly. Ford has developed reliable and efficient factory systems, and there is little need for anything other than a stock ignition for most street applications. However, if your truck has high-performance driving in its future, there are some ignition system upgrades that can make the sparks more meaningful to the air/fuel mixture.

Distributors

For 302-cid V8 applications, the Ford Motorsports SVO Performance

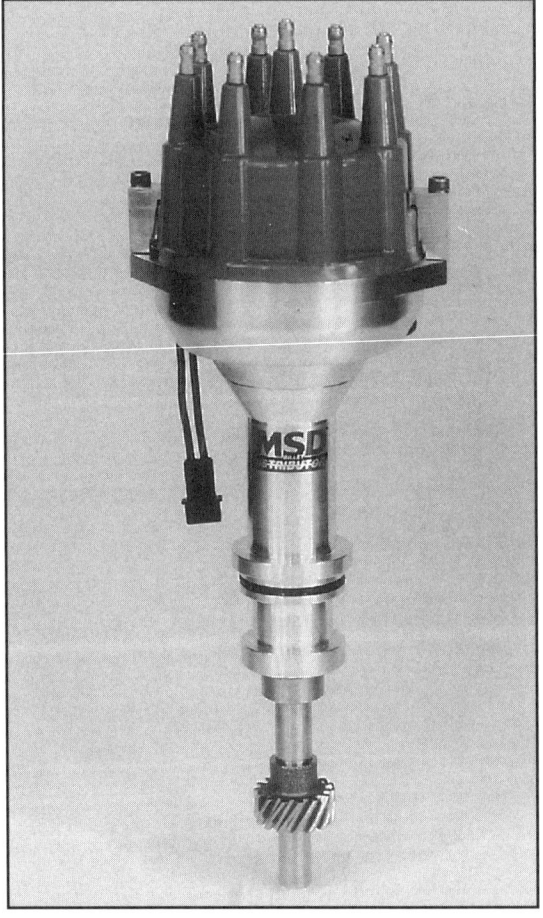

Equipment catalog lists an EEC-IV distributor kit, **part number M-12127-C302**, that includes a steel gear for use with a hydraulic roller camshaft, a distributor cap and ignition module.

Part number M-12127-A304 is a competition distributor assembly that has been prepared and calibrated for high RPM application. The shaft is plated, the weight pins strengthened and vacuum advance is locked out. It is not compatible with steel roller camshafts, and the gear must be changed for this distributor to be compatible with a steel camshaft.

A selection of distributor gears are available for varying applications. Cast iron gears are compatible with cast iron hydraulic or solid flat tapped camshafts. Steel gears are compatible with billet steel hydraulic roller tappet camshafts. And bronze gears can be used with either cast iron or billet steel camshafts, and are recommended by manufacturers of aftermarket billet steel, solid roller tappet camshafts. Bronze, being softer than steel or cast iron will wear more quickly than either of those other types of gears.

Part number M-12390-A is a

cast iron distributor gear for use with 289 to 302-cid V8 hydraulic flat tappet engines that are equipped with a point-type or Duraspark distributor.

Part number M-12390-B is a steel distributor gear intended for use with 302-cid V8 steel billet and production roller camshaft engines that are equipped with a point-type or Duraspark distributor.

Part number M-12390-C is a bronze distributor gear intended for use with 289 to 302-cid V8 engines that are equipped with a point-type or

Ignition Timing

MSD Pro-Billet Ford Distributor was designed for applications where distributor clearance is tight due to tunnel rams, blowers or exotic ignition setups.

For an engine to operate properly, ignition timing must be allowed to vary as RPM changes. For this reason, ignition systems employ three different stages of timing advance. Adjustable timing control units allow the driver to alter initial advance, distributor kits allow alteration of centrifugal advance, and adjustable vacuum advance kits permit modification of vacuum advance. Here are definitions of the three different types of ignition timing advance, and a description of total ignition advance.

Initial Advance

Initial timing is the amount of ignition advance that is necessary for the engine to be able to idle and run up to the RPM level at which the distributor's centrifugal advance begins to have an effect. Initial timing is set by rotating the distributor housing. Measuring initial timing is done by using a timing light aimed at the crankshaft damper and viewing the timing mark as the engine is running at idle speed. The timing light should be fired by impulses from the #1 spark plug cable, and the vacuum advance hose should be disconnected and sealed.

Centrifugal Advance

Centrifugal advance is controlled by springs and weights inside the distributor. As the distributor rotates, centrifugal force acts upon the rotating mass, and by adjusting weights and spring strength, the total amount and the rate of advance can be altered. Centrifugal advance is designed to match the ignition spark to the increasing engine speed, to ensure that the spark arrives at the combustion chamber at the precise moment for optimum performance.

Vacuum Advance

The vacuum portion of ignition advance is designed to match ignition spark to the engine load conditions. It is intended to govern ignition advance under part-throttle operation. At part-throttle, less air/fuel mixture is delivered to the combustion chambers, and more spark advance is needed to efficiently burn the mixture. For this reason, maximum vacuum advance occurs at closed throttle, and none occurs at wide-open throttle.

Total Ignition Advance

Total ignition advance is calculated by adding together all of the numbers from initial advance, centrifugal advance and vacuum advance.

Duraspark distributor.

Part number M-12390-D is a cast iron distributor gear intended for use with all 302-cid V8 hydraulic flat tappet engines that are equipped with EFI, and also all 351W engines.

Part number M-12390-E is a bronze distributor gear for use with all 302-cid V8 hydraulic flat or roller tappet engines that are equipped with EFI, and also all 351W engines.

Part number M-12390-F is a steel distributor gear for use with all 302 to 351W hydraulic roller tappet engines that are equipped with EFI.

Part number M-12390-G is a cast iron distributor gear intended for use with all 351C, 351M, 400, 429 and 460 engines.

Part number M-12390-H is a

bronze distributor gear intended for use with all 351C, 351M, 400, 429 and 460 engines.

Ignition Control Modules

The ignition control module (the magic box) is what commands the high-performance ignition system. The SVO catalog lists **part number M-12199-C301**, which is a self-supporting Extra Performance Ignition Module that replaces Ford Duraspark II units with "blue" or "yellow" wire strain relief. The unit fits most 1976 and later 4-cylinder, 6-cylinder and V8 engines, and provides increased spark energy over production Duraspark II modules and coils. It is built to endure the heat, shock and vibration requirements of high performance applications, and includes a built-in Rev Control. Three RPM limiter modules (6000, 7000, and 8000 RPM) are included. This control module must be used with coil **part number M-12029-A302**, and cannot be used in conjunction with electronic engine control (EEC) systems.

Part number M-12199-C302 is an Extra Performance Ignition Module that replaces the Ford Duraspark III unit with "brown" wire strain relief. It is built to meet the heat, shock and vibration requirements of high performance applications, and includes a built-in Rev Control. Three RPM limiter chips (6000, 7000 and 8000 RPM) are supplied. This unit must be used with coil **part number M12029-A302** and requires input from the EEC III module and cannot be used as a self-supporting ignition system.

The SVO catalog also lists an "Ultra" High Energy Capacitive Discharge "CD" Ignition System that consists of four components. The ignition control module is **part number M-12199-E351**, and is described as an "Ultra" high energy CID ignition module with rev control, for all-out racing applications. Three rev-limited chips (6000, 7000, and 8000 RPM) are supplied. This system provides improved capability to fire wet, fouled spark plugs over non-CD systems. Must be used with either coil **part number M-12029-A351** or coil **part number M-12029-E351** that are listed as part of this system.

Part number M-12029-A351 is a high energy oil-filled coil for CD ignition systems. This unit will accept the Ford "horseshoe" coil connector, and features low primary resistance and heavy-duty construction.

Part number M-12029-E351 is a high energy E-Core coil designed to produce maximum performance from the **M-12199-E351** ignition control module. This unit will accept the Ford E-Core coil connector, and features low primary resistance and heavy-duty construction.

Part number M-12071-B351 is a race-quality wiring harness that includes connectors and adequate wire length to install the ultra high energy CD ignition system, and permits direct plug-in installation of Ford Motorsports tachometers.

Mallory, Accel, MSD and others have developed a variety of performance systems that are ideal for installation on Ford engines. Just to mention two products that are especially applicable, there is the MSD 6AL (**part number 6420**) and MSD 6 BTM (**part number 6462**). Model 6AL is a capacitive discharge multiple spark unit with the added feature of an integral Soft Touch Rev Control circuit that protects the engine from over-revving. Plug-in modules for 3000, 6000, 7000 and 8000 RPM operation come with the unit, and other modules are available. The Soft Touch system monitors engine RPM, and when it reaches the predetermined limit set by the plug-in module, the system begins dropping the spark to some of the cylinders. On the next cycle, these same cylinders are fired

PROMs and Performance

PROMs (programmable read only memory) are computer chips that are designed to control such things as fuel metering rates and ignition timing. Modern trucks come from the factory with electronic fuel injection and electronic ignition systems that are controlled by factory PROMs. A factory PROM is admittedly calibrated to deliver good fuel economy and street performance, because the people who buy and use stock trucks are generally pretty well satisfied with the factory's definition of performance.

Factory PROMs are calibrated, not so much to control engine functions at wide open throttle, but to manage fuel and ignition performance during part-throttle operation, because this is where emission control restrictions are based by the federal government and state air pollution control agencies. For this reason, PROM replacement does not promise improved top-end performance. Any improvement derived from installing an aftermarket PROM will only affect part-throttle performance. In the process, the engine will be de-optimized from a fuel efficiency and emissions standpoint.

Installing aftermarket PROMS is essentially just trading one set of controls for another. Instead of relying on the factory calibration to determine what optimum performance is, you are substituting someone else's calibrations. Factory calibrations are based on precise data regarding the exact vehicle in question. An aftermarket PROM may or may not be so precisely focussed, but may deal more in generalities. The results may or may not be an improvement in performance.

On the other side of the coin are driver-adjustable fuel injection and driver-adjustable ignition curve systems. These allow the driver to change fuel metering and spark timing as conditions demand.

Supercharged or turbocharged engines, or those operating with nitrous oxide injection systems, need to have the ignition timing advance carefully controlled, to avoid detonation. This unit retards timing advance as boost pressure increases, thereby automatically protecting against detonation.

Timing control modules are important for use in conjunction with turbochargers, superchargers and nitrous oxide systems to minimize destructive detonation in the combustion chamber caused by the increased boost pressure. MSD offers several timing control devices, including **part number 5462** which is a Universal Boost Timing Master. This unit controls ignition timing according to the boost pressure, retarding timing as boost pressure increases. The only adjustment the driver needs to make is to match the amount of retard according to the boost pressure, which is done by using a dash-mounted knob.

Another unit is the Adjustable Timing Control, **part number 8680**, which allows the driver to control ignition timing via a dash-mounted knob to compensate for altitude changes, fuel octane, and heavy loads. Timing can be advanced or retarded to prevent engine ping and to optimize performance and fuel economy.

to prevent loading up with fuel. The whole process takes place smoothly, without roughness or backfires.

Model 6 BTM is designed with an integral Boost Timing Master circuit that progressively retards timing in relation with increased boost pressure from a blower. This effectively protects against the damaging effects of detonation in the combustion chambers. By electronically controlling the spark advance, a blown engine can operate on the threshold of detonation to produce maximum power and efficiency, without actually stepping over into dangerous detonation territory.

Timing Control Modules

Rotors

The Ford Motorsports SVO Performance Equipment catalog lists a V8 distributor cap and rotor replacement for all 1957 through 1993 distributors, except EEC. **Part number M-12106-A302** is a high performance replacement for high energy OEM rotor and cap in 1977 through 1993 V8 distributors. Installation on 1957 through 1977 distributors that had a small-diameter cap reduces the possibility of crossfire between terminals at high RPM.

Ford rotors that serve in Duraspark and other high energy ignition systems can suffer erosion, resulting in a short to ground through the rotor to the top of the distributor shaft. This will cause misfire, so the rotor should be inspected for evidence of arcing or heat damage, and replaced if necessary.

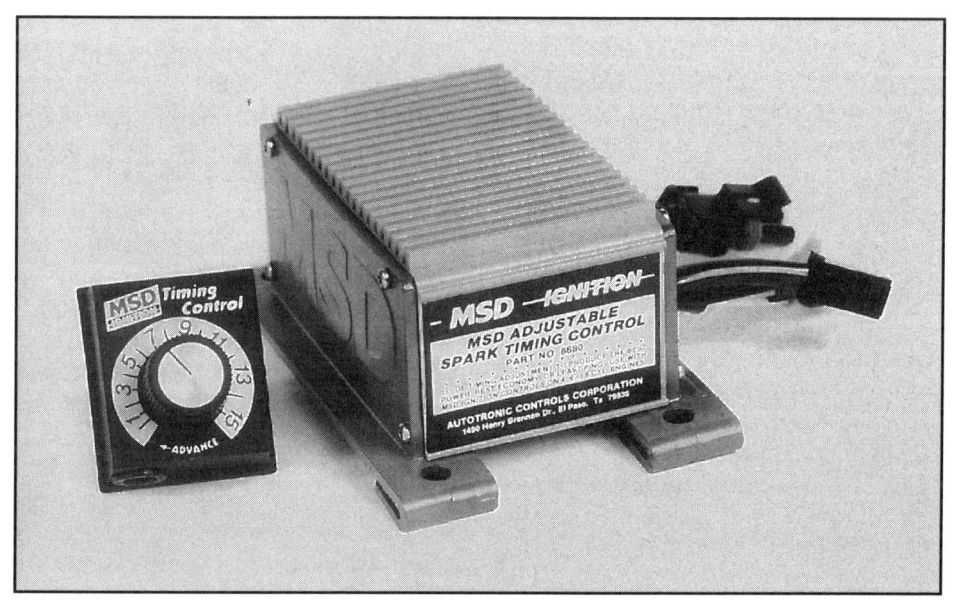

MSD part number 8680 is an adjustable timing control module that permits the driver to dial in the desired ignition timing advance from the driver's seat. This is especially useful when heavy loads, poor quality fuel, or high temperatures cause the engine to ping, requiring the timing to be retarded to prevent damage to the engine's internal components.

Spark Plug Cables

Spark plug cables must be able to carry and contain the electrical current from the distributor to the plugs,

Ignition System

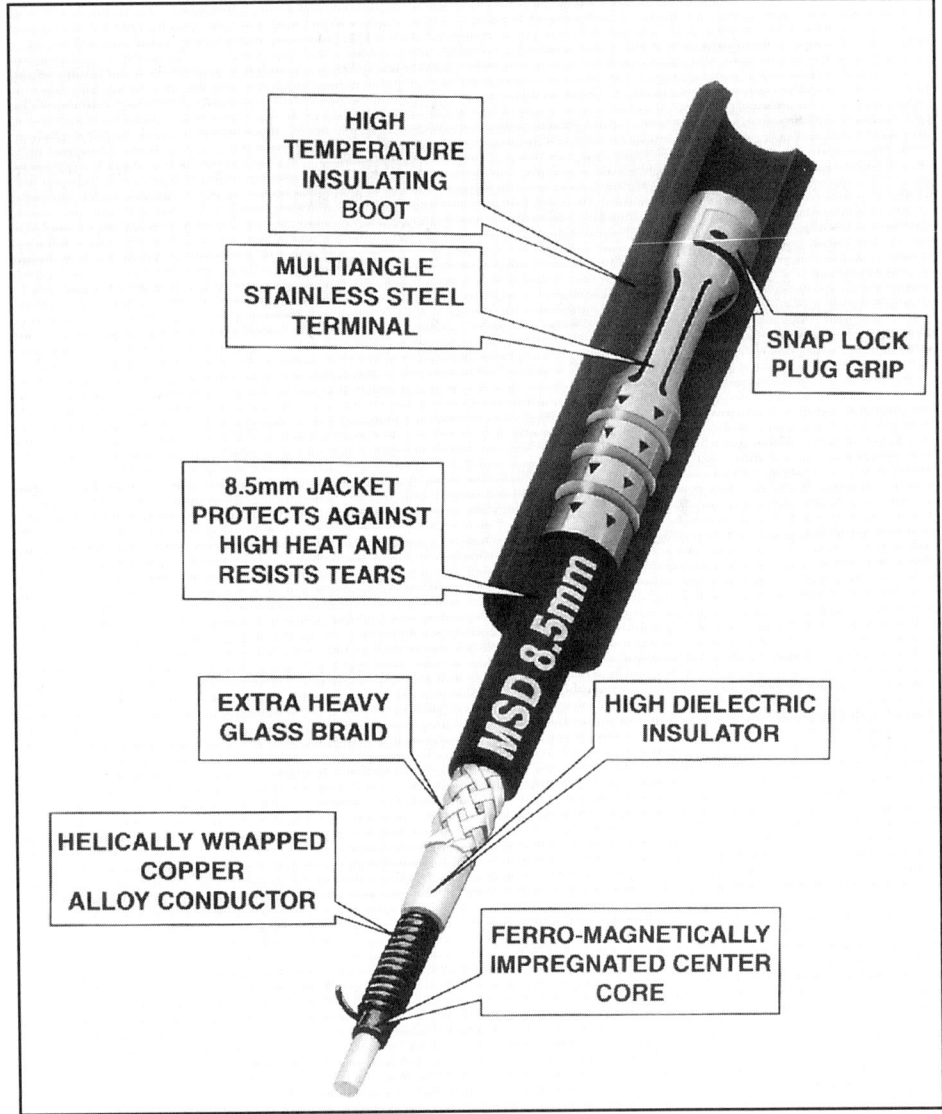

There's a vast difference in spark plug cables, and if you're trying to optimize your truck's ignition system, there's no sense having poor quality spark plug cables. Ideally, you want cables that can withstand high temperatures and vibration, have low electrical resistance and a high level of radio frequency noise suppression capability.

and they must also be able to withstand the extremely high temperature and vibration caused by the engine. Truck engines, especially those in off-road trucks, are likely to experience higher levels of vibration than car engines, so the spark plug cables need to be durable. An additional feature that is highly desirable is that of radio frequency (RF) noise suppression. Without this, you may have a problem enjoying your truck's sound system. It is difficult to come up with a wire that offers low electrical resistance and great radio frequency noise suppression at the same time, but some products come close to perfection in this area.

Original factory cables should be replaced with high-performance cables that are available from the SVO catalog, or from MSD, Mallory, Moroso or similar company that is in the performance ignition business. What you want is something on the order of an 8mm to 8.5mm silicone-jacketed cable with solid cores (for racing applications), or a carbon fiber or helical wound core for street performance applications. Be careful about buying cables that are advertised as having silicone insulation, because some manufacturers make that claim when their product has only a minimal amount of silicone in the insulation layer. These cables won't protect as well against heat damage.

Because heat is the most prominent cause of spark plug cable failure, you may want to encase your cables in glass cloth tubing that is available from MSD, Mallory and a few other companies. In fact, MSD makes performance cables that are already insulated in glass cloth tubing, and sealed at the terminal ends with self-vulcanizing silicone rubber tape. Heat from the exhaust manifolds or headers will permanently bond this tape to the cables, providing excellent protection.

The SVO catalog lists the following spark plug cable sets that are suitable for high-performance applications. These are 8mm wire-wound cables that offer low resistance and minimum spark loss. Silicone insulation and boots withstand high temperatures and are resistant to fuels, oils and solvents. The sets feature stainless steel terminals for "post" type distributor caps, and a coil wire for a socket-type coil. **Part number M-12259-B301** is for 5.0-liter and 5.8-liter V8 applications, and the spark plug boots are angled at 45 degrees. **Part number M-12259-B460** is for 7.0-liter and 7.5-liter V8 engines, and the spark plug boots are angled at 45 degrees. There is also a universal set for 8-cylinder engines, which allows the owner to cut the cables to length and crimp on the terminal ends. The set includes the cable, terminals and crimping tool. The universal set is listed as **part number M-12259-B302**.

The cables need to be routed in such a manner that they are protected from contact with the hot exhaust system, and so each cable is kept separate from the others to reduce the potential for cross-firing. To assist in this, there are spark plug cable dividers and loom holders. In the SVO catalog, the Motorsports versions of these holders can be ordered under **part number M-12297-A4**, which is the cable loom for small-block engines. **Part number M-12297-B2** is a cable divider for two cables, **part number M-12297-B3** holds three cables, and **part number M-12297-B4** will accommodate four cables.

Spark Plugs

The plugs themselves can make a lot of difference. Platinum tip plugs deliver measurable improvement over OEM plugs, giving longer service life and more reliable performance under adverse conditions. Available at considerably higher cost are Split-Fire plugs, which give indications through dyno testing that they deliver performance improvement over regular plugs. We have not heard the last word in exotic spark plug engineering. Research and development are ongoing in the pursuit of other unusual spark plug designs, and we may see some of these hit the market. Hopefully, there will be honest performance gains, as a result.

On engines using pre-electronic, point-type ignition, using a spark plug that is one heat range hotter than specified in the owner's manual may help eliminate carbon fouling during cold-weather start-up and warm-up periods. It is important to use the correct heat range and gap size for best performance. If the stock ignition system is upgraded to a more powerful unit, it is possible to drop to one heat range cooler plug and to open the gap very slightly to improve performance. Increasing gap clearance by 0.010" to 0.020" over factory specification will sometimes result in marginal performance improvement, but don't go any wider than that or the excessive secondary voltage needed to jump the gap may cause damage to ignition components.

Coils

The aftermarket offers coils to replace original equipment, and some of them are very powerful. MSD, for example, offers ignition coils that range higher than 50,000 volts, and several in the 45,000-volt range. Whether or not you need to upgrade to a more powerful coil than came as standard equipment on your truck depends upon the type of driving you will be doing. If high-RPM forays into the world of competition events are in your future, consider upgrading.

Replacement coils from the SVO catalog include the following items. **Part number M-12029-A201** for 1957 through 1974 breaker point ignition systems, and **part number M-12029-A202** for 1975 through 1985 Duraspark Electronic Ignition systems. Both units are manufactured to original equipment specifications and fit non-computer controlled vehicles with round coils. They have 40,000-volt output capacity for improved performance, and a chrome finish dresses up the engine compartment.

Also from the SVO catalog is the Performance Ignition Coil **part number M-12029-A200** to replace 1975 through 1985 Duraspark coils, **part number M-12029-A203** for 1983 through 1993 EEC-IV systems, and **part number M-12029-A204** for use on 1957 through 1975 vehicles. These are blue-finned aluminum-case coils that replace the square coils. They output 40,000 volts for improved performance, stronger low-end torque and easier starting.

Starter

The SVO catalog lists **part number M-11000-A50** for their Hi-Torque small-diameter mini-starter. The smaller size provides added clearance for headers. This is a performance unit that weighs 5 pounds less than a stock starter, yet delivers more cranking power. It comes will integral solenoid and cables, and fits most 289, 302, 351W and 351C engines.

Typically, stock Ford starters, with their remote solenoid, don't suffer hot start syndrome. But with the integrated solenoid on the Hi-Torque mini-starter listed above, the potential exists, especially in hot weather or under high-stress conditions when the engine gets hotter than normal.

If this problem crops up, it is caused by the fact that the starter and solenoid are in close proximity to the exhaust system, which allows the starter and solenoid to become heat soaked. Electrical components suffer an increase in resistance as the temperature rises. As resistance increases, effectiveness diminishes. Pretty soon, the starter just won't work any more. And it's a pretty poor showing if a performance truck won't even start.

To solve the problem, take a three-step approach.

1. Use the heaviest battery

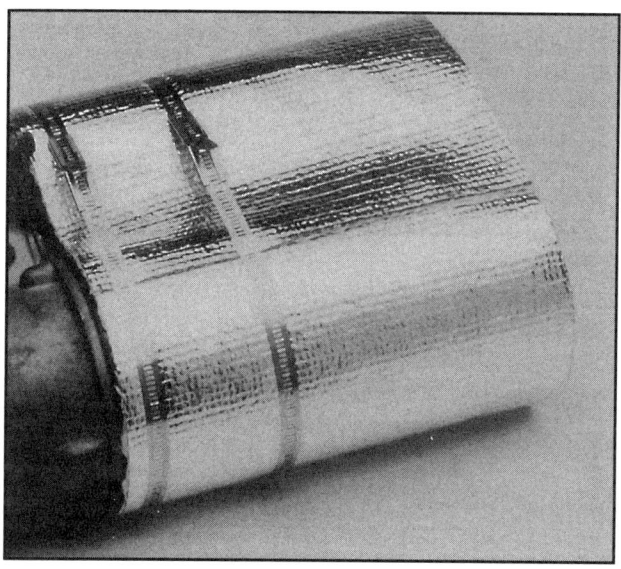

Reflective heat shielding for the starter helps prevent heat soak that can cause the starter to lose efficiency or fail to operate at all. This easy-to-install and highly efficient Starter Heat Shield is a member of the Thermo-Tec product line.

cables possible, and make sure the battery terminals and the cable ends are free of corrosion.

2. Relocate the starter solenoid to a position away from the heat source. This can be done by using a remote Ford starter relay, which is designed as a stand-alone unit.

3. Install heat shielding material between the starter and the exhaust manifold.

A well-designed ignition system will make a lot of difference in the performance level of your truck. Take the time to make things right, and you will enjoy the rewards.

Performance Modifying Ford Trucks

Electrical System

It was a dark and stormy night ... really, it was! It was storming as I left my office, and it started getting dark and cold as I made my way home. The problem was that my alternator had decided to go on vacation without notifying me in advance, and I was about to discover by personal experience what happens when the charging system goes on the blink.

Luckily, there was enough juice in the battery to get the engine started, so I pulled out of the parking lot, relatively ignorant of my impending fate. A gentle rain started to fall, so I switched on the windshield wipers. They ran slowly. As darkness closed in, I switched on my headlights. They looked kind of dim to me, but I didn't pay much attention. It was getting cold, so I turned on the heater. The wipers slowed down a lot, and the headlights looked dimmer than ever. Then the engine started running rough. That's when I noticed my volt meter looking pretty slack.

I had to make some choices, none of which were very pretty. To keep the ignition system operating, I had to start turning things off. First went the heater, and the situation improved for a while. Next, I had to turn off the windshield wipers and strain to see through the rain streaked windshield in the dark. About two miles from home, I had to turn off the headlights in order to keep the engine running long enough to reach my destination.

The moral of this story is that electricity is important. And the more electrical goodies you install, the more important it is to have an uninterrupted flow of power. When the power supply goes down, you don't last long, no matter how much performance muscle you have built into your truck.

How Much Power Do You Need?

Electricity for a pickup comes from two sources — a battery (maybe two) and an alternator. The battery is in charge (no pun intended) of initial power to start the engine and to operate electrical accessories while the engine is turned off. The battery also supplies additional power to the electrical system when demand overwhelms alternator output. This might happen when the engine is running, but the accessories being used draw more amperage than the alternator can produce, or when the engine is running at slow idle and the alternator is not outputting enough to operate the accessories. And finally, the battery serves as a buffer to smooth out the "bumps" in the electrical charging system while the engine is running.

For it's part, the alternator supplies a continuous flow of electricity to the ignition system to keep the engine running, to power electrical accessories while the engine is running, and to recharge the battery while the engine is running.

The real question about building a performance electrical system is: How much power do I need? That question breaks down into two more: How much battery power? How much alternator? And a third question is: Are all batteries and alternators compatible?

Batteries

Let's start with the battery. There are several factors involved in determining the amount of power a new battery has.

1. Ampere Hours: This testing procedure is no longer used by the automotive industry as the standard reference point for battery strength, and it has been replaced by other testing criteria. But if you run into the term, you should know what it means. The ampere hours rating is a way of stating the capability of a battery to deliver current. When this rating system was used, the method was to rate the battery's amps over a given number of hours (usually 20 hours). Multiply the number of amps times the number of hours, and you have your ampere hour rating. For example, 10 amps for 20 hours = 200 ampere hours.

2. Cold Cranking Amps (CCA):

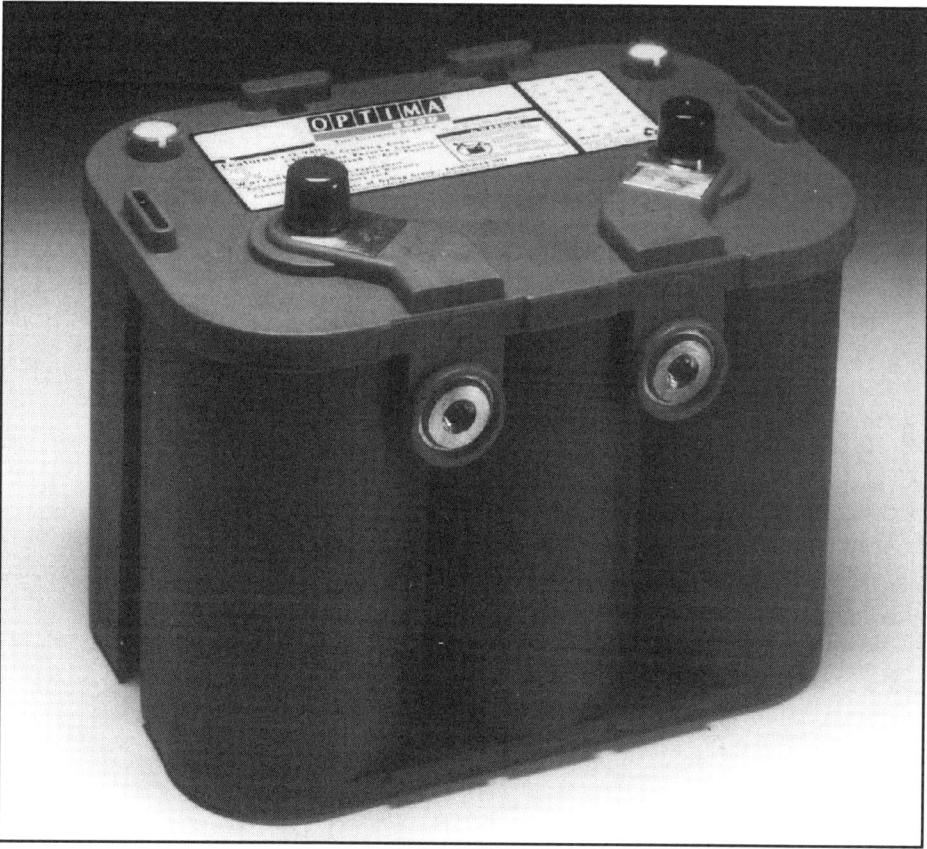

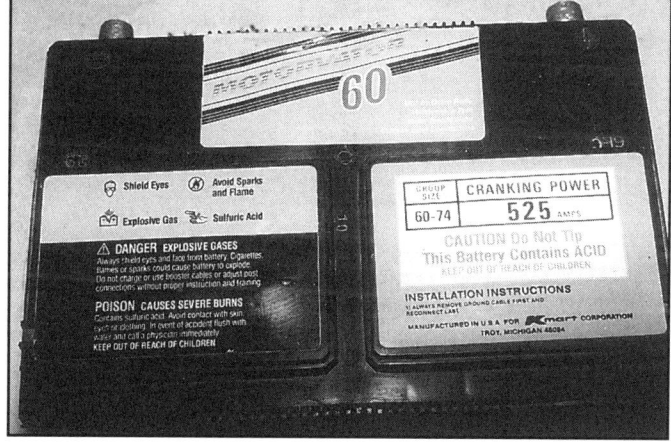

The battery pictured above is unique in its construction. Manufactured by Optima Batteries, it features a spiral wound construction, with high-purity lead grids separated by microporous glass separators. It is designed for rugged use, climactic extremes, fast recharging, and a long life. Notice the two different types of terminals, to accommodate a variety of installation formats. To the left is a photo of the critical information typically found on modern automotive batteries.

By its name, you might guess that this is a system that rates batteries for their ability to deliver current under cold conditions. Testing for CCA is performed with the temperature of the electrolyte in the center cell of the battery at zero degrees F. During the test, current is drawn from the battery for 30 seconds while maintaining 7.2 volts at the terminal posts. Whatever amount of current is necessary to maintain that voltage during the 30 second test period is the CCA for the battery. Although a high CCA rating is wonderful for operation in cold weather, it doesn't work for hot climates. A high CCA can

Electrical System **71**

Performance Modifying Ford Trucks

Battery Charging

There are two ways to test a battery to determine its state of charge. One method employs a hydrometer to physically check the specific gravity of the battery electrolyte. This works for batteries with removable caps that are provided to allow the owner to add distilled water when needed. However, sealed batteries (such as maintenance free) don't allow the use of a hydrometer. In these cases, use of a digital voltmeter to check the open-circuit voltage is the recommended method.

To test specific gravity, use the following values:

CHARGE LEVEL (%)	SPECIFIC GRAVITY
100%	1.265
75%	1.225
50%	1.190
25%	1.155
Discharged	1.120

For testing open-circuit voltage, use the following values:

VOLTAGE	STATE OF CHARGE (%)
12.6 volts or higher	100%
12.4 volts	75%
12.2 volts	50%
12.0 volts	25%
11.7 volts	Discharged

Using a digital voltmeter, it is easy to check a battery's state of charge very precisely. This battery shows 12.66 volts, which indicates 100% charged.

actually reduce battery life in hot weather because of the high ambient temperatures. So, buy the battery that's right for your region's weather, not just the one with the highest numbers.

3. Reserve Capacity: This is the term used to define a battery's endurance characteristics. How long can the battery supply power without the charging system in operation. This is what got me home on that dark and stormy night. Testing for reserve capacity determines the battery's ability to deliver 25 amps and maintain 10.5 volts at the terminals. The number of minutes the battery is capable of doing this is the number used as the reserve capacity rating. The higher, the better regardless of weather conditions.

4. Deep Cycling: The battery's ability to endure repeated discharge and recharge cycles and still perform up to established standards is what determines a battery's deep cycling capability. The test indicates the number of times a battery can pass the discharge/recharge test and maintain an adequate charge. This test is not normally applied to automotive batteries, but is mainly used for marine and RV batteries.

Because we're dealing with automotive batteries, rather than marine or RV units, we will restrict our analysis to those batteries that are most suitable for starting an engine. There are basically three types of batteries used for this purpose: lead-acid, low-maintenance, and maintenance-free.

Lead-Acid: On the positive side, lead-acid batteries offer high CCA ratings, excellent recycling characteristics, and are suitable for deep cycling. On the negative side, they use a lot of water, generate a lot of gas when charged, and undergo a high level of corrosion at the terminals. This last characteristic leads to self-discharge and short shelf life. These batteries generally do not hold up well to high temperatures.

Low-Maintenance: These units generally require little or no maintenance during when operated under normal conditions. They consume less water and create less gas during charging cycles, and exhibit excellent deep cycling characteristics. Low-maintenance batteries provide excellent buffering to protect sensitive electronic equipment from damage from surges and spikes during the charging cycle. The only down side is the moderate shelf life if the battery sits idle for long periods of time.

Maintenance Free: These batteries are capable of very long life — perhaps as much as 250,000 miles — before the need for any maintenance. However, if the battery is subjected to long periods of severe operation, as would happen during extensive overcharging or repeated deep cycle discharges, there may be some water loss. The trouble is that these batteries have no provision for adding water to replace that which is lost.

After being deeply discharged, this type of battery may never fully regain its complete charge again. In order to maintain a maintenance-free battery, it is necessary to charge it with higher voltage, because the calcium grids are more resistant to accepting a charge. But this can result in higher electrical system voltages during periods of charge, creating more heat that can be detrimental to sensitive electronic equipment in the truck.

Zero maintenance: Perhaps you haven't heard of this category. That's okay, because it really isn't a widely accepted category in the automotive world. But Optima is calling their battery "zero maintenance" and the Optima battery is different enough that we decided to put it into its own little slot. Technically, the Optima is a lead acid battery. But where it differs from most lead acid batteries is in its unique construction, that incorporates spiral cells consisting of a lead grid and microporous glass fiber sandwich. There is no free liquid, because the acid is bound within the fiberglass floss. That means there can be no leakage, even if the battery case is broken, which also means no corrosion on the terminals. The battery can operate in any position, even upside down. Rough use, such as in an off-road race truck, doesn't bother the Optima battery. No water is ever needed (zero maintenance). Hydrogen gas cannot build up, even under conditions of overcharging. Extreme high and low temperatures do not appreciably affect starting power.

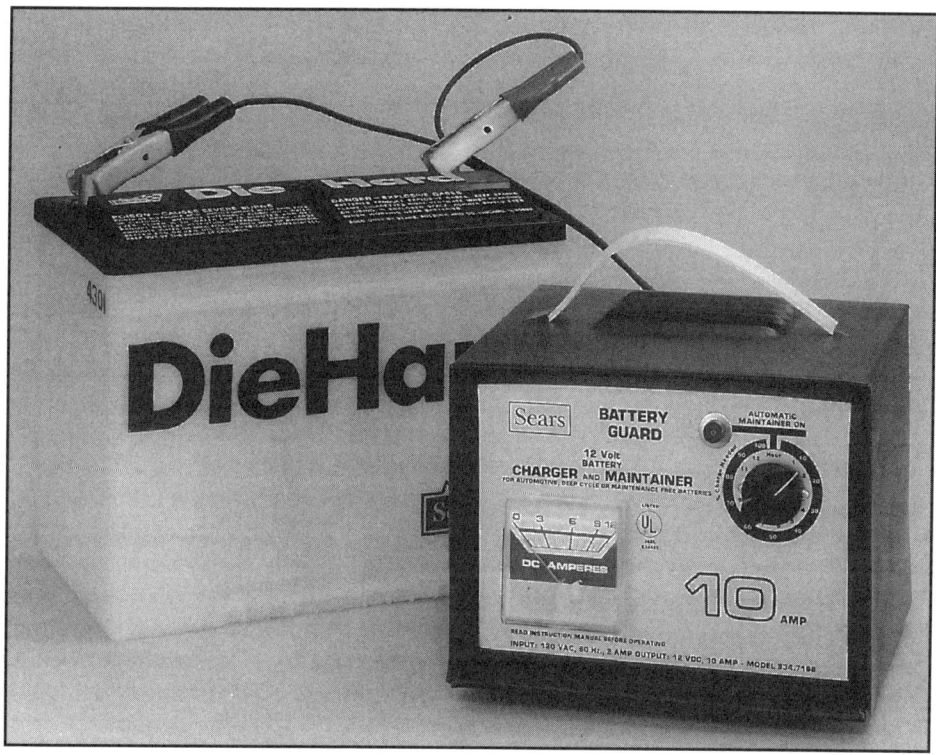

Using a battery charger that has a built-in regulator ensures against overcharging and boiling out the electrolyte. A small variable amperage charger such as the one pictured above allows the owner to dial in the exact amount of time the charger will be operating. A gauge indicates the amount of amperage being drawn by the battery during the charging process.

Alternators

Not all alternators are created equal. There are units that output less than 30 amps, and others that put out well over 100 amps, and ratings in between. How much alternator do you need? The answer to that question depends upon the amount of electrical goodies you have installed in or on the truck, and the type of battery you are using.

Unless you are using a maintenance-free battery, a high-output alternator may cause damage. Maintenance-free batteries require higher charging rates that older lead-acid batteries, so they can withstand (and actually require) the higher output provided by a bigger alternator to keep them properly charged.

Put into terms all taxpayers can understand, satisfying a truck's electrical need is somewhat like running a bloated federal government. The more pork spending there is (electrical goodies), the more the taxpayers (alternator) have to fork over. If the taxpayers (alternator) can't keep up with the pork spending (electrical demand), then you run into a deficit and the government goes bankrupt (truck chugs to a halt at the side of the road).

So, why doesn't everyone just go out and buy the biggest alternator possible, so deficit spending won't happen? Because alternators cost

Performance Modifying Ford Trucks

Circuit Breakers For Charging Systems

ALTERNATOR RATING	EXPECTED LOAD	RECOMMENDED BREAKER
Up to 90 amps	40 amps	50-amp
Up to 120 amps	70 amps	80-amp
Up to 150 amps	110 amps	120-amp
Up to 200 amps	140 amps	150-amp

Electrical System

The function of an alternator is to supply all the electrical current necessary to run the ignition system, operate all the electrical accessories in the vehicle, and to keep the battery fully charged. If a truck has too many thirsty electrical accessories, it is possible to overpower the stock alternator, in which case it is necessary to install a high-amperage aftermarket unit.

horsepower to operate. The larger the alternator, the larger the horsepower drain. And if you're interested in running a performance truck, things need to be kept in balance. Figure out what you need, then run with that.

It doesn't make any sense to be driving around with Hoover Dam on wheels when you don't need that much electrical generating power. Think about it — most of the time you probably won't be operating every last piece of electrical equipment you have on board. How often will you have all the driving lights turned on, headlights and turn signals and emergency flashers lit up, the stereo system blasting, windshield wipers going, a winch in operation, running the electric windows up and down continuously, and punching in the cigarette lighter every few seconds? Probably never.

To calculate how much alternator power you need, remember the purpose of the alternator is to supply power to the accessories and to charge the battery. Add up all the potential electrical demands from accessories, converted to amps, figure out how many of these accessories are likely to be in operation at any given time, and make a logical choice.

Because some accessories are rated in watts, you'll need to know how to convert watts to amps. The formula is watts divided by volts = amps. In a 12-volt DC system, simply divide the watts by 12 to arrive at the amps. An example would be a 100-watt driving light — the amperage draw to power the light would be close to 8.4 amps. So, if you have a light bar filled with half a dozen 100-watt off-road driving lights, when you turn them all on, the alternator will have to put out more than 50 amps just for those lights alone.

One key to successfully designing your truck's electrical system is to use wisdom when buying accessories. Winches and driving lights, for example, do not all have the same electrical requirement. Shop carefully to get what you need, but be aware of the ramifications of adding too many electrical accessories that have too much appetite.

Dual Battery System

In some cases, it may be desirable to install a dual battery system. This comes in handy when you might anticipate a need for more electrical power while the engine is not running, and therefore the alternator is not producing power, or when there may be a need for more power than the alternator alone can produce. For example, if you are operating an electric winch, it is possible that the alternator alone may not be able to keep up with the demand made by the winch, so the reserve capacity of the battery will be called upon to supply the additional power. But if the winch is operated too long, the battery may become substantially drained. In a case like that, you may want to have one battery hooked up solely for the purpose of operating the winch, and the other battery just for starting the vehicle.

In that kind of set-up, a battery isolator allows both batteries to be charged by the alternator when the engine is running, but isolates one battery as a "work" battery while the other one is used for starting the engine. This ensures that one battery will be protected at all times from being drained as a result of the winching operation.

This same concept works when you want to operate a sound system to keep the beach party hopping, but you don't want the engine running. Since the alternator is out of the loop in this situation, one battery can be used to power the stereo system, and the other battery would be protected from depletion so it can still be used to start the truck when the party is over.

Wiring

How you go about wiring accessories is a critical matter that can result in good performance or a meltdown, depending upon how well the wiring job is done.

One of the most common wiring errors related to performance is to run long stretches of wire without considering the current loss caused by resistance due to the increased length. As wire length increases, wire size needs to increase (gauge needs to decrease in number because wire gauge numbers are inverse). Using the accompanying chart, you can see that an 18-amp circuit can be handled by a 16-gauge wire that is as much as 10 feet long. But that same circuit will require a 14-gauge wire if it's going to run 15 feet. And if that same circuit will have a wire that is 25 feet long, you'll need to use a 12-gauge wire to carry the current load.

So, the longer the run of wire, the larger the gauge (smaller number) that will be necessary. Other than becoming cumbersome to work with, there is no drawback to using a wire gauge that is too large. But if you use too small a wire, you are setting the stage for electrical trouble.

When it comes to building a safe electrical system, one of the most common and most dangerous wiring situations is when a length of wire is run directly to the battery positive terminal to supply power to an accessory such as a sound system amplifier. The problem arises when the fuse is positioned close to the accessory and the long stretch of wire is left unprotected all the way to the battery. This sets up a potential for electrical fire along the wire, even though the fuse may blow out due to a short.

The best practice is to wire accessories to available spots in the fuse panel, and make sure the fuse panel is as close to the battery as possible. But if you decide that it is absolutely necessary to run the wire directly to the battery, install an appropriate fuse in the wire as near to the battery as possible so that if a short occurs, the fuse will blow and the major portion of the wire will be at no risk of fire.

Wire terminals make connections easy, but there is a lot of difference between terminals. Automotive wire terminals are available with no insulated barrel, or with either PVC or nylon insulation. Nylon is generally easier to work with, but PVC is more durable against abuse. Some terminals are made with an insulating barrel of shrink tubing, and these are preferred where moisture may be a problem. However, small quantities of shrink tubing of various diameters may be kept on hand so you can seal terminal connections. In addition to sealing out moisture, shrink tubing also stabilizes the area where the terminal has been crimped, making it less prone to pulling loose.

Terminals are color coded: red being used for 22- to 18-gauge wire; Blue for use with 16- to 14-gauge wire; and Yellow for 12- to 10-gauge wire. Always choose the proper color terminal for the wire size being used. If the wrong terminal size is selected, problems will occur with the wire pulling out of the terminal, or it may be difficult to insert the wire and crimp the terminal properly.

When possible, route wire inside conduit or wire looms, and use grommets to protect against abrasion when the wire passes through the firewall or other sheetmetal panels.

Performance Modifying Ford Trucks — Wire Gauge

Total Circuit Amperes	Total Circuit Watts	Gauge / Feet							
		3'	5'	7'	10'	15'	20'	25'	30'
4 amps	48 watts							18	18
5 amps	60 watts						18	18	18
6 amps	72 watts					18	18	16	16
7 amps	84 watts					18	18	16	16
8 amps	96 watts					18	16	16	16
10 amps	120 watts				18	16	16	16	16
11 amps	132 watts				18	16	16	14	14
12 amps	144 watts				18	18	16	16	14	14
15 amps	180 watts				18	18	14	14	12	12
18 amps	216 watts			18	16	16	14	14	12	12
20 amps	240 watts			18	16	16	14	12	10	10
22 amps	264 watts	18	18	16	16	12	10	10	10
24 amps	288 watts	18	18	16	16	12	10	10	10
30 amps	360 watts	18	16	16	14	10	10	10	10
40 amps	480 watts	18	16	14	12	10	10	8	8
50 amps	600 watts	16	14	12	12	10	10	8	8
100 amps	1200 watts	12	12	10	10	6	6	4	4

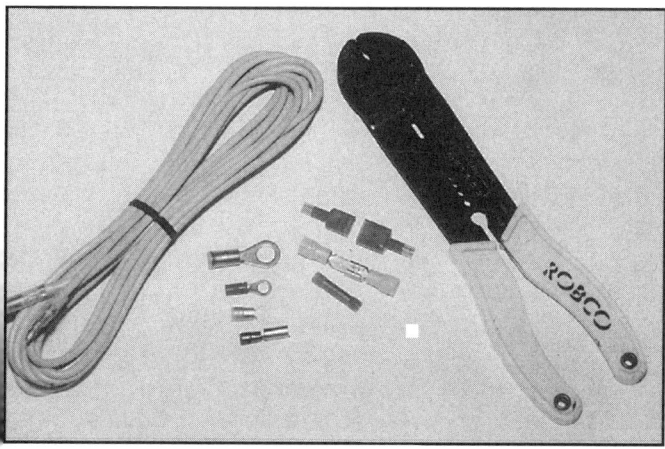

Selecting the proper gauge of wire to handle the current is very important. The same current load requires a smaller number gauge (larger wire diameter) for longer runs of wire. Terminals come in all shapes and sizes, to accommodate a variety of wire gauges and applications. Some terminals are uninsulated, while others have their own built-in protection. A quality crimper is vital to making good electrical connections.

Performance Modifying Ford Trucks

TIRES & WHEELS

When a truck is undergoing performance alteration, or even just cosmetic modification, tires and wheels are often the first aftermarket accessories that are purchased and installed. This is for a very good reason; installation of custom wheels and aftermarket tires results in an immediate cosmetic change. It's a quick and easy path toward getting started on the new image that is being sought.

But making the proper choice of tires and wheels for your particular truck, and for your chosen application — whether that be street cruiser, off-roader, or whatever — is a very complex subject. Swapping from stock tires and wheels to something of a different size may require significant modifications to other parts of the vehicle, notably the axles, gear ratios, brakes, suspension system, steering components, and perhaps even the body itself.

In this section, we will cover the subject of how to select the right tires and wheels to accomplish your purposes, and will also discuss the essential chassis and body modifications that may need to accompany certain tire and wheel selections.

Tires

Tires are extremely important items of performance equipment. No matter how much horsepower you have under the hood, no matter how great the suspension modifications, if the tires can't stick to the ground and do their job, the truck won't perform well. But it's not just sticking to the ground — if it were, we'd all use Indy-type tires on-road and gnarly mudders off-road. Tire performance is a complicated subject, and making the wrong choice can cost you performance in a big way.

How a tire performs through the

corners, in wet weather, and with a heavy load are serious performance issues. How does the tire hold up to heat, how long will the tread last, how high of speed is the tire rated to withstand? Answers to these questions are found in such things as the tire's aspect ratio, section width, load rating, speed and temperature ratings. All of this performance-related information is printed on the tire's sidewall, but unless you understand what the numbers and letters mean, tire selection remains a mystery.

Passenger Car Tires

Although we are dealing with trucks in this book, it is still important to understand passenger car tires. The reason for this is that some people install passenger car tires on their truck, to give it a special appearance — a cosmetic aspect that cannot be achieved by using truck tires.

Three different sizing systems are currently utilized for passenger car tires: P-Metric, European Metric, and Alpha-Numeric. All these systems evolved from the now obsolete tire sizing system known as the Numeric Sizing System, which was used when all tires were designed with the same aspect ratio. That system included only the tire's cross section width and the rim diameter in inches.

These days, aspect ratio is an important factor. Aspect ratio is the dimensional relationship of the tire's section height to section width. Low aspect ratio indicates a short sidewall, which translates into lowered center of gravity and quicker steering response. When aspect ratio is listed in the tire size information, it precedes the construction designation, except in the Alpha-Numeric system.

Here are examples of the three current tire sizing systems:

P-Metric

Based on the metric system, the P-Metric system was developed during the 1970's for small tires used on economy cars. Most U.S. passenger car tire manufacturers now employ this system. An example would read P215/65R15.
P — Passenger Car Tire
215 — Section Width in Millimeters
65 — Aspect Ratio
R — Radial Construction
15 — Rim Diameter in Inches

European Metric

High-performance passenger car tires like this BFGoodrich Comp T/A (above) would be a good choice for hot street trucks that don't need or want the gnarly off-road look in tires. Rated for sustained speeds in excess of 149 miles per hour, these tires also provide all-weather performance.

European Metric is simply a conversion of the old Numeric System from inches to millimeters. In most instances when the aspect ratio is other than 82, it appears in the size designation just prior to the speed rating. If no aspect ratio is listed, it is assumed to be 82. An example of this would be 155SR13.
155 — Cross Section Width in Millimeters
Aspect Ratio Assumed 82
S — S Speed Rating
R — Radial Construction
13 — Rim Diameter in Inches

If the aspect ratio is other than 82, the sidewall information would read something like 185/70SR14 and would be translated as follows:
185 — Cross Section Width in Millimeters
70 — Aspect Ratio
S — Speed Rating
R — Radial Construction
14 — Rim Diameter in Inches

Performance Modifying Ford Trucks — Tire and Rim Association Ratings for Typical Light Truck Tires

TIRE SIZE	Radial PSI	25	30	35	40	45	50
	Diagonal (Bias Ply) PSI	20	25	30	35	40	45
31x10.50 15LT		1400	1595	1775(B)	1945	2100	2250(C)
31x11.50 15LT		1455	1660	1845(B)	2020	2185	2340(C)
32x11.50 15LT		1575	1795	1995(B)	2185	2360	2530(C)
32x12.50 15LT		1755(B)	2000	2225(C)			

Alpha-Numeric

The Alpha-Numeric system was developed in the late 1960's, and is load-based. The load/size relationship of the tire is indicated by the first letter of the designation. Letters range from "A" to "N", and the lower the letter, the smaller the tire size and load carrying capacity. An example is BR60-13.
B — Load Capacity
R — Radial Construction
60 — Aspect Ratio
13 — Rim Diameter in Inches

Light Truck Tires

Three separate light truck tire sizing systems are commonly used today — Light Truck Metric, Light Truck High Flotation, and Light Truck Numeric.

Light Truck Metric

Light Truck Metric is very similar to the P-Metric system that is used for passenger tires. One common example is LT235/75R15/C.
LT — Light Truck Designation
235 — Section Width in Millimeters
75 — Aspect Ratio
R — Radial Construction
15 — Rim Diameter in Inches
C — Load Carrying Capacity

Light Truck High Flotation

As lower aspect ratio tires came into popularity on light trucks in the mid-1970's, Light Truck High Flotation tires were developed. This tire design resulted in better traction on sand and soft soil commonly found in off-road driving situations. Here's an example: 31x10.50R15LT/C.
31 — Tire Diameter in Inches
10.50 — Section Width in Inches
R — Radial Construction
15 — Rim Diameter in Inches
LT — Light Truck Designation
C — Load Carrying Capacity

Light Truck Numeric

Light Truck Numeric is an older tire size designation system that is still in use, mostly on tires for commercial vehicles. An example of this size designation is 7.50R16LT/D.
7.50 — Section Width in Inches
R — Radial Construction
16 — Rim Diameter in Inches
LT — Light Truck Designation
D — Load Carrying Capacity

Speed Rating System

Speed rating is an indication of the range of speeds at which a tire can carry a load under specified service conditions. A letter designation ranging from A to Z indicates the certified speed rating, ranging from 3 mph to over 149 mph. the most common speed ratings for truck tires are as follows: S to 112 mph; T to 118 mph; H to 130 mph; V to 149 mph; and Z over 149 mph.

Speed rating is part of a tire's sizing or service description. As part of the tire's sizing designation, it appears as follows:

Under the old system, the H speed rating in 205/60HR15 would be part of the sizing designation, and is translated as follows:
205 — Section Width in Millimeters
60 — Aspect Ratio
H — Speed Rating
R — Radial Construction
15 — Rim Diameter in Inches

Under the new system, S, T, H and Limited V tires list the speed symbol and load index in the service description as follows: 205/60R15 89H
205 — Section Width in Millimeters
60 — Aspect Ratio
R — Radial Construction
15 — Rim Diameter in Inches
89 — Load Index
H — Speed Symbol

In the service description, the load index ranges from 0 to 279, with the number corresponding to the tire's load capacity. Most passenger car tire load indexes range from 75 to 100, although some T/A passenger tires have a higher rating. In the previous example, the load index of 89 indicates a load carrying capacity of 1279 pounds at maximum inflation pressure.

Uniform Tire Quality Grade Labeling

The Uniform Tire Quality Grading System (UTQGS) is directed by the government to provide consumers with information about three specifics of the tire: treadwear, traction, and temperature. Tire manufacturers perform their own evaluations for these characteristics, following government prescribed test procedures. Manufacturers label tires according to grade. This is known as Uniform Tire Quality Grade Labeling (UTQGL).

Treadwear

Treadwear grades range from 50 to 400, in ten point increments. Naturally, tread life is affected by the

One of the most popular tire styles used on light trucks is reflected in this BFGoodrich Radial All-Terrain T/A, which features a tread design that is rugged enough for serious off-road travel, yet quiet and comfortable enough for everyday highway use.

78 Performance Modifying Ford Trucks

Performance Modifying Ford Trucks

Recommended Rim Widths For Different Tire Sizes

Recommendations provided by BFGoodrich

TIRE SIZE	RECOMMENDED RIM WIDTH
LT215/75R15	5.5 to 7.0 inches
LT235/75R15	6.0 to 7.5 inches
LT225/75R16	6.0 to 7.0 inches
LT235/85R16	6.0 to 7.0 inches
LT245/75R16	6.5 to 8.0 inches
LT265/75R16	7.0 to 8.5 inches
LT285/75R16	7.5 to 9.0 inches
27x8.50R14LT	5.5 to 7.5 inches
30x9.50R15LT	6.5 to 8.5 inches
33x9.50R15LT	6.5 to 8.5 inches
31x10.50R15LT	7.0 to 9.0 inches
32x11.50R15LT	8.0 to 10.0 inches
33x12.50R15LT	8.5 to 11.0 inches
35x12.50R15LT	8.5 to 11.0 inches
31x10.50R16.5LT	8.25 inches
33x12.50R16.5LT	8.25 to 9.75 inches
35x12.50R16.5LT	8.25 to 9.75 inches

Warning: Never mount a 16-inch tire on a 16.5-inch wheel.

quality of road surface, as well as routine service and maintenance such as inflation, alignment and rotation. When the tires are tested for treadwear grade, those tests are performed under controlled conditions on a government prescribed course which does not necessarily replicate "real world" conditions. Because of this, there is no reliable way to guarantee an absolute minimum number of miles of wear when assigning treadwear grade points. The numbers are relative, so higher numbers indicate greater tread durability.

Traction

Traction grades range from A to C, with A being the best. These grades indicate the ability of a new tire to stop in a straight line on wet pavement. Testing is performed under government supervision, and is only for straight-line sliding on concrete or asphalt with a specific amount of wetting to simulate a road surface in a rainstorm. Test ratings do not apply to traction while cornering or to straight line braking in nonskid braking tests.

Temperature

Temperature grades are also indicated by a range of A to C, with A being the highest. This rating relates to the ability of a properly maintained tire to dissipate heat under controlled indoor test conditions. Ratings are determined by running tires on an indoor drum. Successive 30-minute runs are made in 5-mph increments between 75 and 115 mph, or until the tire fails. All tires must meet the 85 mph minimum speed requirement of Federal Motor Vehicle Safety Standard 109. If a tire fails between 85 and 100 mph, it is graded "C"; if it fails between 100 and 115 mph, it receives a "B" grade; and if it exceeds 115 mph, it get a grade of "A."

Max. Load and Max. Inflation

Sidewall information indicates the maximum load that can be supported by a tire that is inflated to maximum recommended air pressure. To show how much load a tire is rated to carry at maximum pressure, the Alpha-Numeric tire sizing system uses a letter on the sidewall to indicate load range. An Alpha-Numeric tire with a Load Range of B is restricted to a load that can be carried with a maximum inflation pressure of 32 psi. Greater load carrying capacity can be obtained by selecting tires with a load range of C, D or E. (Note: most tires with a load range of C, D and E are for light truck applications). This load range information appears at the end of the numbers and letters which indicate size of the tire as follows: LT235/75R15/C

P-Metric tires are rated as either Standard Load or Extra Load. Standard Load tires are limited to the weight that can be carried with a maximum inflation pressure of 35 psi. Extra Load tires are limited to the amount of weight that can be carried with a maximum inflation pressure of 41 psi. Extra Load tires are designated with "XL" on the sidewall, while a Standard Load tire has no special designations. (Note: Tires with a normal inflation pressure of 35 psi may also be labeled with a maximum inflation of 44 psi, indicating the tire's ability to meet special performance requirements. However, this does not increase the tire's load capacity).

Passenger Car Tires On Trucks

Due to the demanding conditions typically experienced by trucks, if a passenger car tire is installed on a light truck, the tire's rated load carrying capacity must be lowered. If the

Wheels & Tires

truck's tire placard indicates that passenger car tires were installed as original equipment, the vehicle manufacturer already lowered the tire load rating to what appears on the placard. However, if the truck's tire placard indicates that light truck tires were installed as original equipment, and you want to use passenger tires as replacements, the load rating information on the tire sidewall must be reduced.

The amount of the reduction is:

Rated load x .91 = Reduced load for light trucks

For example, if you want to install P235/75R15XL tires with a rated load of 2183 at 41 psi on a light truck, reduce the load rating by multiplying it by .91.

Example: 2183 x .91 = 1985 at 41 psi

If the vehicle was originally equipped with load range "D" or "E" light truck tires, it may be impractical to consider passenger tires as replacement, because they will fail to support the load unless you upsize substantially.

Siping Tires For Improved Traction

Traction is a funny thing, because all too often a tire that delivers excellent traction in one kind of terrain proves nearly worthless under other conditions. For example, if you love to go mud bogging, there's a tire for you. But if you take your mudders for a spin in the sand dunes, that's exactly what they'll do — spin, and dig holes. So, there are clearly some limits to what you should expect your tires to do when conditions change.

Which is why so many off-road truck owners have installed all-terrain tires for year round daily driving, and for most off-roading situations. They deliver adequate traction almost everywhere. In fact, most off-road conditions are perfect for all-terrain tires, and as a bonus they are relatively quiet and comfortable on the road.

But winter introduces a new set of challenges to traction. In many parts of the country, ice and snow and slush, or all of the above, make driving a real adventure. Tires that used to stick to the ground, now refuse to display anything resembling traction. When this happens, some people swap their tires for a set of studded snow tires. But there is no need to have special snow tires sitting around just waiting for winter. There is another alternative, called siping.

Siping is the process of cutting hundreds of tiny slits across the lugs of a tire to improve traction in wet and wintry conditions. This technique works very well on passenger car tires that are popular on street trucks, as well as on light truck all-terrain tires that are so popular on off-road trucks.

If you look closely at a stock tire, you'll see that each lug of the traction surface generally includes several little sipes already from the factory. These sipes are molded into the tire to change each lug from a big, immovable block of rubber into a textured unit that can move around a bit to get a better bite on the road or trail surface. When the road is wet, this becomes very important. There isn't much that is slipperier on a wet surface than a solid block of smooth rubber. So, when additional sipes are cut across the traction lugs, they provide extra gripping edges.

Keep in mind that the sipes we're talking about, the ones you can have your tire dealer cut across the tread, are completely different from the big channels that make up the normal

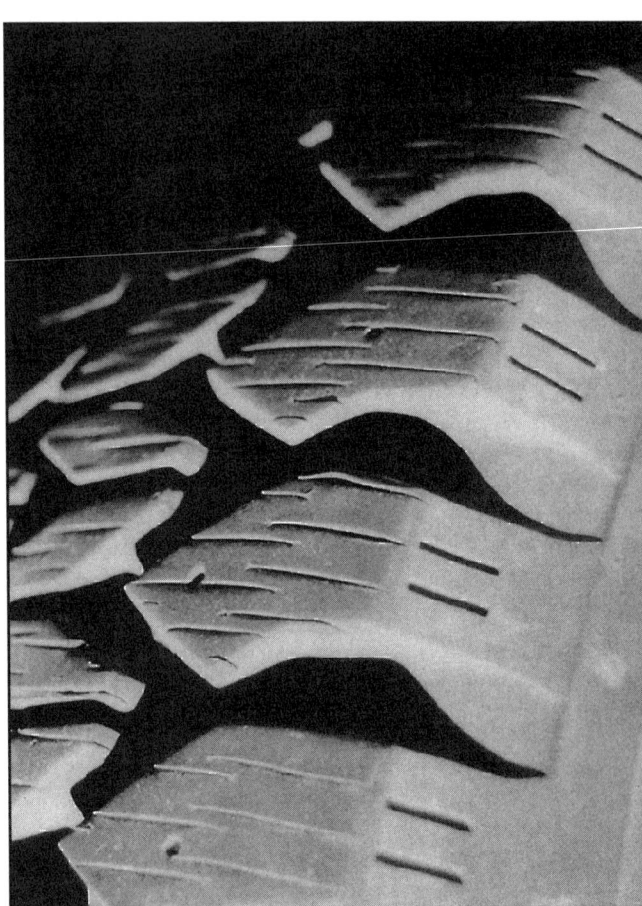

For added traction, especially in wet or snowy conditions, siping has proven to be very effective. The sipes are the tiny slits cut across the tread lugs, which add hundreds of gripping teeth to the tread.

tread pattern. Those are designed to move large amounts of water away from beneath the tread so the tire doesn't "hydroplane" on a thin liquid film and lose traction altogether. The sipes you can have custom cut across your tread won't move any water from under the tire. They are only intended to add teeth to the tread, little gripping edges that make the difference between slipping and having traction in those marginal conditions resulting from wet weather and winter.

I've had my past two sets of tires siped by the local tire dealer, at a cost of a few dollars per tire. The work takes only a few minutes per tire on a special siping machine, and having the tires siped does make a difference when road conditions are bad. It doesn't hurt the tire, and both on and off-road the little teeth are getting a good bite on the ground, and helping me get where I want to go. When winter comes, I don't have to swap tires, and the rest of the year I don't have to store a set of winter tires.

Effective Axle Ratios

A change of tire size can have a dramatic impact on a vehicle's rate of acceleration, towing capability, and fuel economy. To keep the engine

A siping machine quickly makes hundreds of precision cuts across the tread, enhancing traction in wet or snowy conditions.

within the desired rpm range for optimum performance, specific gear ratios must be chosen. If the diameter of the replacement tire is different from the original tire, it will turn a different number of revolutions per mile. This changes the effective gear ratio in the axle, which will affect performance.

Tire Revolutions Per Mile

To calculate tire revolutions per mile (rpm), use the following formula: 20,178 divided by Overall Tire Diameter = Tire rpm. Just in case you're curious, the number 20,178 is only a shortcut. The longer way around this formula is to multiply the number of feet in a mile (5,280) times 12 to discover the number of inches in a mile (63,360). Then take the diameter of the tire and multiply it times 3.14 (pi times the diameter = circumference). Then divide 63,360 by the tire circumference to find out how many revolutions the tire will make in a mile. Shortcutting the formula, 63,360 is divided by 3.14, which equals 20,178. For the nit pickers who want to use 3.1416 for pi, go ahead. The shortcut number is then 20,168. But by the time you go through the rest of the formula work, it doesn't really matter. It all works out the same in the end.

Example: 20,178 divided by 32" = 630 tire rpm.

To determine how changing tire size will alter a vehicle's effective axle ratio, use the following formula. These are just rough examples, using the sidewall information as if it were actually the tire diameter. For more precise calculations, physically measure the tire diameter, then plug that figure into the formula. But for here, we're going to pretend that a 32x11.50R15LT really measures 32 inches in diameter.

Formula:
New Tire rpm x Original Axle Ratio divided by Original Tire rpm = Effective Axle Ratio.

As an example, let's see what would be the result if the tires on a pickup with a 3.73:1 axle ratio were changed from 32x11.50R15LT to 35x12.50R15LT tires?

Example: $\dfrac{576 \times 3.73}{630} = 3.41:1$

A tire swap of this type will result in a numerically lower effective axle ratio. This will cause the truck to accelerate more slowly off the line, and it will reduce towing capability. However, it may help the truck achieve slightly better highway fuel economy when driven solo at highway cruising speed. A change in the opposite direction would result in a numerically higher axle ratio than original. The truck would then accelerate more quickly off the line, and enjoy improved towing ability (especially uphill). But the change might decrease the truck's highway fuel economy when driven solo at highway cruising speed.

Choosing Optional Axle Ratios

What about changing your truck's tire size but retaining the original acceleration, towing ability and fuel economy performance levels? Basically, you have only two choices. If you are planning ahead about tire size changes before buying a new truck, you can either order a numerically higher axle ratio to begin with, or if you already own the truck, you can install a ring and pinion set with the appropriate gear ratio. The following formula shows how to select the correct alternate axle ratio.

Formula:
Original Tire rpm x Original Axle Ratio divided by New Tire rpm = Effective Axle Ratio

Using the same truck from the preceding formula, here's how it works:

Example: $\dfrac{630 \times 3.73}{576} = 4.07:1$

In other words, you have to upgrade to a ring and pinion set with close to a 4.07:1 ratio in order to maintain the same equivalent gear ratio you had with the original 3.73:1 ring and pinion set before the tire size was changed. The obvious ring and pinion choice that is close to a 4.07:1 would be a 4.10:1 set.

Wheels

With a change in tire size, it may be necessary or desirable to swap to some new wheels. Although most people think of wheels as merely ornamental, there are some very definite performance factors involved in wheel design. Not all wheels, of course, are engineered with performance in mind. There are manufacturers who are happy to simply crank out wheels to please the current visual fad, without much consideration for special performance factors beyond those which are required by the Department of Transportation for safety purposes.

Very wide tires, like the Mickey Thompson Baja Belted 35x17.50-15LT require installation on rims in the range of 13 to 15 inches in width. This can involve special considerations as far as clearance in concerned. The rims will undoubtedly have negative offset to move the tire outboard to provide adequate clearance between tire/rim and suspension components or body panels.

On the other hand, there are wheels built for racing. Racing is the laboratory for development of "real world" performance products. And when it comes to winning races, there is hardly anything more fundamental than having wheels that remain intact. Off road racing, in particular, is a brutal test bed for discovery of what works and what doesn't.

Racing in Arizona, I once had a cast aluminum front wheel disintegrate as I was flying down a rock-strewn sandy wash on approach to the finish line. Steering control vanished, as did my chance for a win.

Obviously, the ability to endure the slings and arrows of racing is a priority. Over time, wheels get a reputation for durability, as well as other performance characteristics. Watch what type of wheel is being used in the kind of competition events that represent the type of performance you're most interested in. If you're building a drag truck, you don't necessarily want what the off road racers are using, etc. Keep in mind that racers will often use certain components because of sponsorship and contingency money that is paid by product manufacturers. But still, no racer in his right mind is going to use a piece of junk, regardless of sponsorship or contingency money, because that money only comes when the truck wins. And if the components fall apart before the finish line, there won't be much in the way of income for the racer.

Besides holding together, performance wheels must do other things as well. They must be true on both the horizontal axis and the vertical axis. In other words, they must be as nearly perfectly round as possible, and they must not wobble side to side as they rotate. Alloy wheels that are machined, by the nature of their method of manufacture, are generally pretty close to perfect when they come off the lathe. Cast or stamped wheels may or may not be so true.

Wheel size must be matched to the size of tires you will be using. Tire manufacturers publish charts with engineering data that indicate, among other things, a range of rim widths suitable for any given tire size. Most tire dealers should have these charts for the brands of tires they handle.

It is popular, these days, for some truck enthusiasts to install super-wide rims and then put skinny little tires on them, forcing the tires to bulge unnaturally in order for the tire beads to mate with the rims. This is done in an effort to make the truck look low and wide. Although this may be a popular cosmetic trend, it in no way improves truck performance, and can radically reduce performance, so we cannot condone the practice. One problem is that when you put skinny tires on a wide rim, it's easy to accidentally unbead the tire, resulting in immediate and catastrophic air pressure loss, and possibly loss of vehicle control. Another problem is that these tiny tires are not rated to carry the load that is imposed on them.

Another important factor to consider when buying wheels is offset. In an attempt to increase the truck's track (the distance between the centerlines of tires at opposite ends of the same axle), some people will install wheels with a negative offset.

Offset is defined as the distance between the centerline of the rim and the surface of the bolt flange that makes contact with the hub. The bolt flange may be quite thick, depending upon wheel design, so make sure you measure to the inner surface of the bolt flange — the part that contacts the axle hub when the wheel is installed.

Negative offset moves the

wheels outward, widening the track. Positive offset moves the wheels inward, narrowing the vehicle's track. Zero offset is when the centerline of the rim is on the same plane as the surface of the bolt flange that contacts the axle hub.

To calculate offset, place the rim face down on a level surface. Measure the total rim width. Then, using a straightedge across the rear surface of the rim, measure the distance from that point to the center of the bolt flange. This measurement is called rear spacing. Using these measurements, the formula for calculating offset is: Offset equals rear spacing subtracted from half the total rim width.

Extreme negative offset increases leverage on axle housings, wheel bearings, spindles, suspension components, and steering geometry. If wheels with negative offset are installed, it may be necessary to install a full-floating rear axle to help counter the stress imposed by the offset wheel. A full-floating axle lends better support to the axle shaft and bearings.

Negative offset may move the tire out enough to create a hazard of contact between the tire sidewall and the lip of the wheel opening in the fender, requiring some body modifications. Before changing to a wheel with a different offset, study the situation carefully. Take measurements to discover any potential clearance problems in advance of making the change.

Realize also that there are laws requiring that the face of the tread be covered by the truck's body. If you decide to go ahead with a wheel swap that results in a significant increase in negative offset, you may have to install fender flares to give you not only the necessary clearance but also legal coverage for running fat tires on wide wheels, or a wider track than came from the factory.

Increasing Tire/Wheel Diameter

For those who are interested in lifting their truck, one of the easiest ways to do this is by increasing tire and wheel diameters. In fact, to gain ground clearance under the axles, there is no other method than increasing the diameters of tires and wheels. A suspension lift only raises everything from the frame up. A body lift only lifts the body, not even the frame. So the only way to gain true ground clearance from the axle and above is to install bigger tires and wheels.

We'll discuss the dynamics of various types of lifting techniques later, but for now, it is important to understand that when you increase tire and wheel size you are making a gigantic modification that impacts the entire drivetrain, suspension system, steering geometry, and perhaps even the body of the truck. This is not a

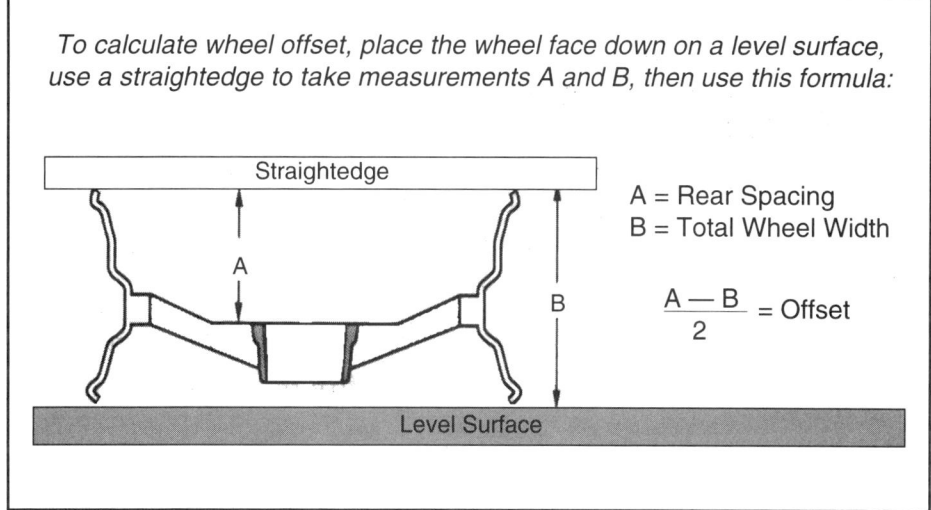

To calculate wheel offset, place the wheel face down on a level surface, use a straightedge to take measurements A and B, then use this formula:

A = Rear Spacing
B = Total Wheel Width

$$\frac{A - B}{2} = \text{Offset}$$

modification to be taken lightly.

Increasing wheel diameter (going from a 15-inch wheel to a 16.5-inch wheel, for example) in an effort to give the truck a little lift, can have some dramatic side effects. As we discussed in the section on tires, increasing the circumference of the tire numerically decreases the axle ratio, which lowers engine RPM for any give road speed. It's like running in Overdrive all the time, in every gear. This will wreak havoc on performance, as the engine lugs and struggles to reach an RPM level that allows for optimum torque production. To overcome this negative side effect, it will be necessary to make gearing changes in the differential(s).

Swapping to larger tires and wheels increases the unsprung mass (unsprung mass is essentially the weight of everything below the springs), and this puts a whole new set of stresses on the suspension system as it tries to maintain control over the movement of that mass.

In order to fit larger tires and wheels under the truck, it may be necessary to perform a suspension lift or a body lift. Either of these options may include the necessity of altering some steering components, usually the pitman arm, to maintain proper steering geometry.

Increasing the rolling mass of the tire/wheel combination imposes additional stress on the brake system, requiring possible modifications to the brake system to maintain the appropriate level of safety.

Tires and wheels are often the first place a truck owner looks when considering cosmetic alterations. But making these seemingly simple changes can force the door open to a lot of other substantial modifications. It is a serious mistake to think that you can just swap tire and wheel sizes without considering the impact on other aspects of the truck's performance and safety.

Performance Modifying Ford Trucks

Axles

At the receiving end of the torque and horsepower supply are the axle assemblies. There must be adequate strength here, or the power created by the engine will not be usable. If the axle assembly is the weak link in the power chain, all that thunderous horsepower and torque will be wasted, most likely because when the full complement of power is applied, something in the axle assembly will break.

For the purposes of this discussion, the axle assembly consists of the housing, axle shafts, and everything comprising the differential. These are the components that can be properly selected, modified, or upgraded to handle the power delivered by a high-performance engine, withstand stressful driving conditions, and deliver maximum traction.

Depending upon vintage and duty rating, Ford trucks come from the factory with one of two different types of axles — semi-floating, or full-floating. Semi-floating axles offer less strength and ruggedness than full-floating axles, but are generally suitable for the majority of light-duty truck applications for the average driver. Semi-floating axles are designed so that the entire load on the outer end of the axle shaft is supported by a single outer wheel bearing. Support for the inner end of the axle shaft comes from the differential side gear. To hold the axle shaft in position, the semi-floating design relies on the bearing retainer plate at the outer bearing. With this design, if the semi-floating axle shaft should break, it is possible for the wheel to leave the vehicle, trailing the broken shaft behind it.

Full-floating axles, on the other

84   Performance Modifying Ford Trucks

hand, are designed so that the shaft is nothing more than a bar that transfers torque from the differential to the wheel hub. The wheels are not directly connected to the axle shaft, but are bolted to spindles, much like those supporting the front wheels. The spindles are integral components of the axle housing, so the load on the wheels is transferred directly to the axle housing, rather than being supported by the axle shaft. With this design, the axle shafts are under much less stress, because their only job is to transfer torque, not to carry the weight of the vehicle. If the shaft should break, the wheel won't leave the vehicle. All that happens when a full-floating axle shaft fractures is that power is no longer transferred from the differential to the wheel on the side where the broken shaft exists. A truck with a broken full-floating axle shaft can still be driven, but if the broken shaft belongs to the front axle, it is necessary to remove the broken segments to ensure that steering control will not be affected. To remove the broken sections of shaft, you don't even need to jack up the truck. All that is required is to remove the flange from the wheel hub, pull out the broken shaft, replace the flange and drive on. Of course, the truck will have lost all traction effort on the side that is broken, so more careful driving may be in order.

In high-performance applications a full-floating axle is generally preferred over a semi-floating unit, because it is stronger, more reliable, more durable, and easier to work on in an emergency. However, one school of thought is that for optimum performance, you should use the smallest axle that will safely handle the maximum amount of torque the engine produces. The theory behind this is that you should minimize weight if you want to go fast. On the other hand, there are those who believe that to win races, first you have to finish. If, in the effort to save weight, you end up with a marginal component that ultimately fails, that is not how races are won. And this applies to axles that are utilized in performance street or strip work, and off-road. The off-road environment is probably the most hazardous to the health of an axle assembly because there are times when a wheel may leave contact with the ground and spin wildly in mid-air. When that wheel regains contact with the ground, still spinning, and suddenly grabs traction, the axle shaft or differential gears may break. This is not a time to be running with the lightest axle possible.

To determine the amount of torque a truck engine can put to the ground, there is a simple formula. Multiply the maximum torque output of the engine times the ratio of the transmission first gear. Take that number and multiply it times the differential gear ratio. Now, multiply that times 90 percent (to compensate for friction loss). The final number should be the maximum torque output that can reach the axle assembly. Ideally, this torque will be equally divided between the two axle shafts, but there may be times when one shaft may carry the load. An example of this would be in off-roading when one wheel leaves the ground, and the other wheel receives the full torque load. For that reason, there is wisdom in having axle shafts that are rated for at least double the maximum torque output figure that results from using the above-mentioned formula. Then you can have confidence when the going gets rough.

When making the choice of which axle assembly to install, first decide what the truck is going to be used for and determine how much torque the engine produces. There is a tremendous difference in the amount and type of axle strength needed for street/strip events as opposed to running off-road. The one requires a lot of torque strength, but bearings and housing don't take much of a beating. The other may require enormous strength in the housing and bearing arrangement. A semi-floating assembly may be fine for street and strip, whereas a full-floater will be preferable for the most demanding off-road, towing and heavy hauling applications.

Over the years, one of the differences between a 1/2-ton and 3/4-ton Ford pickup has been the rear axle configuration. F-150 trucks are equipped with semi-floating rear axles, while for several generations prior to 1980, 3/4-ton Ford trucks were equipped with easily distinguishable full-floating rear axles. But since that time, the 3/4-ton trucks built by Ford have been equipped with heavy-duty semi-floating rear axles. Larger than Ford's 9-inch or 8.8-inch axles that are employed on the F-150 trucks, the F-250 semi-floating rear axles can be identified by the 8-lug wheel pattern. Since 1980, full-floating rear axles have been reserved for service under the F-250 HD models and the F-350.

Performance Modifying Ford Trucks — Torque To The Axles

The formula for calculating how much torque can reach the ground is found by multiplying engine torque output, times the ratio of the transmission's first gear, times the differential gear ratio, times 90 percent. Here's an example:

```
    485      (engine torque output)
 x 1.86     (transmission first gear ratio)
 x 4.10     (differential gear ratio)
 x  .90     (friction loss)
 3328.749 ft. lbs. of torque to the axles
```

Corporate axles for F-150 pickups, from 1957 through the mid-1980's, were the venerable and rugged 9-inch axle. After the mid-'80's, the 9-inch was replaced with the currently-used 8.8-inch unit.

Dana/Spicer axles that have been utilized for application under Ford trucks include the Model 44, Model 60, Model 60-HD, and Model 70, as well as their front axle counterparts for four-wheel-drive applications: Model 44, Model 44-IFS, Model 50-IFS, and Model 60-F.

Ford began incorporating independent front suspension for F-150 and F-250 4x4 trucks in 1980, and the design of the Twin Traction Beam design has been a major difference between Ford full-size 4x4 pickups and the trucks made by other manufacturers. Spicer independent carriers for Model 44-IFS and 50-IFS offer strength and flexibility for these front drive units.

Rear axle assembly Model 44 is a semi-floating unit that can be ordered with a Trac-Lok limited slip differential as an option. Tube diameter is 2.75 inches, and the ring gear diameter is 8.5 inches. Model 44 axle assemblies carry a maximum torque output rating of 3460 ft. lbs, and a continuous torque rating of 1100 ft. lbs. Brake options include both drums and discs. The nominal gross axle weight rating of this assembly is 3500 pounds, and the nominal gross combination weight rating is 11,000 pounds. Model 44 is a good axle for street trucks that aren't producing massive amounts of horsepower and torque, and for off-road applications that don't include serious racing or abuse. It's a very good assembly for most light-duty trucks that aren't being pushed to the limits of hauling enormous payloads or towing heavy trailers. The full range of standard and non-standard ratios available from Spicer for the Model 44 axle include 2.55:1, 2.72:1, 2.87:1, 2.94:1 3.00:1, 3.07:1, 3.23:1, 3.31:1, 3.42:1 3.50:1, 3.54:1, 3.73:1, 3.92:1, 4.09:1 4.27:1, 4.55:1, 4.78:1, 4.89:1, 5.38:1 and 5.89:1.

Front axle assembly Model 44-IFS is a steerable full-floater with a nominal gross axle weight rating of 3500 pounds. The center section weighs 87 pounds in iron, and 66 pounds in aluminum form. Ring gear diameter is 8.5 inches, and maximum torque output ratings for both short duration and continuous modes are identical to the Model 44. Available ratios for Model 44-IFS include 2.72:1, 2.87:1, 3.07:1, 3.31:1, 3.54:1 3.73:1, 3.92:1, 4.09:1, 4.27:1, and 4.55:1. Trac-Lok is the optional limited slip differential.

Model 50-IFS is a steerable full floating front axle assembly with a

Dana/Spicer Axle Ratios

Model 44 & Model 44-IFS	Model 50-IFS	Model 60 (60-HD) & Model 60-F	Model 70 & Model 70-F
2.55:1			
2.72:1			
2.87:1			
2.94:1			
3.00:1			
3.07:1			
3.23:1			
3.31:1		3.33:1	
3.42:1			
3.50:1	3.54:1		
3.54:1		3.54:1	
3.73:1		3.73:1	3.73:1
3.92:1			
4.09:1	4.10:1	4.10:1	4.10:1
4.27:1			
4.55:1		4.56:1	4.56:1
4.78:1			
4.89:1		4.88:1	4.88:1
5.38:1		5.13:1	5.13:1
5.89:1		5.86:1	5.86:1
		6.17:1	6.17:1
		7.17:1	7.17:1

nominal gross axle weight rating of 4000 pounds, and an aluminum center section weight of 85 pounds. Ring gear diameter is 9 inches. Short duration maximum torque output is rated at 5000 ft. lbs., and continuous maximum torque output is 1200 ft. lbs. Available ratios for the Model 50-IFS are 3.54:1 and 4.10:1. Naturally, this limited selection of ratios will have an impact on the rear axle ratio that is chosen, because both front and rear axles need to have matching axle ratios.

Model 60 is a heavy-duty axle, yet is still quite a ways down the list from the strongest assemblies produced by the Spicer Axle Division of Dana Corporation. Model 60 is a semi-floating axle assembly with housing tube diameter of 3.125 inching is 1500 ft. lbs. Brake options include both drums and discs, and the wheel bolt pattern is eight 1/2-inch diameter bolts on a 6.5-inch diameter circle. Optional limited slip differential is the Trac-Lok unit. Available axle ratios for the Model 60 rearend include 3.33:1, 3.54:1, 3.73:1, 4.10:1, 4.56:1 and 4.88:1.

Model 60-HD is the first place that a full-floater is available from Spicer. Many of the specifications for this assembly are identical to the Model 60, such as the axle housing tube diameter at 3.125 inches, and the ring gear diameter of 9.75 inches. But some of the weight and torque ratings increase. Nominal gross axle weight rating is 6000 pounds, and the nominal gross combination weight rating is 13,500 pounds. Short duraweight of the vehicle, but are only serving as a medium to transfer torque from the differential to the wheel hubs. Available ratios for the Model 60-HD rear axle include 3.33:1, 3.54:1, 3.73:1, 4.10:1, 4.56:1, 4.88:1, 5.13:1, 5.86:1, 6.17:1 and 7.17:1.

Front axle, Model 60-F, is a steerable full-floater that weighs 305 pounds without brakes. Housing tube diameter is 3.125 inches, and ring gear measurement is 9.75 inches. Nominal gross axle weight rating is 4500 pounds (1000 pounds lower than the Model 60 rear axle), and torque output ratings are identical to those of the Model 60 rear axle. Maximum steering angle is 40 degrees, and brake options include both drum and disc assemblies. Eight

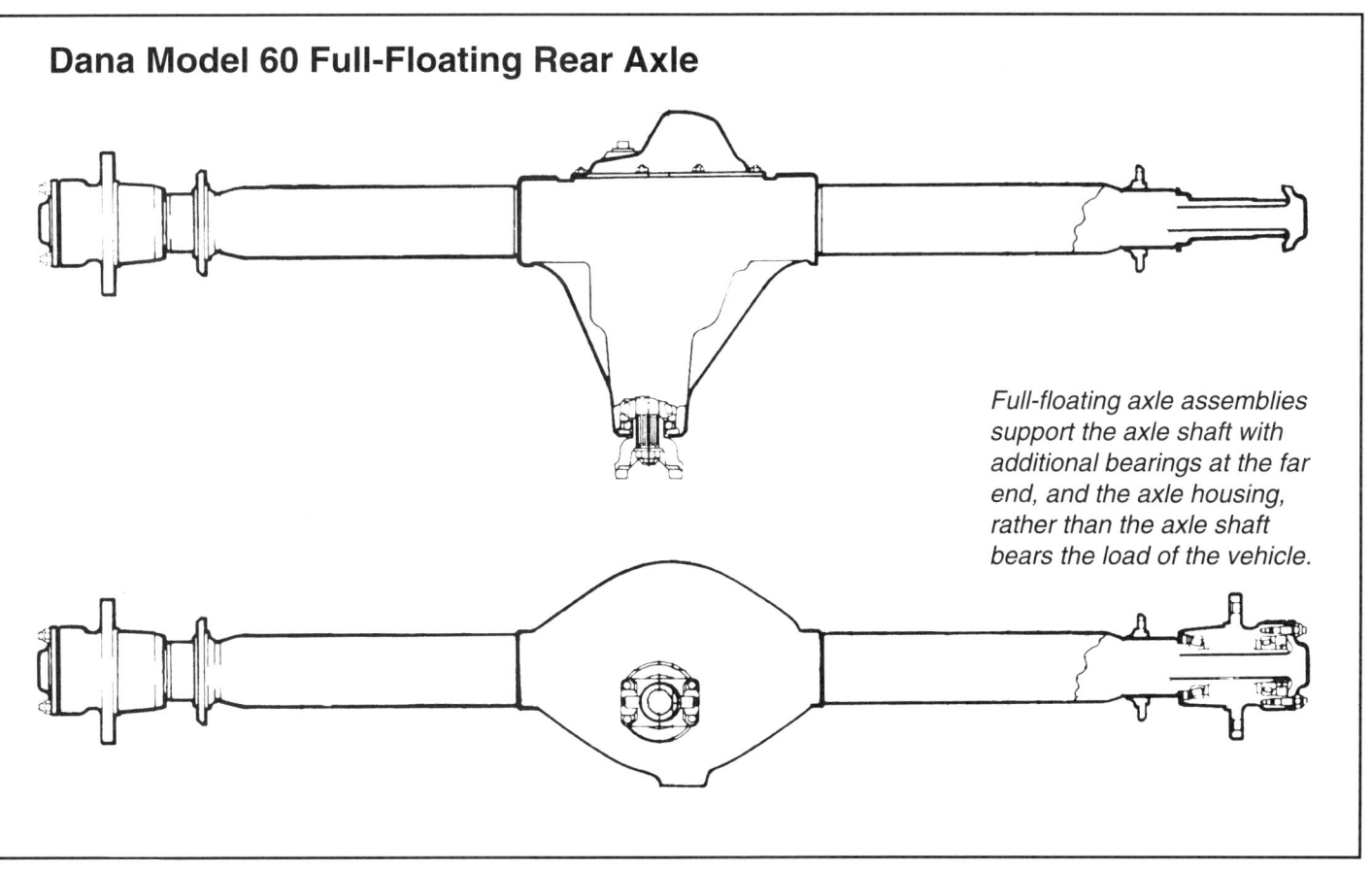

Dana Model 60 Full-Floating Rear Axle

Full-floating axle assemblies support the axle shaft with additional bearings at the far end, and the axle housing, rather than the axle shaft bears the load of the vehicle.

es. The differential ring gear has a diameter of 9.75 inches. Nominal gross axle weight rating is 5500 pounds, and nominal gross combination weight rating is 13,500 pounds. Maximum torque rating for short duration use is 5550 ft. lbs., and the maximum continuous use torque rattion maximum torque rating is 6000 ft. lbs., and continuous torque rating is 1500 ft. lbs. So there are some increases in ratings. But the biggest improvement is in the way the axle is supported by additional bearings at the outer end, and the fact that the axle shafts are not supporting the .50-inch bolts in a 6.5-inch circle hold the wheels, and the optional limited slip unit is the Trac-Lok, and ratios are identical to those listed under the Model 60-HD rear axle.

When talking about strength and durability, at the top of Spicer's truck axle line is the Model 70 assembly.

Dana Model 60-F Full-Floating Front Axle

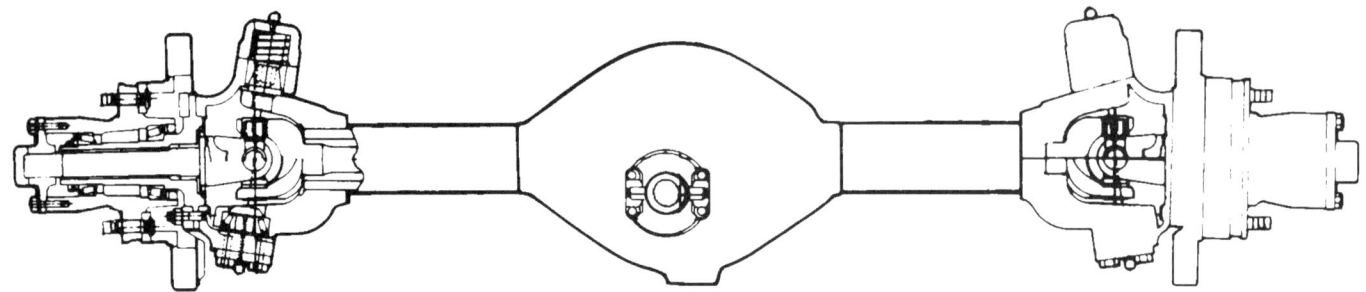

It's important to match the front axle to the rear, when building or modifying a four-wheel-drive truck. This ensures that components are well balanced from a strength standpoint, and gearing is compatible.

We're talking heavy-duty here, with emphasis on the word heavy. At 260 pounds, this unit weighs almost twice as much as a 140-pound Model 44 assembly, and it is 50 pounds heavier than a Model 60. This is a full-floater with housing tube diameter of 3.562 inches and a ring gear diameter of 10.5 inches. Nominal gross axle weight rating is 7500 pounds, and nominal gross combination weight rating is a massive 18,500 pounds. This is the kind of axle that you can find under some motorhomes, so it stands to reason that it will hold up to just about any kind of demand placed on it by a high-performance truck. Maximum torque rating for short duration is 8000 ft. lbs., and continuous torque rating is 2000 ft. lbs. Drum brakes or discs can be installed on this assembly, and the wheel lug pattern is eight .625-inch diameter bolts on a 6.5-inch circle. The optional limited slip differential for the Model 70 is the Powr-Lok unit. Available ratios include 3.73:1, 4.10:1, 4.56:1, 4.88:1, 5.13:1, 5.86:1, 6.17:1, and 7.17:1.

When building or modifying a high-performance four-wheel-drive truck, it's important to match front and rear axle assemblies. There isn't much sense in trying to save weight or money by, let's say, installing a Model 60 rear axle and a Model 44-F front axle. The differences in weight ratings and torque ratings are so substantial that you would be intentionally building in a weakness where strength is demanded. Not only that, but front and rear axle ratios should be identical. Model 44-F offers 20 different possible gear ratios and Model 60 offers only half that many — and only two of those are the same as the Model 44-F, and those two ratios are not considered performance gearing.

For those who must have axles made to non-standard dimensions, Spicer Axle Division of Dana Corporation can accommodate you. What you need to provide them are the following bits of information about the axle assemblies you want built: Load Capacity, Torque Requirements, Tread Requirements, and Spring Location. One of the important elements when having axles made is to properly lay out the dimensional design. While rear axles can have the differential centered, front axles for 4x4 trucks have to have the differential offset to one side to provide clearance for the engine oil pan. Knowing the dimensions of wheels and tires is vital. If the wheels have a lot of offset either positive or negative, that will have an impact on total axle width. Exact location of spring pads is critical. These are just a few of the considerations when designing replacement axles as you move toward high-performance chassis components.

Strengthening the Housing

The axle housing is subject to

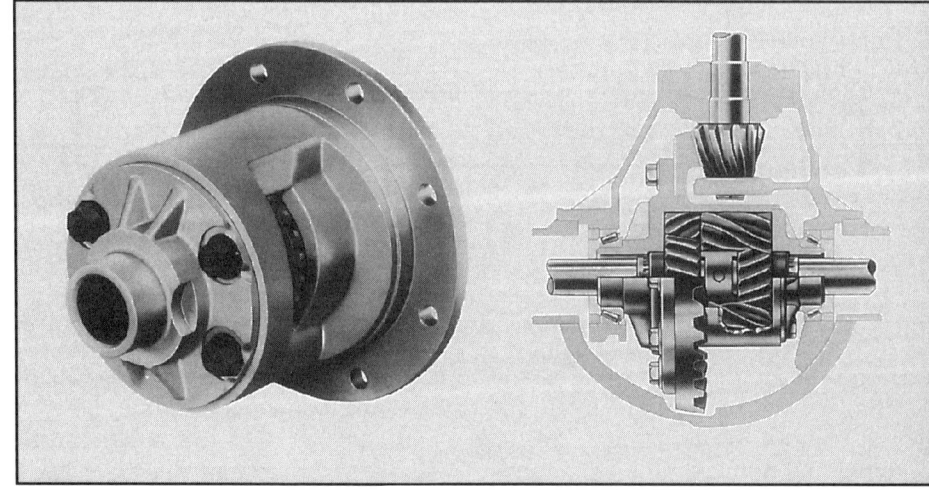

Detroit's TrueTrac is a limited-slip differential that operates through direct gear to gear contact, rather than through the use of clutch packs, as other limited-slip units do.

This cutaway view of the Detroit Soflocker shows the two dog clutch assemblies that engage for straight-line driving, and disengage when turning corners to allow for differential action as the outside and inside tires travel through paths of different lengths. The Detroit locker is one of the most rugged positive locking differentials available.

truss. Over the years, these trusses have evolved from simple steel rods with brackets on each end, to massive bridge work complete with skid plate under the differential. Some of these units are so heavy and so large that they end up adding unnecessary weight to the unsprung mass, and they eliminate much-needed clearance beneath the axle. They look macho, and they may even provide some justifiable protection against bending the axle, but you have to ask if they are really worth it.

Custom-Made Performance Axle Shafts

There are companies that specialize in manufacturing high-performance replacement axle shafts to fit many different applications. Moser Engineering is one of these companies, and their Custom Alloy axles are made of forged steel, induction several different kinds of forces. Under hard acceleration, the entire axle assembly tries to twist. In off-road conditions, where the trail is rough, the housing can take a lot of abuse from being hammered on rocks or stumps, or just from having the tires suddenly jump or drop when obstacles get in the way.

While the twisting motion of hard acceleration isn't particularly hard on the axle housing, damage can be done to the suspension system. I have broken two sets of leaf springs during hard acceleration, and the U-joint angle becomes so radical under these conditions that damage can result. The answer is either to stop accelerating quickly (sorry, unacceptable) or install a set of traction bars.

Off-road axle abuse is often the reason for people installing an axle

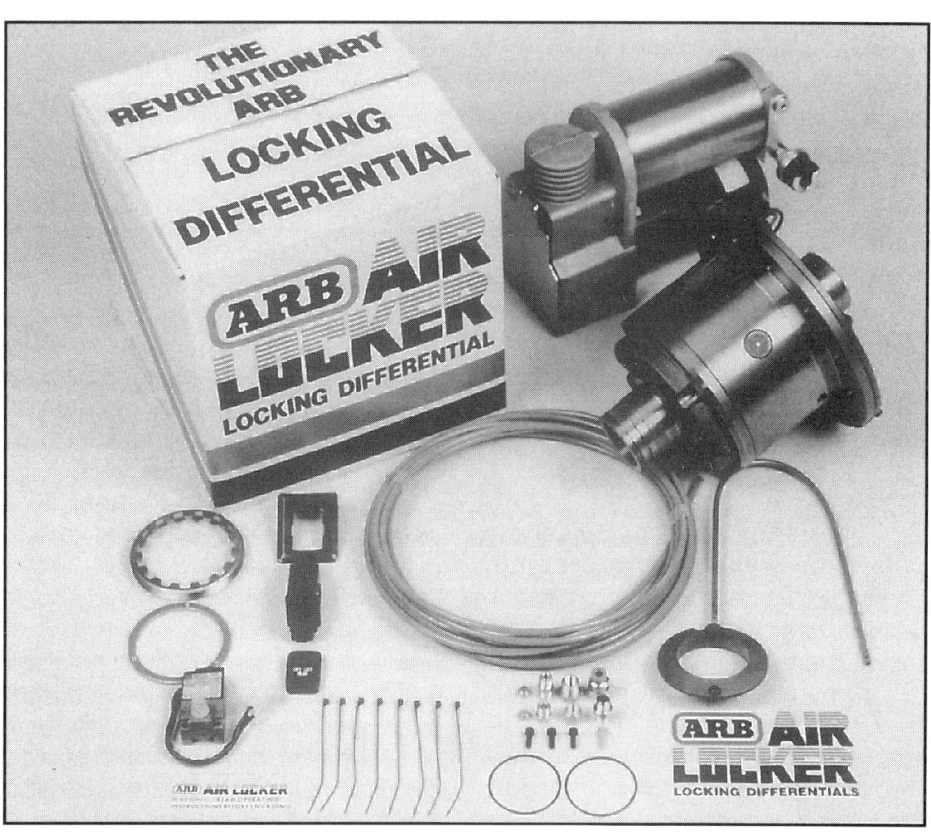

The ARB Air Locker is a unique approach to offering a driver-controlled positive locking differential. When the extra traction effort of a locked differential is not necessary, the ARB unit remains unlocked and operates like an open differential. When additional traction is required, the driver can actuate the locker by pressing a dash-mounted button, and the differential locks up and delivers equal torque to both axles.

heat treated, and then 100% Magnafluxed. These axles can be used for street applications, but they are especially engineered to handle the rigors of racing. Shafts are made of non-tapered stock, so they can be shortened and resplined later if necessary. Available spline counts and torque ratings include: 30-spline 6200 ft. lbs, 31-spline 7000 ft. lbs, 33-spline 8200 ft. lbs., 35-spline 9600 ft. lbs., and 40-spline 12,000 ft. lbs. Moser also carries a variety of other axle related components for high-performance applications.

Dutchman Motorsports, Inc. is another prime manufacturer of aftermarket axle shafts for high-performance applications. Available axles include replacements for Ford 7.5-inch, 8.8-inch and 9-inch, as well as for the Dana Model 60, and they can cut shafts to any popular spline count. Dutchman deals in shafts that have a non-tapered body so they can be shortened and resplined later on if necessary. They can deliver double splined or flanged axles, as well as C-clip style axles, and they can also supply related small parts for building a custom axle.

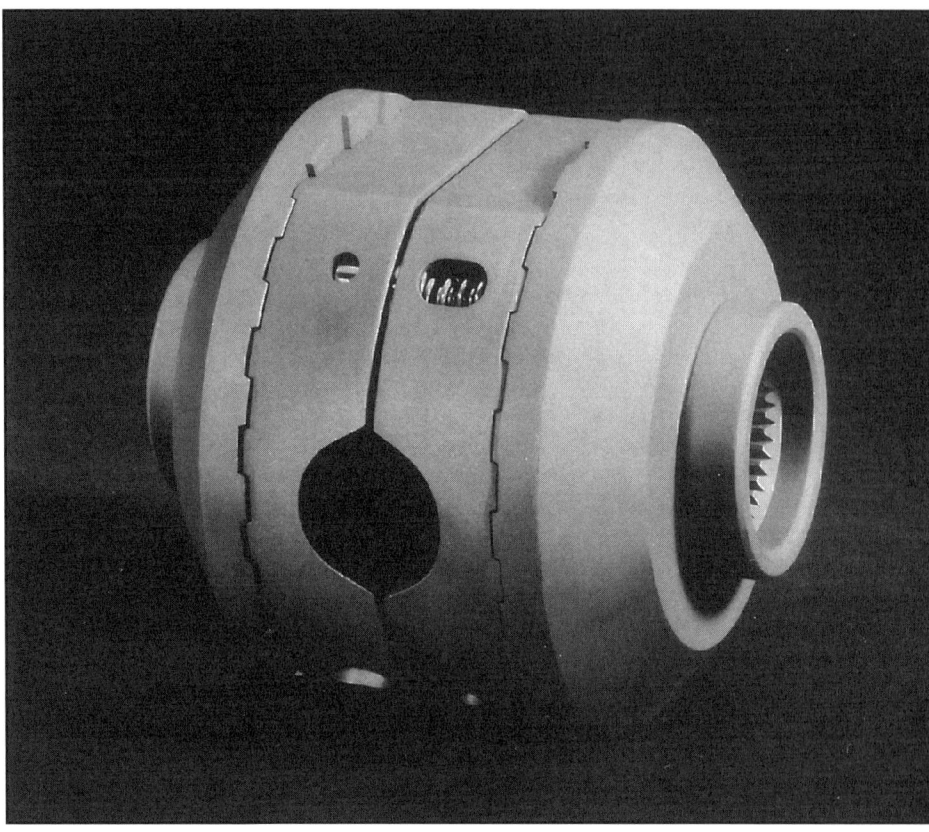

PowerTrax manufactures the Lock-Right positive locking differential that is installed in an otherwise stock axle, replacing the original spider gears with the assembly you see in this photo. When driving straight, the locking drivers are engaged. When turning a corner, they disengage to allow differential action to take place between the two sides of the axle assembly.

Maximum Traction Differentials

There are three different types of differentials — open, limited-slip, and lockers. Standard from the factory are open differentials, although some can be ordered with optional factory limited-slip units. None come from the factory with lockers.

Differentials are necessary to allow the truck to turn a corner smoothly. During cornering, the outside tires must travel a greater distance than the tires on the inside of the corner. This requires that the outside tires rotate faster, and the inside tires slower. If differential action were not possible, the tires would scrub and hop trying to match each other's speed through the corner, and axle wind-up and maybe even axle breakage would result.

Open differentials allow all the tires to run at whatever speed they want. Torque is delivered to whatever tire has the least traction, and tires that have best traction don't get any torque. This doesn't seem fair, and it certainly doesn't help matters when the tire that's sitting on snow or mud gets all the torque so it spins wildly, while the tire that has excellent bite on dry ground receives no torque effort. With open differentials, even the best four-wheel-drive truck is still essentially just a two-wheel drive vehicle under the wrong conditions.

This is why limited slip and locker units were developed. Limited slip differentials are designed to detect when one tire loses traction, and shift the torque to the tire that still has good traction. Limited slip units have a dual power path from the differential case to the axle shafts, and utilize clutch packs or gears to transfer torque from side to side as needed. When it comes to traction, this is a vast improvement over an open differential. Popular limited-slip units include the Detroit True Trac, Trac-Lok and Powr-Lok units.

Then there are lockers. The ultimate locker is a spool, because it physically locks both axle shafts together and delivers equal torque to both sides all the time with no differential action. This may be great for straight-line drag racing, but it is totally out of the question for any kind of driving that requires cornering. In an effort to provide the full lock-up traction of a spool, and still deliver differential action, positive locking differentials were developed. Among these are the venerable Detroit Locker from Tractech, the Lock-Right by PowerTrax and the ARB Air Locker.

This category of positive locking differentials is interesting from the standpoint of the various directions taken by different manufacturers. The Detroit Locker is very basic and rugged, being fully automatic in operation and as far as Ford trucks are concerned, this unit will fit Dana Model 44, 60, and 70 axle assemblies. The Detroit Locker consists of a pair of dog clutches (one for each side) that engage and disengage automatically as the vehicle turns corners, thus allowing full differential action. When running straight, the massively toothed clutches are fully engaged, delivering full and equal torque to both sides of the axle assembly. It's very positive, very rugged, and also has a reputation for being very noticeable in that there is a ratcheting noise and often a loud bang as the clutches operate. Tractech's "New Improved Detroit Locker" is designed with preload devices between the side gears to eliminate the backlash feel and noise. Because of the extremely positive nature of the Detroit Locker, the recommended setup for a truck is to use the locker in the rear axle and a Detroit TrueTrac limited-slip unit in the front axle. A locker in the front axle produces a nasty hopping and skipping of the front tires during tight turns, so the use of a limited-slip differential up front delivers maximum traction and also decent handling.

The ARB Air Locker is a completely different approach to maximum traction, utilizing an air compressor and storage tank that pneumatically shifts the locker into or out of positive lockup. This system is known as a manually lockable differential. When the locker isn't needed, the unit acts like an open differential. But when conditions demand, the driver can simply push a dash-mounted button and activate the locker. Because it can be activated on-demand, the system can be installed in both the front and rear axles.

Original equipment axles and bearings are retained, there is no special maintenance required, and standard lubricants are used.

Lock-Right is a positive locking differential made by PowerTrax, and is employed in commercial and military vehicles worldwide, as well as in consumer trucks. Installation is quick and easy, operation is smooth and quiet, and the system is completely automatic. The original differential's spider gears are replaced with a pair of Lock-Right driver and coupler gear sets in the existing gear case. Locking is achieved by the camming action of the pinion shaft in the driver's recess. When turning a corner, the coupler rotates the driver away from the pinion shaft, allowing both sets of teeth to rotate past each other to unlock the axles. After the turn is completed, the teeth again mesh to lock the differential.

Hubs

Most of the time, four-wheel-drive trucks don't need the additional traction provided by the front drive axle. To enable the driver to selectively engage or disengage the front wheels from the front axle, there are hubs. In the disengaged mode, the wheels and tires are free to rotate on the spindle, but that rotation is not connected to the axle shaft. This prevents the front axle assembly components from needlessly spinning, soaking up horsepower, and wearing out when not needed for traction. Shifting the transfer cast to 2WD will only reroute torque to just the rear wheels, but it will not eliminate rolling involvement of the front axle components and the front driveshaft. Hubs are needed to idle all these components when not needed.

Hubs come in two versions — manual and automatic. Manual hubs require that the driver hop out of the truck and dial the hub from "free" to "lock" when conditions require use of the four-wheel-drive system. Then, when conditions improve, the driver again must dial the hubs from "lock" back to "free."

Automatic hubs sense when the transfer case has been engaged in the 4WD mode and torque effort is shifted to the front drive axle. They automatically lock the front wheels and axle to each other. When 4x4 is no longer needed, the driver shifts the transfer case back to the 2WD selection, puts the truck in reverse and backs up a dozen feet to disengage the hubs. All this with never the need to step out of the truck.

The reason for all this concern about locking and unlocking the hubs is performance. With hubs in the "free" position, drag on performance is reduced because the front drive components are at rest. Sure, the extra weight of the front axle is still there, but at least friction loss and horsepower drain have been reduced. When four-wheel-drive is needed, the hubs make it happen, and that dramatically improves performance in conditions that call for additional traction. Hubs not only improve the "go" type of performance, but also the "stop" type. Using the hubs in the "lock" position, the truck is provided with four-wheel compression braking ability.

Warn Industries is probably the most famous manufacturer of hubs. Warn hubs feature a limited lifetime warranty, and they never require maintenance. However, these hubs can be easily disassembled for maintenance, if it ever becomes necessary. And service kits are available for those occasions when it becomes necessary to remove the hubs for brake work or wheel bearing service.

Performance Modifying Ford Trucks

Warn Hubs For Ford Trucks

YEAR	VEHICLE DESCRIPTION	WARN PART #'s Std, Manual	Prem. Manual
1976-'95	F-150	9790/25550	20990
1977-'95	F-250 Light Duty	9790/25550	20990
1978-'95	F-250 Heavy Duty	11690	
1988-'95	F-350	11690	

Performance Modifying Ford Trucks

Suspension

When discussing high-performance trucks, the suspension system ranks right up there alongside the drivetrain in overall importance. Without a well-designed and expertly executed suspension system, the truck will be unruly and unmanageable, truly a disappointment to drive.

If the suspension system isn't right, all the under-hood power in the world won't do much good, because the truck will not be able to be driven up to its full potential. It's the suspension system that keeps the tires in contact with the ground, without which all that glorious horsepower and torque fail to translate into traction. When the tires leave the ground, traction is lost, time is lost, speed is lost, and perhaps even control is lost.

The suspension system is generally thought of as consisting of two major components, springs and shock absorbers, although the full suspension system consists of many more components than just these two. There is some misunderstanding about the role of springs and shock absorbers. Some folks believe that springs and shock absorbers do the same job, but their duties are really very different.

Springs vs. Shock Absorbers

The primary function of springs is to support the truck while permitting limited movement between the chassis and the wheels. Traveling along a smooth highway, the suspension system may be largely at rest much of the time, except for its role in supporting the weight of the truck. But as the tires pass over a bump, energy is produced as the suspension system is deflected upward. The spring absorbs this energy by compressing, and then slowly releases some of this energy to the chassis, while the rest of it is released as the springs rebound. The spring action cushions the impact of the bump, and if the bump is small enough, occupants of the truck may not even feel the impact, as most of the energy is dissipated.

Naturally, some energy is absorbed by the tire as it passes over the obstacle and goes through its own compression and rebound cycle. But tires are not supposed to be part of the suspension system. They are only incidental to the whole process, and should not be counted on to provide the ride and handling characteristics that ought to be delivered by a properly engineered suspension system.

When the tire encounters a depression in the surface of the ground, the spring extends, allowing the suspension system to drop. Again, energy is absorbed by the spring before it is gradually released to the chassis and body. When energy is released to the truck's chassis, it will respond by dropping slightly until enough weight is back on the spring to place it in its neutral position.

The funny thing about springs is that they don't just compress or extend. Being springs, they compress, extend, compress, extend, compress, extend, ad infinitum until all the energy is released and they can relax again. Springs, being very resilient, would continue through the compress-rebound cycle for a long time, unless they were acted upon by some force to damp the movement and absorb the energy. This is where shock absorbers come into play.

Unlike springs, shock absorbers are not intended to support the truck. No matter how many or what kind of shock absorbers you have under the truck, you can remove them, and the truck will still sit at the same height as before, and will carry the same load as before (air adjustable shocks are an exception to this rule). Regular shock absorbers are not in the business of carrying weight.

Without the damping effort of shock absorbers, springs would be free to compress and rebound without control after hitting a bump. The function of shock absorbers is to damp the action of the springs, absorbing and dissipating the energy produced by movement of the suspension system, slowing and controlling the motion of the springs.

The function of shock absorbers is to damp the action of the springs. They absorb and dissipate the energy produced by movement in the suspension system, and control and slow the motion of the springs. Were it not for shock absorbers, the springs would compress and rebound completely uncontrolled, sending the pent-up energy to the chassis and body, making life miserable for occupants of the truck, and destroying ride and handling quality.

Springs

Okay, now that we have sorted out the differing functions of springs and shock absorbers, let's have a look at their individual characteristics. Hopefully, this will help you decide what modifications will be appropriate for your particular truck.

Ford truck springs come in two varieties — leaf and coil. Both of these types of springs are available in various spring rates, ride height, and total suspension travel. The style, spring rate, ride height, travel, and strength of springs your truck has depends upon several factors, including its vintage, whether it is a two-wheel-drive or four-wheel-drive truck, and the truck's duty rating.

The spring rate (stiffness — or rate at which a spring deflects a given amount under a given load) of leaf springs is controlled by several factors, among which are eye-to-eye spring length, the number of leaves in the pack, leaf thickness and taper. These elements are all inter-related. If you take a spring pack with eight leaves and reduce the number to five, there will naturally be more deflection under load. Likewise, if you take leaves of a given thickness, and lengthen them, they will be more resilient than the shorter leaves would be under the same load. Thinner leaves, or those that taper more quickly will also display softer characteristics.

In addition to adding more or thicker leaves, the suspension can be stiffened by installing springs that are made with a more aggressive arc. Slightly arced springs are often used as a means of lifting a truck a few inches, but caution must be used because springs of this type are stiffer than stock springs, and the owner may be disappointed in the harsh ride quality that results. I have seen this taken to extremes, with over-arced springs that offer virtually no suspension travel. The result is virtual elimination of suspension travel. The truck may look macho, but it can't be driven with any measure of ride comfort, handling or control.

If soft suspension is your goal, one possible method is to install longer spring packs to soften the ride. Of course, this would require careful repositioning of the spring hangers on the frame rails, taking care to prevent a shift of axle position either fore or aft. If the spring pad is positioned at the center of the spring pack, lengthening the pack means that both the front and rear hangers must be moved. Consider the difficulty of moving the forward hanger of a front leaf spring any farther forward, if it is already positioned at the extreme front of the frame rail. It is possible to lengthen the front of the frame to accommodate the spring hanger move, and this is something you must think about before modifying leaf spring length. Just about anything can be done, but sometimes the complications exceed the benefits.

Whenever the suspension system is altered in the direction of softness, it is important to consider the potential for bottoming-out on bumps. Because the springs are engineered to support the weight of the vehicle under what the engineers calculate will be the most probable driving conditions, softening the suspension may result in the truck more easily exceeding total suspension travel and hitting the bump stops more often.

Coil springs are made of heavy spring wire that is wound into a coil. Spring rate, overall suspension travel, ride height and capacity are all controlled by the diameter of the wire. Once a coil spring is made, it is not as easy to modify as a leaf spring to increase spring rate or load bearing capacity. You can't just add an extra coil. However, stiffer or softer, longer or shorter coils can be installed to modify ride height and spring rate.

Eventually, springs wear out, lose resiliency, sag, break or otherwise require replacement. If the truck isn't too old, factory stock replacements are available through dealerships. But if you decide that is the time to step up to something a little different, there are aftermarket companies that specialize in custom components for those who want to alter the suspension characteristics of their truck.

Shock Absorbers

The function of shock absorbers is to control spring movement. One area where this is so obviously applied is in the category of off-road racing. If you watch the suspension under an off-road race truck, you will notice that it moves easily. There is lots of suspension travel, and it doesn't take much of a bump to put the suspension into action. These trucks sometimes have as many as four shock absorbers at each corner to control the springs.

The trick is to achieve a soft but well controlled suspension. The springs must be allowed to move easily, but the shock absorbers must maintain control of the springs. When the truck settles back to earth after flying over a jump, the tires must stay on the ground so control and traction are maintained. One reason why race trucks have so many shocks is that each shock absorber is fairly soft, but the combination of four of them at each corner adds up to ample control. Shock absorbers heat up due to friction, so having more units means the overall heat load can be shared, and each unit suffers less. Also, multiple shocks give added protection in case one unit fails.

When building the suspension system for an off-road vehicle, a soft suspension allows the tires to stay in contact with the terrain, delivers superior handling and ride characteristics, and protects the truck from damage that would otherwise result from driving over a brutal trail. If there is a fear that soft suspension will permit the tires to make contact with the body when the springs are compressed, then other steps such as body modifications should be taken to provide tire clearance. Ideally, the suspension system should not be compromised just to keep the tires from moving up and contacting body panels.

For street trucks, multiple shocks are not needed, except for appearance. Unfortunately, I've seen some people who, in an attempt to emulate a race truck, have installed lift kits and quad shocks at each corner, only to discover that the truck then has virtually no suspension action and is uncomfortable and unmanageable to drive. The problem is that, in looking at race trucks, these owners have only counted the shocks and measured the ride height, but they haven't paid attention to overall suspension engineering, and they don't understand that race shocks are specially-made, rebuildable, and quite soft. Off-the-shelf shock absorbers are generally too stiff for multiple shock installation.

The way shock absorbers work is by moving a piston up and down inside a cylinder that is filled with oil. The piston is designed with valving that permits the oil to pass through

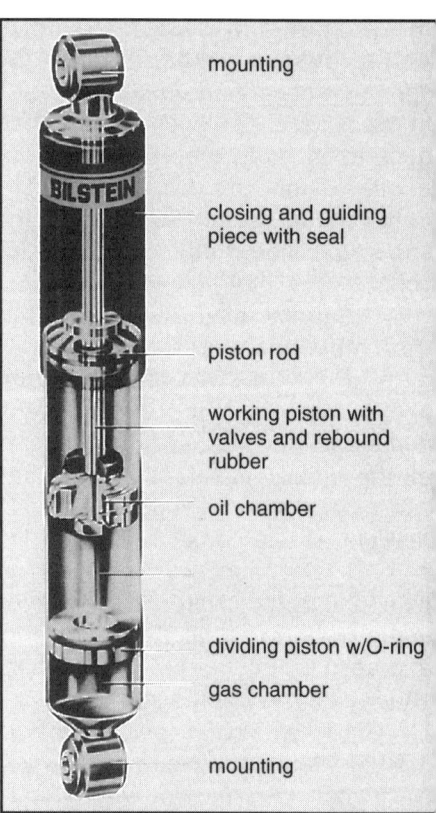

This cutaway of a Bilstein gas pressure shock absorber shows how the oil chamber and gas chamber are divided by a floating piston. This type of design provides excellent suspension control and reduced cavitation.

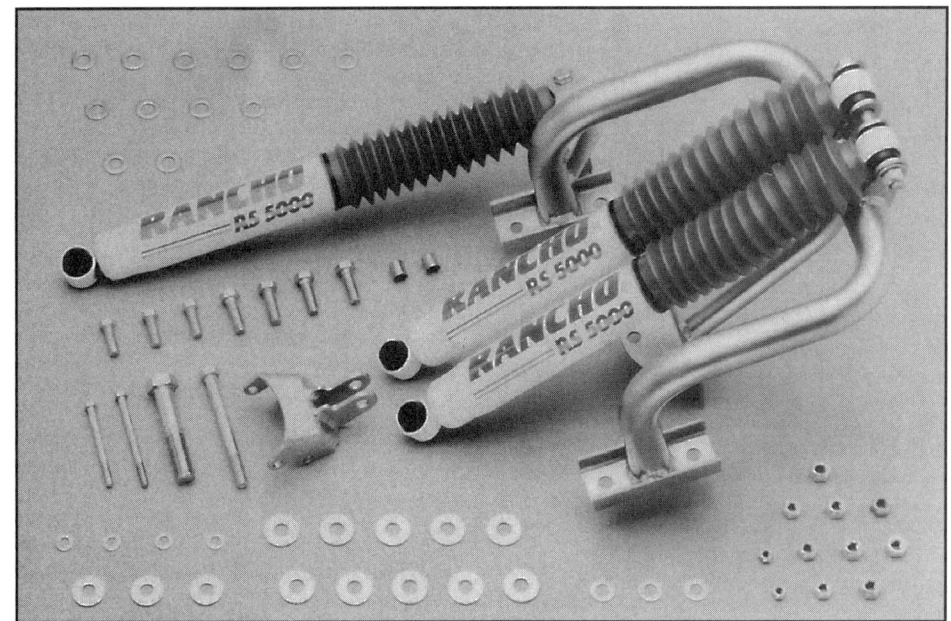

Multiple shock kits, such as this one from Rancho Suspension, are popular among some off-road enthusiasts, perhaps as much for appearance as for function. Race trucks use multiple shocks for very good reasons, but street trucks don't need them, and unless the shocks are selected carefully, suspension characteristics suffer under their influence.

the piston at a controlled rate. Some shock absorbers are designed so the piston can move easily in one direction, but there is greater resistance in the other direction. In other words, the shock absorber may collapse quickly under compression, but rebound more slowly and with greater control. Some shocks feature adjustable valving, so the driver can customize the ride and control characteristics. And technology has even brought us shock absorbers that can be adjusted from the driver's seat, on the fly, with separate controls for front and rear shock absorbers.

As the piston and oil interact, not only is heat is built up but the oil can foam, which causes a loss of efficiency. This is caused by cavitation as the piston moves rapidly through the oil under normal pressure. This is why gas pressurized shocks were developed. Under pressure, the oil is less prone to foaming.

And one other type of shock absorber that should be mentioned is the adjustable air shock, which features an air chamber that can be pressurized from an air compressor. These are designed to actually raise or lower the vehicle ride height and support a load, such as when towing a trailer that has a heavy tongue weight.

Lifting and Lowering

With leaf springs, it is fairly easy to either raise or lower truck ride height. If the spring pack is located on top of the axle tube, and you want to raise the truck without changing spring rate, it is an easy matter to install a set of riser blocks between the top of the axle housing and the bottom of the spring pack. If the springs are slung under the axle housing, several inches of lift can be obtained by simply moving the springs to the top of the axle housing. The amount of lift depends upon the diameter of the axle housing tube and the height of the spring pad. This will require cutting away the spring pad from under the housing and carefully welding it in place on top of the housing. If welding is done on the axle housing, extreme care must be taken to prevent the housing from suffering heat warp.

Any time a spring pad is being installed, care must be exercised to ensure that the pinion angle of the differential is absolutely correct. The best way to do this is to use a level and protractor to get the angle of the spring pad in its original position, and then transfer that angle to the top of the spring pad as it is being welded on top of the axle housing.

Aftermarket lift kits are available, and they are normally bolt-on units

Strength and stability can be added to truck suspension by installing an Air Lift air spring system, which is controllable from inside the cab. The springs can be inflated whenever additional strength is required, such as when carrying a heavy load, towing a trailer, or additional ride height is needed.

Suspension **95**

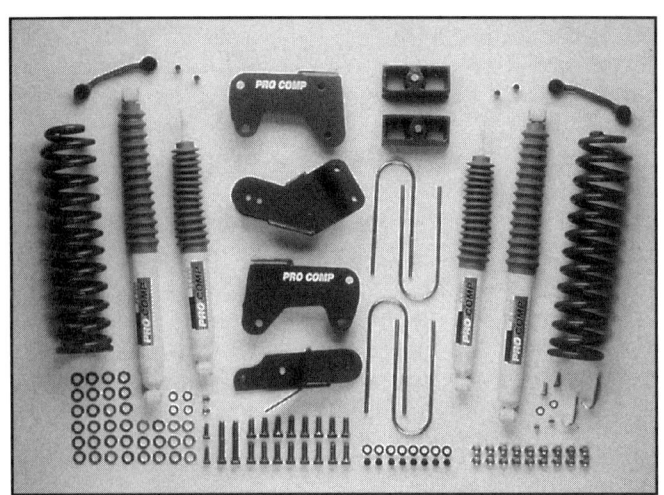

Explorer Pro Comp offers this complete 5-inch lift kit for the two-wheel-drive Ford Ranger. Pictured above is the Stage I kit, which includes coil springs, shock absorbers, and all the rest of the hardware to complete the lift.

that supply all the necessary hardware and instructions. Part of the kit may be new leaf springs that are designed with more arc than the originals, or new coil springs that are longer than what they are replacing.

Be aware that lifting can cause complications with the driveline and steering linkage. When a truck is lifted, the transmission and/or transfer case is raised along with the chassis, while the axle remains in its original position. This has the effect of separating the two from each other, increasing the U-joint angles at the transmission or transfer case output shaft and the differential pinion, and lengthening the driveshaft. These issues will have to be addressed, in order to prevent damage to the driveline. If the output shaft and pinion angles become too severe, the U-joints can suffer.

I have seen many examples of trucks that have had their axles rotated so that the pinion angle is reduced to almost nothing, in an effort to save the U-joints. But this causes problems with vibration in the driveline, as the output shaft U-joint rotates through its normal angularity, while the pinion U-joint has virtually no angle to work with. When the truck is at rest, the output shaft angle and the pinion angle should be equal. U-joints are made to work through angles, and they function best if the output shaft angle and the pinion angle match, so long as the angles do not exceed the manufacturer's recommendations.

Because lifting stretches the driveline, a new set of driveshafts will need to be made. As the axles move up and down in relation to the body, the driveshaft alternately lengthens and shortens. This is permitted by the driveshaft slip-joint, so careful measurement must be taken to ensure that the slip-joint has sufficient room to slide as the suspension permits the axles to move up and down. One other item of concern is that the driveshaft be installed with the U-joints in phase with each other. If they are installed out of phase, vibration will result. Being in phase means that the yokes at both ends of the driveshaft line up with each other.

Lowering a truck with leaf springs is relatively simple. If the springs are mounted atop the axle housing, they can be shifted to a position below the housing. If the springs are already below the axle, a lowering block between the spring pack and axle housing will space the suspension downward.

Lifting a truck the right way involves more than just installing lift blocks. This photo shows the Explorer Pro Comp Stage 2 lift kit for raising a two-wheel-drive Ford Ranger five inches, taking a comprehensive approach to suspension modification.

This complete bolt-on suspension system is the F-150 Stage II package from Explorer Pro Comp that is designed to raise a full-size Ford truck four inches to provide increased wheel travel or the ability to install taller tires

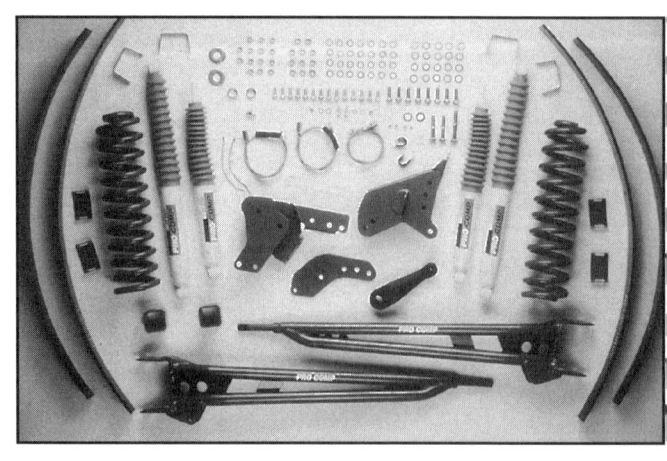

Some people try to alter the characteristics of a stock coil spring by applying heat to cause the coil to sag. This was the quick and dirty method for lowering the suspension of a custom car back in the '50's, but it is not a technique that we can endorse. First of all, heating a spring to make it sag is not a precisely repeatable process. You may end up with one spring that sags more than the other. What is really happening is that the quality of elasticity is being removed from the coil wire, and the overall suspension suffers. What has been carefully engineered into the coil spring is instantly tossed out, and nobody can guarantee the strength or integrity of a coil spring that has been altered by heating.

Another lowering technique is to simply cut off one or more of the coil loops, essentially shortening the spring. But the problem with this is that the suspension characteristics depend in part on the number of loops in the coil. Removing loops results in a stiffer ride, because there is less spring length to soak up the impact of bumps. So this method may work as far as lowering the truck is concerned, but it may also ruin ride and handling quality.

When it comes to springs, the best method for lowering a truck is to buy springs that are made to accomplish the task. However, this is not the only way to lower a truck. Popular these days are lowered spindles and lowered control arms, which can be installed for an instant drop in stance. These spindles and control arms are offset to drop the chassis in relation to the center of the wheel. Of course, this results in less clearance in the wheel well for the tires, so it is common to see lowered truck running smaller tires. And naturally, that plays havoc with the effective gear ratio, fuel economy and overall performance.

Be aware that lowering will result in the same complications that are created by lifting, in addition to a few problems that are unique to lowering. Depending upon the amount of lift or lowering, it may also be necessary to make alterations to the brake lines and steering linkage. Driveline angles

Lowered trucks enjoy a more favorable aerodynamic profile, allowing them to slip through the air with less resistance. The lower stance also improves cornering dynamics. But reduced ground clearance can sometimes be a drawback, such as when entering a steep driveway or negotiating speed bumps in a parking lot.

and driveshaft lengths may need to be adjusted to fit the new profile. There will be less clearance for tires, less clearance below the truck's body, and less clearance below the axles where the springs and lowering blocks are installed. If the lowering job requires installation of smaller tires for clearance purposes, that will also result in less clearance below the body and axle housings. Some trucks are lowered to the point that they become almost undrivable on any road surface that is rougher than a skating rink. Entering a driveway can cause body contact with the ground, and driving over a speed bump is out of the question. Although the outward appearance may follow a particular popular styling trend, that doesn't mean the vehicle has actually been improved from a performance standpoint. Quite the contrary, performance may decline dramatically.

You may surmise from this discussion that lifting and lowering are not high on my list of good performance moves. That is only partly true. There are situations in which performance can definitely be enhanced by lifting or lowering. But most of the radical lifts and lowering jobs we see on the streets today are counter productive to performance. They are done primarily to make a visual statement, not to improve vehicle performance. Perhaps that is all some people want, a visual statement, but if that is the case we need to recognize this and not confuse the issues.

If built properly, a lowered truck will enjoy improved aerodynamics and increased cornering capability as a result of the lower profile and lower center of gravity. This will improve performance for such high-speed activities as drag racing, gymkhanas, or road racing. But it takes more than a shorter coil spring or underslung leaf springs to make a good race truck. All things must be balanced — suspension, steering, brakes, drivetrain. A true race suspension is firm but supple. It sticks the tires to the ground, and yet yields to irregularities in the road surface. It delivers excellent road feel and control to the driver's hands and seat of the pants, but it intercepts punishment.

Likewise, a lifted truck has an honest performance purpose, but many lifted trucks that are raised solely for cosmetic purposes miss by a mile when it comes to engineering. Lifting a truck is beneficial to some aspects of performance in the off-road setting, where obtaining sufficient ground clearance is a challenge, but it also raises the center of gravity and can result in lack of vehicle stability during cornering and side-hill driving situations. Race trucks in particular need to have massive amounts of suspension travel, and this means lots of clearance for the tires to work up and down without hitting the body. Lifting the truck gives the needed clearance for tires. It also increases approach and departure angles, as well as ramp breakover angle to permit the truck to travel over truly nasty terrain without hanging up on the big bumps and drop-offs. Other than that, and ego, there is no reason to lift a truck. In fact, there are many off-road race trucks that are not lifted. Tire clearance for the massive suspension travel is achieved by removal of the inner fender panels, but the truck itself may sit fairly close to the ground.

If a lift is desired, the best suspension is the one that remains soft and well controlled. The Monster Truck category is at the radical extreme of lifted trucks, but they serve as a perfect example of suspension evolution that has resulted in tremendously improved performance. In the beginning, the car-crushers were lifted by just about any means possible to enable the driver to install big tires. And the trucks then crawled ever so carefully over a line of old derelict cars, crushing them to the delight of a stadium full of spectators. It was all the drivers could do just to keep the trucks under control while gingerly maneuvering over the line of cars. The trucks would bounce hard as they drove over the cars, and they were a handful to control. But now, Monster Truck drivers are involved in full-out drag races over the line of cars, often flying their trucks many feet in the air and landing at the far end of the course. But notice that the winning trucks don't really crash down. They settle softly, and stick to the ground once they've made contact, because the suspension systems have evolved into hydraulic cushioning devices of wonderful engineering that can absorb and dissipate an enormous amount of impact.

Lowering and lifting satisfy some very specific performance demands. Done poorly, the truck will become a disappointment. But done properly, a radically altered suspension system will deliver reasonable comfort and superior handling characteristics. Be aware that lowering and lifting are not legal for street use in many places around the country. Before launching into this type of project, you should check with local law enforcement authorities to find out what restrictions are in effect in your area.

Bushings

One of the suspension components that is easy to overlook, yet needs periodic attention are the bushings that cushion the space between spring eyes and shackles and the mounting points of shock absorbers. High quality aftermarket bushings are made of urethane, which is more firm than stock rubber bushings. They are quite durable, so they hold up well, and because of their firmness they do a better job of eliminating free-play and controlling movement between suspension components than original equipment rubber bushings. With free-play eliminated, shock absorbers and springs react more quickly and precisely to terrain changes.

Over time, even the best bushings wear out and require replacement. Life span depends largely upon the type of driving that is being done. Naturally, the more abuse the suspension suffers, the faster the bushings will wear out or break down. When ordering new suspension components, such as springs and shocks, from aftermarket companies like Rancho Suspension, they often arrive already equipped with urethane bushings. But even if you aren't replacing your stock suspension, if you're still running around on stock bushings, some noticeable performance improvement can be obtained by simply swapping over to urethane bushings at the springs and shock absorbers.

Add-A-Leaf

If your truck needs extra strength in the suspension department to permit the hauling of heavy loads, an add-a-leaf kit may be just the ticket. This is a method to raise the ride height of a truck, and increase the spring rate without replacing the entire spring pack. Most often, add-a-leaf kits are installed when a truck is relegated to hauling heavy loads on a fairly regular basis. This would include carrying a camper or towing a trailer with a heavy tongue weight. The add-a-leaf fits between the stock overload spring and the rest of the spring pack. A normal overload spring is flat, and doesn't come into play until the load on the suspension is great enough to flatten the spring pack against the overload spring. But an add-a-leaf is curved to match the contour of the spring pack, so it is in operation at all times. This naturally stiffens the ride and reduces body sway under all driving conditions, whether or not a heavy load is being carried.

Rancho Suspension offers a system called Lev-A-Load, which, unlike an add-a-leaf kit, is installed on top of the stock spring pack. The Lev-A-Load system permits variable adjustment of ride height and spring rate increase by tuning the tension on U-bolt brackets. The system is a simple bolt-on design, and does not affect ride quality when the truck is unloaded.

Traction Arms

Way back in the early days of street racing, hot cars would typically be equipped with traction bars to control axle hop and spring wind-up during hard acceleration. Nobody ever thought about putting traction bars on trucks, but that was because trucks were just for farming and construction work. Nowadays, trucks are the hot street machines, and traction bars for trucks are available for the same reasons that performance cars use them.

Under heavy acceleration, torque twists the rear axle and places a lot of strain on the springs. As a kid, I managed to break two sets of rear leaf springs this way. A set of traction bars would have prevented the breakage and probably would have improved my times in the Saturday night stoplight drags.

Traction bars are connected to the rear axle and to some point on the frame or floor ahead of the rear axle. As the truck accelerates, and the axle tries to twist, the traction bars prevent that twist and tend to keep the tires more firmly in contact with the road surface. The result is improved suspension control and performance.

Explorer Pro Comp markets their Ground Attack Lateral Trac Bars, consisting of race-style, double-tube main bars that are ready to receive a pair of Pro Comp ES3000 Series shock absorbers to complete the package. The units are finished in Hammerstone Grey powder coat, and the design of the mounting system keeps the equipment up and away from trail hazards.

Rancho Suspension sells traction bars under the name Torque Arm Traction Systems. They also market Kicker Shocks, that act like a cushioned version of the Torque Arm traction System. Kicker shocks reduce axle wrap-up, increase traction, and control suspension movement. They work especially well on trucks with large tires and high-performance engines.

Shock Boots

It used to be that shock boots were used only for function, but these days they are also a fashion statement. Available in many colors, people install shock boots as part of the color coordination of the overall truck.

But from a function standpoint, shock boots are intended to protect the piston rod from dirt, rocks, muck and corrosive elements. The piston rod of a shock absorber passes through a rubber seal that acts like a squeegee to clean stuff off the rod before it enters the sanitary confines of the shock absorber's inner chamber. Boots simply help prolong the life of the shock absorber by preventing corrosion of the piston rod and resultant damage to the oil chamber seal.

Naturally, shock boots should also be installed on steering stabilizers. And in an effort to prevent damage to the driveshaft slip joint, there are now also drive shaft boots that cover the slip and spline section of the shaft, protecting against dirt, mud, water and rocks that may come in contact with this sensitive part of the driveshaft. They look just like shock boots.

Bump Stops

When the suspension system is altered, new bump stops become an integral part of the modification. On a lifted or lowered truck, it may be necessary to install new bump stops of a different height than the stock units, to maintain the proper amount of suspension travel.

Bump stops limit suspension travel in the direction of compression. This prevents harsh contact between axle housing and frame when the suspension is fully compressed, as when hitting a bump hard or when an airborne off-road truck settles back to earth after flying over a jump. Without bump stops of proper dimensions, the axle housing would continue moving toward the frame as the suspension compresses under the impact.

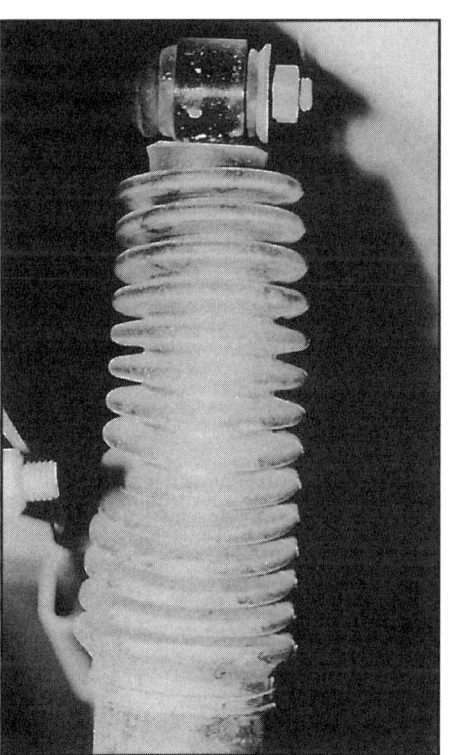

Shock boots protect the fine machined surface of the piston rod from dirt, rocks and other stuff that can destroy the oil chamber seal and render the shock absorber useless.

Factory bump stops are fine for stock suspension systems, such as seen here, but it may be necessary to install aftermarket bump stops if the suspension is lifted or lowered.

Limiting Straps

Used for off-road performance driving, limiting straps do the opposite of what bump stops do. They limit the amount of suspension movement that is allowed under full extension, such as when a truck takes a jump and the axles hang beneath the suspension system. These straps prevent damage to shock absorbers and other suspension components that would result from over-extension.

Summary

Designing a custom suspension system can be a challenge, but one that is very rewarding as the performance of the truck improves dramatically. Some aftermarket companies have solved most of the problems by engineering all the components for a complete suspension swap, either for lowering or lifting, or even for retaining the stock ride height but improving suspension performance.

Performance Brakes

It's no accident that trucks are some of today's most popular vehicles. They come from the factory with a distinct personality that seems to escape the vast offering of automobiles. Then the very nature of a truck begs for modification to personalize it to fit your own taste. The aftermarket has responded by supplying parts and pieces that range from tires and wheels to suspension and body modifications, allowing an owner to truly customize a truck.

But as soon as you decide to make modifications that affect handling, ride height, top speed and other such characteristics, an entire game plan becomes necessary because these modifications have a direct effect on performance and safety. In this chapter, we will discuss how and why this planning becomes essential before you can begin to design the brake system.

Designing a good brake system requires that you evaluate many of the other modifications you are planning for your truck. Before designing a brake system, it is necessary to know as much about the nature of the finished truck as possible. Some of the data needed to make brake calculations include: tire size, total vehicle weight and weight distribution, top speed, suspension travel, wheel size, and road surface, to name a few.

How the truck will be used — whether for street/strip performance, towing or hauling, or off-road recreational driving — will also determine your brake needs. For example, if you intend to drive your truck fully loaded on the highway to the desert for a weekend of enjoyment, then take it off-road for hard use in the sandy desert, then return home again on the highway, your brake system can't be designed for only one application, but must be a compromise in several respects.

What we will do here is to present some ideas of the things you'll need to consider in order to properly develop the brake system, once your truck has been fully planned.

In this book, we are discussing a wide range of trucks that span the decades from the mid-1970's to the present. As you begin your project, evaluate the existing system components and values your truck is now equipped with. Then decide what you can keep and what needs to be changed.

Trucks, by the very nature of their design, impose a high percentage of overall weight on the front wheels. This is done to allow a widely varying amount of weight to be placed on the rear of the truck in the form of cargo. This, in itself, creates a problem for installing a brake system. Ideally, a brake system should work under fixed conditions. Changing the weight bias, either by adding passengers or loading cargo in the rear, changes the ratio of weight on the wheels during deceleration. This condition exists more with trucks than with other types of vehicles that are not subject to such radical changes in cargo weight.

In automobiles, for example, the passengers sit centered somewhere between the front and rear wheels. As additional passengers are added to the vehicle, they sit in front of the rear wheels, which helps distribute the weight more evenly over the four load carrying tires. Also, most vehicle commuting is done with two or fewer people present. So it can be noted, that most vehicle brake systems are subjected to little more work, under normal circumstances, than stopping their own weight, and the weight of an occasional couple of passengers.

A truck, however, is a breed of its own. The possibilities of how the owner of a pickup will use that vehicle are almost limitless, and may range from mild to wild. There are those who modify their trucks for special purposes, such as the low-rider who drops his truck to accent the clean lines, the drag racer who tries to get as much weight as possible to the rear so the tires can grab maximum traction, or the off-roader who raises his vehicle to gain ground clearance.

Pity the poor brake system designer. Since he doesn't really know what application to design the brake system to handle, he does the most logical thing — he designs the brakes for none of them. Because he must try to design brakes suitable for all applications, the only real answer

High-performance and modified trucks, by their very nature, impose greater stresses on the brake system than do stock trucks. A truck that is designed for high-speed operation naturally needs improved braking ability. Also, when larger tires are installed, the rolling mass puts greater stress on the brake system, necessitating component upgrades.

is to design the system for the average load and hope it will work halfway decently for everyone.

As you plan the modifications of your truck, keep in mind that the more radical the changes, the more you must consider the truck's end use in order to develop a good, safe brake system. At one end of the spectrum is the person who intends to do a simple truck restoration. This individual has the easiest job, because a good restoration primarily involves installation of stock components in all areas, and maintaining factory original performance levels.

At the other extreme is the person who intends to raise his truck, install tall tires and drive fast. This builder has a lot of planning to do in order to design a brake system with the capability to handle the stopping requirements of such a radically altered performance truck.

Fortunately, there are solid solutions for both of these builders, and other variations in between. Because this chapter is intended to help you deal with your own personal choices, we will give you some insight into

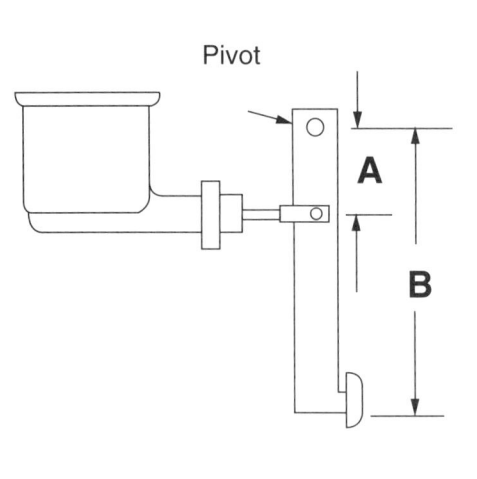

Calculating brake pedal ratio is accomplished by comparing the measurement from the pivot point to the master cylinder pushrod (A), against the measurement from the pivot point to the center of the pedal (B). For example, if "A" measures 3 inches, and "B" measures 12 inches, the pedal ratio is 12 divided by 3, which equals 4. Expressed as a ratio, it is 4:1.

what each of the brake system components are designed to do, and then we'll offer some guidance about how to apply this knowledge to specific situations.

But remember that under no circumstances should you take a modified vehicle out on the street without properly testing the brake system under all conditions that you might expect to encounter. We can help you build a balanced, safe system, but mistakes can happen. It doesn't take very much time or effort after building or modifying a vehicle to test drive it under controlled conditions, and have someone else check your work. Safety is always worth double checking.

To begin the project, first decide what it is you are trying to accomplish with your truck, and then design the brake system accordingly. To help you understand how to arrive at a suitable end result, we are going to discuss each of the components of the brake system according to what they do, how the component would be affected on a full size off-road truck, and then we'll take a look at how the same component would be affected on a performance modified street truck.

Brake Pads

One of the simplest ways to improve brake system performance, believe it or not, is to change your brake pads. The pads that come from the factory have been chosen to work in an environment consisting of the normal demands of everyday use. A common complaint from light truck owners is that their brake pads wear out very quickly. It is not unusual to hear of pads lasting as little as 10,000 miles. If they only last this long under normal use, you can imagine what happens with a highly modified truck.

There are three characteristics of a brake pad. First, and most important, is the coefficient of friction. This has to do with how well the pad "bites" the rotor. If you are now using a pad that has a coefficient of friction of .3, and you install a new pad with a coefficient of friction of .45, you have increased your brake torque by 50%! Obviously, this would be an easy way to solve the greatest percentage of brake problems, but it's not that simple. Many companies claim to have "heavy duty" pads, but unfortunately, this does not describe coefficient of friction.

The second important characteristic of a brake pad is the abrasion factor. This has to do with how the pad wears out the rotor. Many "heavy duty" pads use large amounts of sintered iron to improve coefficient of friction, but in the process they cause severe wear damage to the rotors. Be cautious when considering "metallic" pads. They can cause more problems than they solve. Another characteristic of metallic pads is that they require heat to work and, consequently, do not work well when cold. This means you must use them a few times to get them up to temperature. This is not the most desirable of characteristics.

The final factor for brake pads is life span. It is important to remember that the brake pad is going to experience heat in the system. The harder you use them, the hotter they get. The higher the temperature, the faster they wear. Very simply, some pads are specially designed to handle higher temperature ranges. They normally cost more because of the quality of the ingredients used to improve life span at higher temperatures. In order to truly obtain the best pads, all three factors must be considered.

If most of the modifications to your truck will be fairly mild, and the major emphasis will be on increased speed, an upgrade in brake pads alone may satisfy your needs.

However, keep in mind that in the case of increased speed, high-speed deceleration shifts much of the stopping requirement from the rear brakes to the front, as a result of weight transfer. Upgrading the front pads may be all that is needed, since the rear brakes will now be dealing with less weight to stop.

It is important to understand more about how a brake system functions, even if a simple upgrade of brake pads may be your ultimate solution. So, read on to see how the entire system operates.

Brake Pedal and Master Cylinder

The brake pedal and master cylinder work together to create the system operating pressure, so we will discuss them as a unit.

The master cylinder must be large enough to supply a sufficient amount of fluid to actuate all of the calipers and wheel cylinders that will be feeding from it. And the master cylinder must be able to do this in approximately half of its available stroke, but no more than two-thirds of its stroke.

The second, and most often overlooked requirement of the master cylinder, is that it must have a reservoir with a capacity large enough to hold reserve fluid in a sufficient amount to accommodate the displacement required for total wear of the lining, and subsequent piston movement.

When the linings and/or pads are in a totally worn condition, the reservoir should still have approximately 25% of its reserve remaining in the tank for a safety factor. Failure to make sure that your system meets or decreasing the "A" dimension. If you decreased the "A" dimension to 2 inches by drilling a new hole for the pushrod, the formula would now be (12" divided by 2" = 6") and the ratio would be 6:1. If you used the same amount of pushing effort from your foot, you would have increased the brake pressure by 50% in the second equation.

The problem is that your pushrod

Here it is: Input pressure multiplied times the pedal ratio, divided by surface area of the master cylinder = line pressure in PSI.

Let's try the formula. Input pressure refers to the force from your foot entering the pedal. Most people can push 150 pounds with effort under a maximum braking situation while sitting. This is a good number to use here. If you want to perform a test to

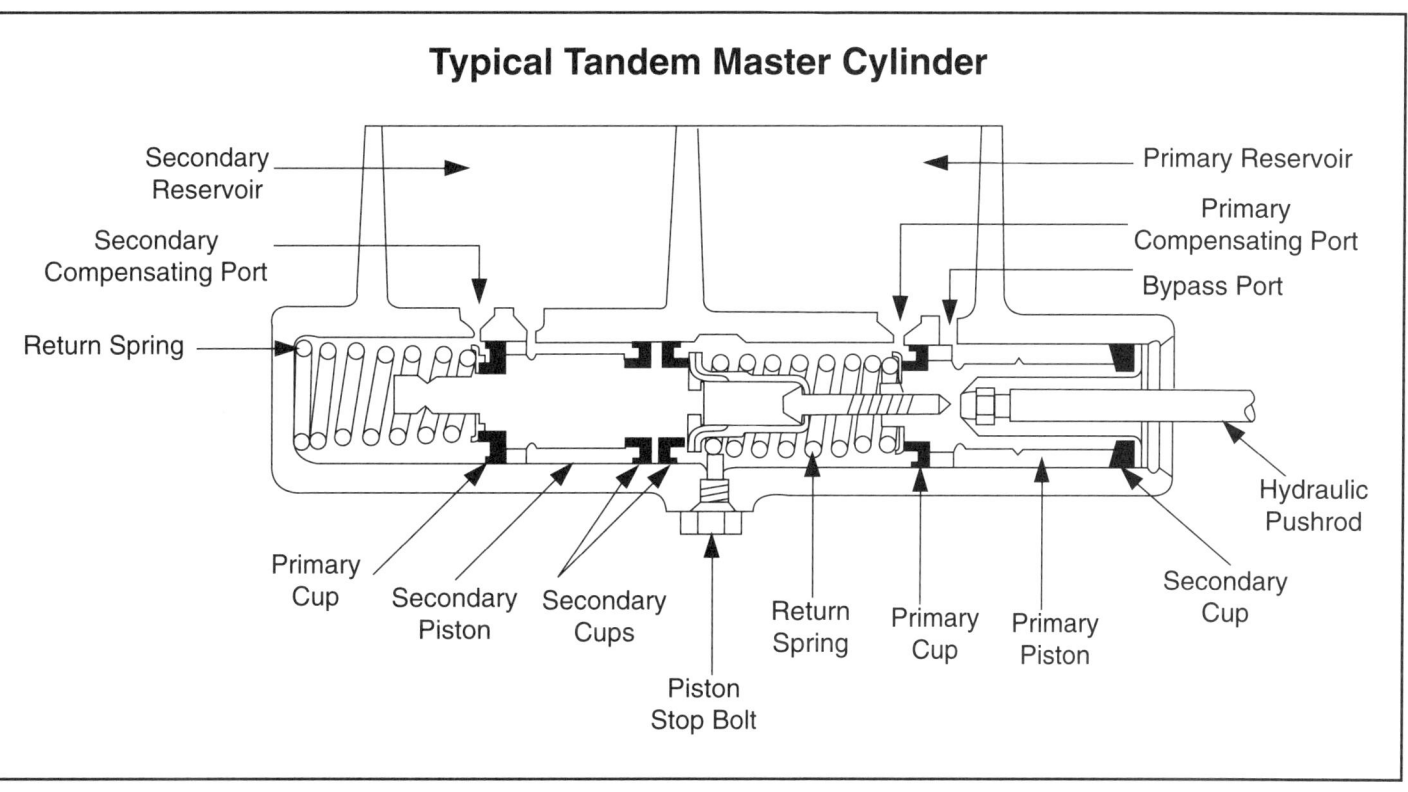

Typical Tandem Master Cylinder

this requirement could result in a partial or complete system failure.

The brake pedal is designed to be in a comfortable position for driver use. But more important, since it is a lever, the pedal must be designed with a proper ratio to give the best results. Pedal ratio is the comparison of the measurement from the pivot point to the master cylinder pushrod point, when compared to the measurement from the pivot point to the center of the pedal.

If the first measurement "A," in this case, 3 inches, is divided into the second measurement "B," in this case, 12 inches, the pedal ratio is (12" divided by 3" = 4") said to be 4:1. As you can see, if you wish to increase leverage, it can be done by either lengthening the "B" dimension will be pushing into the bore on an angle. It will be necessary to relocate the master cylinder closer to the pivot point or premature wear to the master cylinder bore will result. Additionally, this will also increase pedal travel by 50%, creating an uncomfortable and slow reacting pedal. Small changes make a large difference. Be careful to consider all factors before making any modifications in this area.

There is a formula that clearly shows the relationship of the master cylinder bore size and the pedal ratio. If you use it and plug in different values, you will be able to determine what your system is doing and whether it is in proper proportion. This will also allow you to explore the best way of making system modifications that achieve all your goals.

verify your input pressure, place a bathroom scale on top of the brake pedal and see what you can do. (We don't want the brakes too touchy or they will lock easily, which will hurt stopping distance). The ideal pedal ratio for a truck with a manual brake system (no power booster) is about 6:1.

The surface area of the master cylinder refers to the surface area of the bore size. (7/8" diameter = .60 square inches, 1.00" diameter = .79 square inches, 1-1/8" diameter = 1.01 square inches etc.)

Okay, let's plug in some values: 150 pounds (input pressure) multiplied times 6 (pedal ratio), divided by 1.01 (surface area of a 1-1/8" bore master cylinder) = 891 (pounds per square inch line pressure).

A number around 900 pounds per square inch line pressure, when used to supply adequate components (calipers or drum brakes), will result in a proper operating effort for most trucks. On heavier trucks, you may want the system pressure a little higher, and on lighter trucks, you may want it a little lower, but the example supplied here should help you understand the relationship of the numbers. Never exceed the maximum suggested operating pressure of the system. This is usually 1200 PSI, but always check with the manufacturer of the components first.

If you increase the input pressure or pedal ratio, the PSI increases. If the master cylinder bore size increases, the PSI drops. System pressure can be increased by decreasing the bore size of the master cylinder, but don't forget about its primary duties mentioned earlier. This is only an option if the other criteria can be met.

If your system has a problem of requiring too high an effort to make the brakes work, the trouble may lie with what you have just learned about developing line pressure. It doesn't make any difference how big the calipers or drum brakes are, if they don't receive sufficient pressure, they will not do what they are capable of doing.

It is not only important that the master cylinder create pressure, it is also important that it relieve the pressure when you take your foot off the brake pedal. If the master cylinder has an internal residual valve which is made to operate with drum brakes by maintaining about 10 pounds of line pressure (not enough to overcome the drum return springs, but helps to substantially reduce pedal travel), it will not release the pressure sufficiently for disc brake calipers. This will cause a serious brake drag problem, resulting in extreme wear. This in turn, causes overheating of the brake system and an unnecessarily high load on the drivetrain. If you do n't allow the brake pedal to return all the way, it is possible that the piston inside the master cylinder will not return far enough to open the pressure-compensating port. This would also result in serious brake drag.

In most cases, factory stock components will work even for the full size off-road pickup and performance street truck, unless major modifications have been made. The most important time to look closely at these components is when you change the existing calipers or master cylinders. That's when you must be sure that the fluid capacity and line pressure requirements are met.

If your truck had drum brakes on the rear and you have changed the rear end to one that has disc brakes, you must take a close look at the combination valve and master cylinder. Drum brakes require a 10-pound residual valve to work properly. Since the drum brakes have large return springs pulling the shoes back, they are more than capable of pulling the shoes back in spite of the valve.

The disc brake caliper, however, has nothing pulling its piston back after brake application, and any residual pressure will cause the brakes to remain applied. This valve must be removed, if you install rear disc brakes. Failure to do so will result in premature wear of your disc pads, possibly in as little as 50 miles. This will cause excessive drag to the vehicle. If you notice your vehicle does not roll easily, this may be the cause.

One note of caution: If you plan to reroute any brake lines, make sure to keep them well away from the exhaust system. Failure to do so will result in heat transfer to the brake fluid, causing the fluid to boil, resulting in potential brake failure. If you must run the exhaust system near brake lines, use a heat shield or insulation material to prevent unwanted heat transfer.

Never attempt to design a brake system around a single bore master cylinder. In the late 60's, the tandem master cylinder was developed, which is simply two masters in one. On the old fruit jar master, if there was an internal failure, the brake pedal went to the floor and you had no brakes. On the later tandem cylinders, if an internal seal goes bad, it will probably only result in a loss of half of the system. This will still allow the truck to be stopped, although not as quickly, with the other two wheels.

A good rule of thumb is to use the stock pedal and master cylinder that came on the truck, but only if it is capable of meeting the pressure requirements outlined in this section. If you need smaller components because of a space limitation, try to make the mounting match what you are removing so that new mounting holes will not be necessary. The less you are required to modify insofar as mounting position is concerned, the better.

Calipers and Wheel Cylinders in Drum Brakes

Wheel cylinder or calipers (they both perform the same function) take the pressure in the system and turn it into force. The force is the push on the shoes or linings, as the case may be, and is determined by the size of the piston. The larger the piston, the greater the force.

Keep in mind that the job of the front brakes is to handle the biggest portion of the braking requirement and they need to be powerful enough to handle the worst situation. If you intend to carry heavy loads, the brake system design needs to be sufficient for the highest load. If you intend to drive the vehicle at a high rate of speed and want to attain high deceleration rates, then your system must be prepared to handle the weight that will transfer to the front wheels from the rear during that deceleration.

In the case of a truck with larger tire diameters, it may be necessary to install larger calipers and wheel cylinders to improve brake torque. As tire size increases, so does the requirement for brake torque to stop the tire from turning. The best way to think of this is that the distance from the center of the wheel to the ground acts as a lever. The longer the lever, the harder it is to stop it from turning. Many trucks have increased tire sizes to such a degree that the brake system becomes woefully inadequate.

Changing the wheel cylinder in drum brakes has the same effect for the rear that changing the calipers has on the front. If the stock unit was 1-1/8", upgrading to a wheel cylinder with a bore diameter of 1-3/16" wil

When stock brakes are rebuilt with previously used components, the drums and rotors should be machine turned to renew the swept area and provide absolutely true surfaces for the brake pads and shoes to contact. This will help prolong brake life, deliver better braking performance, and eliminate pulsing and hot spots.

result in more force. The amount of additional force increases proportionately with the surface area of the wheel cylinder.

An important point to remember in the case of driving an off-road truck is that soft soil or other marginal traction conditions can make a truck tend to plow straight ahead, even though the front wheels are turned. Because of this, off-road trucks must have more rear brake than normal, to improve steering ability. This is where an adjustable proportioning valve in the line to the rear brakes should be opened to allow additional line pressure to reach the rear brakes. However, don't forget that when you get back on the highway you need to reset the valve to reduce rear brake pressure.

If you have decided to upgrade front disc brakes, you have several things to remember. Obviously, it is necessary to prepare the master cylinder as mentioned. Don't even begin to be concerned about the disc brake adaptation until that portion of the job is completed.

Next, remember that disc brakes require considerably more wheel clearance, which may require installation of different wheels. If you intend to run the stock wheels, be prepared to make major modifications to the new brake components or their mounting location in order to make them fit.

If the plans include situations that will require hard use of the brake system, keep in mind that the system is only as strong as the weakest component. Be sure to compare the bearing diameters on your spindles with the bearing diameters of the new components, to make sure you are not creating a weakness in the system.

Brake Fluid

Brake fluid is the life blood of the brake system. It is best to use heavy duty fluid in vehicles that will be driven harder than normal. Change the fluid at least once a year, and even more often than that, if the type of driving you are doing severely heats up the brake system.

Never use Dot 5 Silicone fluid in any brake system. The problems associated with this fluid are not worth the advertised benefits. Dot 5 Silicone fluid is never used in racing brake systems, contrary to popular belief. Don't let anyone tell you differently.

Testing

Regardless of the size, shape or use of your truck, the final phase in any modifications you make is to properly test to see if the results are suitable to the application. Perform controlled stops, beginning from 30 mph to 0 mph, to ensure proper operation. Increase the speed of these controlled stops throughout the range of speeds you will use normally. If you encounter premature front or rear brake lockup, review your system and make the necessary changes to bring the system into better balance.

If you make the brake system adjustable, as in the case of an off-road truck, install suitable warnings on the dash to remind any potential driver to check and change settings to match the driving conditions that will be encountered. Don't leave anything to chance. If you create a special-use vehicle, make sure other potential drivers understand when it is safe and when it is not safe to drive the truck.

Designing and building a good brake system is the result of successful planning, careful component selection, and precision assembly. Not the least of this overall process is making sure the final product works. After all, in a performance truck, the ability to stop is every bit as important as the ability to go.

Drum brake wheel cylinders will sometimes develop leaks around the seal boots. Inspect the boots for cracks, and pull the boots back to look for signs of moisture or corrosion on the wheel cylinder pistons.

Transmission & Transfer Case

Of all drivetrain components, nothing quite compares with the transmission in its ability to affect performance. This is because it is only by virtue of selecting the proper gearing that the full potential of the engine can be realized.

An engine produces maximum torque at a specific RPM, one of the functions of a transmission is to ensure that the engine can easily operate in the optimum RPM range. To do this, several gears are available in the transmission, and selection of the appropriate gear at any given engine RPM allows the vehicle to produce maximum performance.

Over the years, many different manual and automatic transmissions have come and gone, and some were better than others for particular applications. Knowing which transmission is best for a particular function is important when building a performance truck. Whether you're looking for an automatic or a manual transmission, a rule of thumb for selecting a transmission with the maximum strength and durability is to go with the transmission that was originally specified by the factory for use in trucks with the highest GVWR.

Manual Trannys

Early Ford trucks were equipped with 4-speed manual transmissions made by Warner and designated T-98. This unit eventually developed into the T-18, which has provided gear selection for Ford trucks for several decades. Among the best 4-speed manual transmissions that have found a home in F-series Ford trucks are the T-18, T-19 and the New Process 435. The T-18 and the New Process NP435 are rated tops for durability.

With four gears, these transmissions offered a nice spread between gear ratios, and also a compound low gear. If durability is the most important consideration, these cast iron 4-speed truck transmissions are highly recommended.

Later model 5-speed aluminum-housed manual transmissions deliver good service, as long as they are in excellent condition. Where problems arise is when a builder swaps in a used 5-speed aluminum tranny and discovers that the stamina isn't equal to that of the heavier 4-speeds.

Dedicated truck transmissions feature larger and heavier-duty clutch assemblies, which is an important element in the drivetrain. The function of the clutch is to engage and disengage the engine from the transmission, by means of a system incorporating a flywheel, a clutch plate, a pressure plate, and other components. When the clutch is pedal is depressed, the pressure plate releases pressure that holds the clutch plate firmly in contact with the flywheel. As the pedal is released, the pressure plate pushes the clutch plate into contact with the flywheel. Naturally, as the stationary clutch plate comes into contact with the spinning flywheel, some slippage is necessary. If there were no slippage, the transmission would immediately transfer the full torque load to the driveshafts and on to the axles. The result would be a jerky take-off. Even in drag racing, clutch slip is dialed in to match traction factors offered by the track, to prevent tire spin.

Depending upon your particular application, you may choose a heavy-duty racing clutch, or you may want something a bit more mild that won't strain your leg as you try to keep the clutch pedal on the floor while waiting for the stoplight to change.

The clutch presents one of the problems for using a manual transmission when towing. Recognizing that the clutch is the weak link in the drivetrain, truck manufacturers almost always issue lower tow ratings for manual transmissions than for automatics. This is because it's so easy to burn out a clutch while slipping it in an effort to get a heavy load started moving. People who tow with a manual transmission soon must learn the proper clutch technique, or they will ruin the clutch. Excessive slipping can ruin not only the clutch plate itself, but also the flywheel. When having a new clutch installed, it is frequently necessary to install a new flywheel or at least have the old one machined to give it a new contact surface. Conventional wisdom is to always install a new throwout bearing when doing clutch work.

Automatic Transmissions

Ford has offered a variety of automatic transmissions over the years, beginning with the 3-speed Fordomatic and leading through the 1960's with the cast iron Cruise-O-Matic, both of which saw extensive duty in both cars and light-duty trucks. In 1965, a new light-duty aluminum 3-speed automatic was introduced as Ford's C-4 transmission, and it began replacing the cast iron 3-speed units very successfully. The C-4 was a reliable transmission, when applied to automobiles or light-duty trucks powered by six-cylinder and small V8 engines.

The C-6 aluminum-housed 3-speed automatic came along in the late 1960's, and has seen duty behind some of Ford's biggest and most powerful muscle car and heavy-duty truck engines right up into the 1990's. The C-6 is strong and durable enough for application in heavy-duty applications and in trucks with optional high-output engine packages. The C-6 has been around for a long time, has proven its reliability, is easily maintained and serviced, and parts are easy to find.

In the 1980's, the quest for fuel economy drove the industry into the realm of the 4-speed automatic overdrive transmission. Unfortunately, some of the early units were not entirely reliable, and it was only natural that a bad reputation developed. Ford continued working out the bugs, and the later units were much more reliable. If you happen to have one of the early automatic overdrive transmissions, and are unhappy with the service it has delivered, an overhaul

Shift kits can help solve sluggish shifting problems in automatic transmissions. When preparing a high performance transmission, installation of a shift kit is a common approach.

to replace the weak components will probably result in a satisfactory unit for light-duty applications.

The latest automatic overdrive transmission from Ford is the E4OD, which currently enjoys a good reputation for stamina and reliability, and offers the advantage of an overdrive gear for improved fuel economy.

When preparing the truck's drivetrain for high-performance driving, you may want to look to some of the leading names in the aftermarket for shift kits or even complete transmission rework to suit the intended application. Aftermarket companies such as Art Carr, B&M, TCI, and others offer a multitude of transmission upgrades, and even fully race-prepped transmissions ready for street and strip, towing and strenuous off-road applications.

Torque Converters

Creating a viscous coupling between the engine and transmission is the job of the torque converter.

The stock torque converter that came with your transmission may not be adequate for properly handling the power delivered by a high performance engine. To accommodate a wide variety of applications and driving styles, many different types of aftermarket torque converters are available. Choosing the wrong one can seriously affect the truck's performance.

Bolted directly to the flexplate, the torque converter begins spinning as soon as the engine starts to run. Oil inside the converter follows the spinning motion, and transfers torque to the transmission. Torque converters come in diameters ranging from 7 inches to 13 inches, and can be modified to deliver various stall speeds and torque multiplication to answer a variety of performance needs.

Depending upon your application and planned driving style, there will be a number of options available to you when choosing a performance torque converter. High stall speeds are generally intended to be used in conjunction with high performance engines that can produce sufficient low-end power. Some torque converters, like Art Carr's Heavy Duty Super Torque unit are specifically aimed at the rugged duty required in off-road racing, supercharged and nitrous oxide enhanced engines.

Choice of camshaft has a lot to do with torque converter effectiveness. When building the engine, make sure to get a camshaft that is designed for use with an automatic transmission and will deliver good bottom-end and mid-range torque.

Transfer Cases

A transfer case is the backbone of what makes a four-wheel-drive truck different than a two-wheel-drive. Transfer cases are, in essence, power dividers that route a percentage of the engine's power to the rear driveshaft and a portion to a front driveshaft. When this is accomplished, both front and rear drive axles can put torque to the ground, resulting in improved traction. Of course, not all transfer cases are equal in virtues and vices.

1973 was a turning point for Ford, insofar as four-wheel-drive was concerned. Prior to that year, Ford had employed Spicer Model 21 and Model 24 transfer cases — Model 21 being a single-speed power divider, while Model 24 offered the benefits of dual range gearing. But in 1973, Ford switched over to the New Process 205 transfer case, which is a part-time unit that features a durable cast iron case and extremely rugged gear-drive. It is one of the strongest and most reliable transfer cases ever developed, and the gear-drive eliminates chain stretch problems that have cropped up in lesser transfer cases. This is, however, a heavy piece of equipment, so its application has been somewhat limited to trucks with requirements for strength and durability. Although many people consider the NP 205 transfer case one of the best units ever offered, Ford discontinued use of this transfer case after the 1979 model year.

Overlapping its use of the NP205 transfer case, Ford started to offer full-time 4x4 systems based on the New Process 203 transfer case beginning with the 1974 model year. NP203 was a chain-driven unit, and although it was a reliable and durable piece of equipment, its full-time nature did not interface well with the increasing cost of gasoline and public concerns about fuel economy. Not only that, but as a full-time system, there was concern about excessive component wear, especially in the front drivetrain and steering system. A popular method of overcoming some of the negative aspects of the NP203 was installation of an aftermarket part-time kit to modify the transfer case, as well as installation of free-wheeling front hubs. This allowed drivers to select four-wheel-drive only when needed.

Then in 1980, Ford began offering its four-wheel-drive trucks with the NP208 transfer case. This is a lighter-weight aluminum-housed, chain-driven transfer case that offers superb low-range gearing for excellent low-speed crawling capability. This comes in very handy when negotiating a nasty stretch of off-road trail, and in other situations calling for very low speed operation. However, the New Process 208 doesn't have the reputation for long-term reliability and strength that the older NP205 had.

Ford has more recently employed aluminum-housed Borg Warner 1345 and 1356 chain drive transfer cases. While these perform well, they don't last as long or offer as trouble-free service as the heavier NP205.

If you are looking for the ultimate in strength and reliability, find an NP205 and go through it to restore it to its original glory. If weight is a concern, one of the more recent aluminum units may be more to your liking, but you can expect that it may not last as long as the NP205, and you should pay close attention to service and maintenance.

Adapters

You may want to join a transmission and transfer case that were never designed for each other. While building a Jeep project vehicle, I once wanted to back up a late-model automatic overdrive transmission with a Dana 300 transfer case, considered by many to be the ultimate Jeep transfer case. This transmission and transfer case weren't meant for each other, so I had a special adapter built to allow the marriage. I went to Novak

Enterprises, Inc. to have the adapter housing made, along with a shaft to connect the transmission output and the transfer case input. It worked great for my particular application.

If you have a vehicle project that involves an engine and transmission that don't match, or a transmission to transfer case marriage that doesn't appear to work, contact Novak or Advance Adapters. These are prime sources for know-how and components that allow the joining of mismatched drivetrain pieces.

Automatic Transmission Oil Cooling

When automatic transmissions overheat, delicate components inside can warp, leading to eventual failure. To keep an automatic transmission happy, the fluid should never reach a temperature that is higher than 225 degrees F. Automatic transmissions are quickly ruined by overheating. At 175 degrees, automatic transmission fluid has an expected life of 100,000 miles. At 195 degrees, that life drops to 30,000 miles. At 275 degrees, the expected life of the fluid is only 3,000 miles, and at 295 degrees, it drops to 1,500 miles. But the time the fluid temperature hits 315 degrees, expect the transmission to die in 750 miles.

Some trucks are equipped with transmission oil coolers built into the lower part of the radiator. However, these units are not always adequate, so it is often helpful to install an auxiliary transmission oil cooler. In order to make the decision about whether or not you need to install a transmission cooler, the first step is to discover exactly how hot things are getting. To do this, install a gauge and sending unit. The best place for the sending unit is in the bottom of the transmission pan. This will require drilling a hole and brazing on a threaded receiver, so the sending unit can be screwed into place. Make sure the sending unit and the lines running to the gauges are protected from hazard of being snagged by road or trail debris.

After installation of these gauges, you will be able to monitor transmission temperature when involved in performance driving, climbing a steep hill or towing a trailer. Only then will you be able to make a decision about installing an auxiliary cooler.

Performance Driving

Those who are involved in activities such as drag racing need to learn to use an automatic transmission to squeeze out the maximum performance and to prevent damage to transmission components.

Best results for getting off the line in a hurry can be achieved by "brake starting." This technique involves applying the brake enough to hold the truck in place while simultaneously throttling up the engine to a "high idle" RPM level. Care must be taken not to over-rev the engine. At high idle, pressure builds in the torque converter. When it's time to go, release the brake and tromp the accelerator.

In drag race competition, stage at idle and prepare for the green light. If you time everything just right, floor the accelerator and launch off the line just as the light turns green. Hitting wide open throttle all of a sudden like this causes a surge in the torque converter at stall speed, and the vehicle will launch as engine power continues to build. Using a transmission brake such as the Art Carr Rebel Trans Brake will result in maximum launch capability.

It is important to follow the proper procedure when doing a burn-out, in order to prevent damage to the torque converter. Burn-outs are done to heat up the tires for improved traction, but you want to be able to accomplish this without damage to the drivetrain.

The best method is to do a wet burn-out that is just long enough to heat up the tires and dry off any residual moisture. It is critical that you back off the engine before the tires recover traction. Don't allow the tires to gain traction, thus pulling the engine down. Don't make repeated dry launches before the race, because this will excessively heat up the torque converter. Don't make short, smoky burn-outs followed by a hard, dry burn-out. And finally, make sure you shift to a higher gear before the tires hook up to prevent damage to internal transmission components.

Performance driving is more than just foot-to-the-wood and hang on. It takes skill and self-control to get the most out of the machinery and prevent component damage.

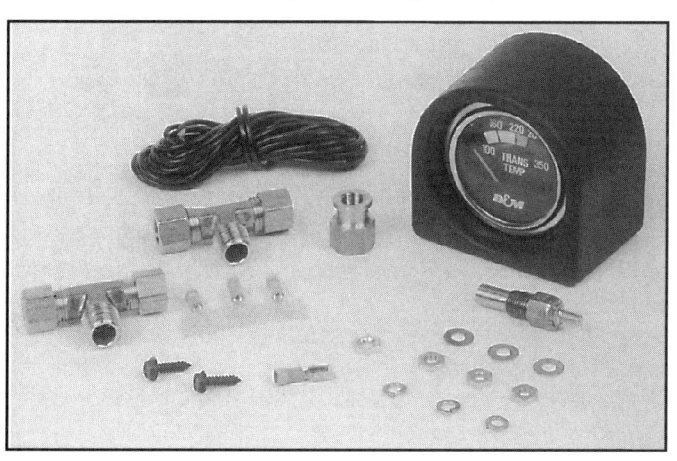

Automatic transmission coolers come in a variety of sizes, as pictured above. These heat exchangers are installed in front of the radiator. Pictured below is a transmission temperature gauge, which is an important item in a high performance truck, or one that is involved in towing or hauling heavy loads.

Building A Performance C-6 Trans

Ford's C-6 automatic transmission is widely recognized as the most bullet-proof unit that is available in consumer trucks built by Ford Motor Company. The C-6 has a good reputation for reliability and longevity in heavy-duty applications. But that doesn't mean that the unit cannot be improved. Since the time when the C-6 was developed, a lot of technology has flowed under the bridge, and some of it is applicable to this venerable transmission.

Take, for example the C-6 thrust washers. Nothing special there. But the kit from Level 10 features a thrust bearing to replace the thrust washer at the extreme rear of the assembly, which significantly reduces the amount of horsepower consumed by the transmission. From a performance standpoint, replacing the C-6 thrust washer with the Level 10 thrust bearing will free up horsepower that can be used to enhance the performance of the truck.

Another component swap that can be considered is replacement of the C-6 low gear with AOD gearing. The AOD low gear ratio 2.75:1, which is lower than the stock C-6 ratio of 2.48:1, so first gear spunk can be improved by exchanging gear sets.

What this swap accomplishes can be a two-fold performance improvement, if you also consider the gearing in the differential. If your truck already has tall rear-end gearing that delivers sluggish low-end performance, the change to lower first gear in the transmission will improve off-the-line performance. If your truck is equipped with 4.11:1 gears in the differential, which can be an economy killer, you may now consider a swap to a taller differential gear set to improve fuel economy at cruising speed, while still maintaining good first gear off-the-line spunk.

The upgrade pictured here employs a Level 10 Super Rebuild Kit, Super Load torque converter and a modified valve body. The rebuild kit includes the latest high-tech friction discs and bands, adjustable vacuum modulator, and all the necessary gaskets and seals. The Super Load torque converter is designed specifically for towing applications, and the valve body has modifications above and beyond what can be accomplished with a conventional shift kit.

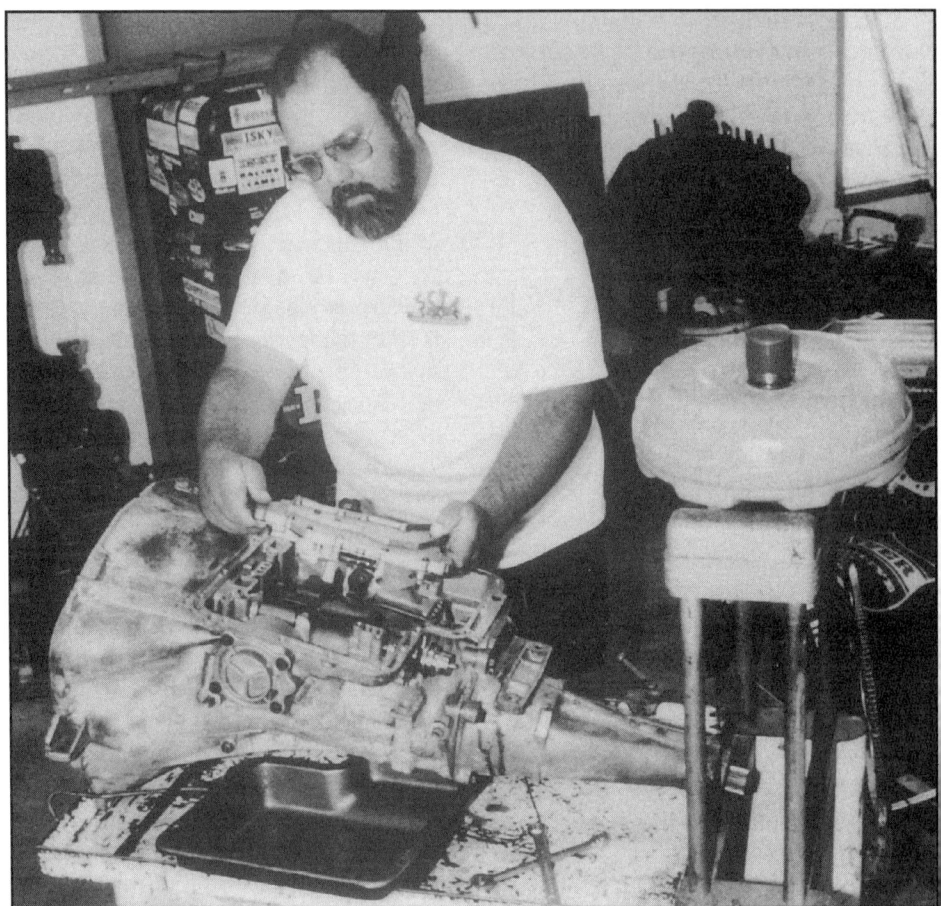

Taking a do-it-yourself approach to automatic transmission overhaul and upgrade is not as difficult as some backyard mechanics believe. Keeping everything very clean and organized is the key. Also essential is an excellent automatic transmission service manual.

It's very important to keep all the parts organized during the building phase, so it's easy to find what you're looking for during reassembly. Laid out in sequence, the internal components of the C-6 include (top row, right to left) the front pump, reverse-high clutch assembly, forward planetary assembly and input shell, low-reverse clutch hub, low-reverse piston, output shaft and governor assembly. The lower row (right to left) shows the intermediate band, intermediate servo, low-reverse clutch plates, parking gear, and governor distributor.

The heart of the Level 10 low first gear kit includes a new forward planetary gear set, sun gear, and input shell. By installing this new gearset, the transmission will go from a 2.48:1 first gear ratio to a 2.75:1 first gear ratio. This will give the truck a quicker start off the line and aid towing.

Here's a graphic comparison of the old sun gear and input shell next to the new Level 10 unit. Note not only the size difference between the two but also how much more beefy the Level 10 equipment is. Strength as well as gearing is improved with this conversion.

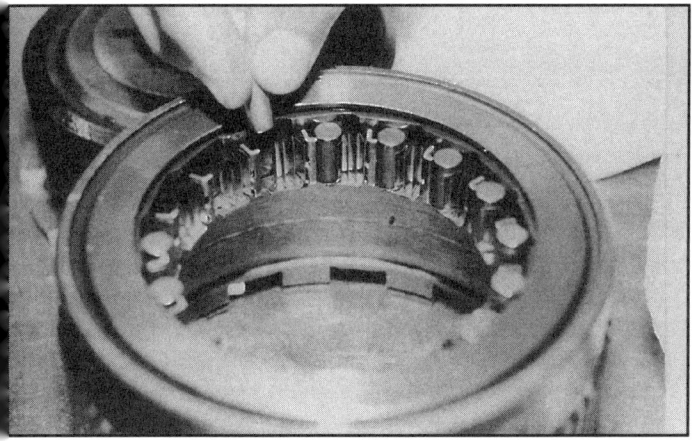

A new one-way clutch that comes with the Level 10 kit is installed in the low reverse clutch hub. Small rollers are secured by springs and held against an eccentric, allowing the clutch to turn in only one direction.

The Level 10 kit includes a new roller clutch hub and needle thrust bearing (right) to replace the original hub and thrust washer (left). Replacement of the washer with the bearing is credited with a tremendous reduction in the amount of horsepower necessary to run the transmission.

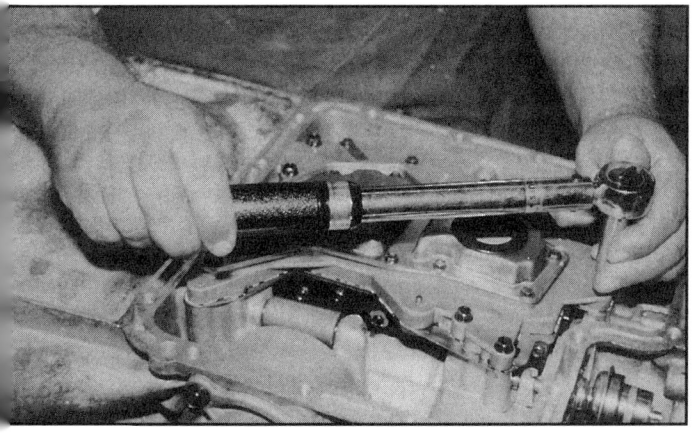

One of the biggest problems with do-it-yourself C-6 rebuilds is torquing the valve body down properly. This valve body is very sensitive to unequal tightening, and is prone to spring leaks if torqued unevenly.

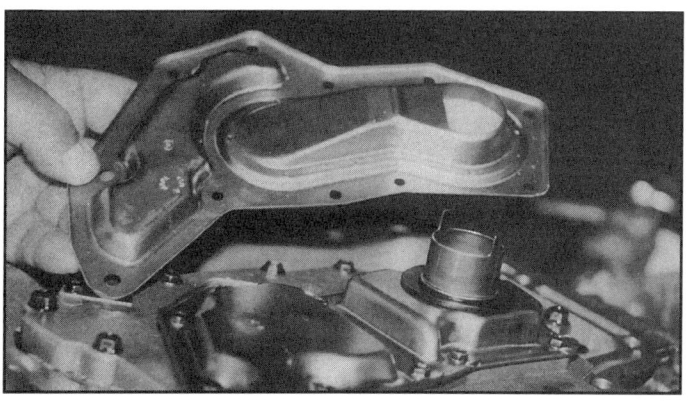

Truck owners need to make sure they get the right filter and extension, because truck transmission pans are deeper than car pans. Note the difference between the installed truck filter and the car filter being held for comparison.

Interior & Exterior Accessories

Performance Modifying Ford Trucks

One of the undeniable factors that has helped make modern pickup trucks so popular with a youthful consumer market is that these vehicles are easy to personalize. Today's market is loaded with products that can be quickly and easily installed to transform a truck into a vehicle that reflects your own personality. I'm talking about what might be considered simple "bolt-on" products, those that don't take an engineering degree and a week of down-time to install. These are items that can make an almost immediate difference in the way the truck looks, feels and sounds.

Elsewhere in this book, we have discussed some things that belong on the list, such as tires and wheels, but we approached the subject more from a technical standpoint, rather than a cosmetic one. Tires and wheels rank among the most popular items that are swapped to upgrade a truck's appearance, as well as its performance.

In our opinion, appearance add-ons are as much a part of building a performance truck as anything else. Once you have all the horsepower, torque, ride and handling characteristics built into your vehicle, you might as well make it comfortable and attractive to look at. So in this chapter we'll investigate some of the things that can be done to personalize your truck, both inside and out. Keep in mind that these are only suggestions, and the market offers much more than we are able to show here. But perhaps these ideas will stir your imagination, and that may help you zero in on the accessories you want.

The interior of a standard cab pickup is quite limited in space, yet it still offers many possibilities for customizing and upgrading. Following is an overview of some of the things that can be done.

Sound System

This is an area that can range from mild to wild. Just about the only thing that places a ceiling on how much audio power can be installed in a truck is the budget. That's because space is almost unlimited. If that sounds contradictory to the statement about there being a shortage of interior space, it isn't, because with truck sound systems the interior is not the only place for installation.

Of course, most of us will restrict sound system installation to the interior, but not everyone is so conservative. With the coming of the boom-boom era, innovative truck owners fell into a competitive spirit regarding woofer size and decibel levels, and the cargo bed was fair game as housing for the biggest speakers one could find. Parking lot competitions attracted trucks that had been converted to essentially one gigantic, rolling sound system.

While this book isn't about promoting the ultimate sound system, you should at least recognize that trucks are an ideal foundation for building as powerful a system as your auditory nerves and wallet can handle.

By virtue of their tight living quarters, trucks are easy to fill with music. However, interior speaker placement is a challenge. Typical dashboard and door panel locations are fine for speakers up to about 6"x9" dimensions, but anything larger generally needs to be installed behind the seatback. The aftermarket has responded to this reality by offering special truck speakers that are housed in tailored enclosures to fit between the seatback and the rear wall of a standard-cab pickup.

But speaker size alone is not necessarily the most important determining factor in producing quality sound. You can have enormous speakers and still be stuck with lousy sound quality. Conversely, you can have 6"x9" speakers that put out some real quality. When we refer to sound quality, what we are really talking about is clarity, lack of distortion, power, tonal range, and characteristics that sometimes even defy description, except that those who truly appreciate a great sound system can pick out the flaws to which most of the rest of us are completely oblivious.

What determines overall clarity, tonal range, freedom from distortion and power of a sound system is a combination of speaker construction and placement, amplifier power, wiring quality and output device (radio, tape player, CD player, etc.) quality. Failing in any one of these areas will compromise the overall quality of sound the system can produce. But naturally, each of us must work within a budget, so it's important to understand what to look for when purchasing components, enabling us to get the best our money can buy.

Let's begin with the power supply. A vehicle's electrical system is 12-volt DC, but to produce high wattage, the components in the sound system amplifier must convert the battery's 12-volt DC to AC so it can be boosted by a transformer. But the output transistors need to be driven by DC power, so the amplifier must convert the higher AC voltage back to DC. The circuitry that performs all this is called a DC to DC converter. If the amplifier in the sound system doesn't have a DC to DC converter, it will be incapable of producing more than 18 to 20 watts per channel.

The amplifier should feature a regulated power supply to maintain a steady supply of power regardless of the demands on the battery by other accessories such as headlights, etc. High-performance transistors called MOSFETs (Metal Oxide Semiconductor Field Effect Transistor), used in the best amplifiers, have higher switching speed and generate almost no heat, so they provide quick and efficient response to musical peaks.

Amplifiers that are rated at more than 20 watts per channel should have discrete output transistors. And some amplifiers feature integrated cooling fans to ensure longer life.

Total Harmonic Distortion (THD) should be as low as possible. Expressed as a percentage, you will be looking for a THD rating below 1%, because less than 1% of THD is undetectable by the human ear. Typical ratings for quality amplifiers will read something like 0.04%.

More power means better, not just louder, music. A low power stereo system produces a lot of distortion when the volume is turned up, and it's distortion, not high power, that ruins speakers. More power produces cleaner sound, stronger bass and crisper treble. When you're looking at an amplifier's power rating, pay attention to the RMS watts, not the Peak Power watts. An amplifier may be rated at 90 x 4 Peak Power watts, but only deliver 40 x 4 RMS watts.

Amplifiers come in a variety of formats. Stereo amps will power left and right speakers. If you are trying to drive four speakers with a single stereo amp, hook up the system so the receiver's internal amp powering one set of speakers, and the external amp powering the other two speakers.

A Tri-Way amplifier is a 2-channel stereo amp that allows you to drive a pair of stereo speakers and a subwoofer at the same time by using a crossover module. This is the least expensive way to power a set of stereo speakers and a subwoofer.

A 4-channel amplifier is needed to power a pair of stereo speakers in front and another set of stereo speakers or a pair of subwoofers in the rear. A 2, 3, or 4-channel amplifier can power four speakers in stereo, or the outputs can be bridged to produce much greater power to two stereo speakers. It is also possible to bridge the rear channels so you can drive a pair of stereo front speakers and power a subwoofer, in the 3-channel mode.

When it comes to speakers, nothing beats the matched component approach. Separate woofers and tweeters (as opposed to full-range speakers that are designed as a combination woofer/tweeter unit) because this allows you to separate the woofers and tweeters. More realistic sound is produced if the tweeters are mounted high, at ear level or on the dash, and the woofers are mounted at some other location.

Many stock stereo speakers are not capable of producing clean bass tones, so they are prone to distortion when the volume is turned up on music that has a lot of low bass. But this can be overcome by using a bass blocking device, which is installed on the speaker's positive input side and filters out the bass. The overall effect is to clean up the music and deliver better mid-range and high tones.

Well, we could go on an on about the ultimate features for a sound system. But hopefully you get the point that a great system is more than just bigger speakers and a lot of volume. Check out the specifications to make sure you get the best equipment your budget will allow.

Seats & Seat Covers

In a truck I built a few years ago, I installed a seat cover that no one who ever saw the interior would believe was simply a seat cover. It was called Sport Seating by Cobra. There is a great distinction between this product and what you might expect to find when you buy seat covers. Cobra's cover features built-in lumbar padding to support the lower back, and side bolsters to support the thighs and upper torso, giving the old bench almost a bucket-seat feel. There is also an air-cushioned back to add a cooling effect, which is appreciated on hot days. A pocket designed into the front edge of the seat below the driver's legs offer a place where maps and such can be stored. Complete installation took only about 15 minutes. The seatback cover is open across the bottom, so it simply slides down over the seatback and fastens together along the bottom with hook/loop fastener strips. The seat bottom cover fits snugly and attaches via nylon straps that run both fore/aft and crosswise beneath the seat. Fit is so good that it looks like a custom bench seat was installed.

But maybe you want more than just fancy covers for a bench seat. Something sporty, like race-quality bucket seats, or perhaps a nice split bench with fold-down console to fill the space between driver and passenger positions. Both are available. But before you buy, sit on the seats and think about how you will feel after driving for several hours in one of these seats. Consider how well your legs are supported, or if there are any annoying aspects to the design. The stock bench seat in my 1990 Ford F-150 SuperCab pickup was very comfortable, except for the fact that support was lacking on the side toward the door, and I always felt like I was tilting that direction. This is the kind of thing that will drive you nuts after a while, so don't overlook these aspects of seat design when searching for the ideal seat for your truck. This is a highly personal matter, and what your buddy has in his truck may suit him fine, but leave you searching for a chiropractor.

Safety Belts

Even the best racing seat won't keep you in place when the going gets rough. Off-roaders who have learned the value of seat belts the hard way (does this sound like experience speaking?) know all too well the feeling of smashing against the roof after negotiating even a little bump too fast. It can result in complete loss of control, not to mention brain damage or other physical harm. Never drive without a seatbelt, even if you're just on your way to the grocery store.

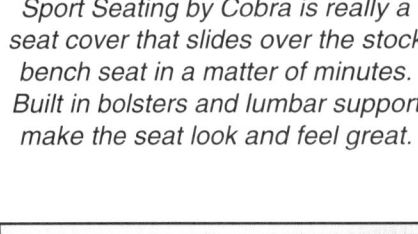

Sport Seating by Cobra is really a seat cover that slides over the stock bench seat in a matter of minutes. Built in bolsters and lumbar support make the seat look and feel great.

With the seat out of the truck, while the interior was being repainted, I slipped the seat cover over the factory bench, pressed the hook and loop fastener strip together, and cinched the straps. At right are the two pieces of the set before installation.

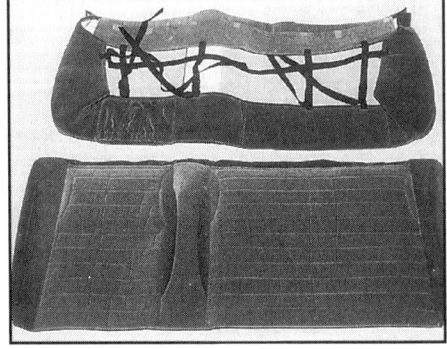

By Cobra Inc., Keiper Recaro Seating Inc., and others make sport seats that are often found in race vehicles, like the one pictured here. These seats are sturdy, and sometimes even comfortable, although their strict rigidity usually takes some getting used to. When racing they are definitely more comfortable than a seat that allows your body to be tossed all over the inside of the truck. Notice the seat belts, which are a five-point racing harness, often referred to as a restraint system.

Unless you're expecting to become involved in serious competitive driving, I see no compelling reason to replace the factory lap belts and shoulder harnesses, unless of course the upgrade to a racing harness happens to fit the motif. However, if racing is in your future, you may actually be forced to swap for a five-point harness (popularly known as a restraint system) by the sanctioning body. If that's the case, get your hands on a Simpson Race Products catalog and you'll find exactly what you need.

Carpeting

Nothing can make the interior of a truck look ragged more quickly than worn out or badly soiled carpeting. When the original carpeting wears out, or perhaps when you're making an interior color change and want to change the carpet to match, you can order factory replacement carpeting from the dealership parts department. Or, you can turn to the aftermarket and find high quality factory-style new carpet for trucks from companies like Auto Custom Carpets.

This type of carpet set is premolded for exact fit over the driveline hump, and to follow the floor contours under the seat. Installation is easy, requiring only positioning the carpet and cutting the holes to accommodate transmission and transfer case shift levers. This aftermarket carpet also features an insulation padding layer to help quiet road noise and prevent heat from the highway, the engine compartment, and the exhaust system from penetrating the interior. On the driver's side, there is a built-in rubber heel plate to bear the brunt of the constant wear caused by the driver's right foot on the accelerator pedal. In addition to this, Auto Custom Carpets can supply you with a matching set of floor mats to increase the life of the carpeting.

Electric Sliding Rear Window

On one of my project trucks, I replaced the rear window with a Powr Slider from C.R. Laurence Automotive Products. This is a tinted electric sliding window that is operated by a convenient dash-mounted switch. When the sun is hitting the rear glass, the dark tint helps keep the driver and passengers comfortable. The power unit fits nicely behind the seat, and a drive-cable runs up to the window drive mechanism. Installation is exactly like replacement of any rear window, the only difference being the power unit that simply bolts to the back of the cab and is then wired to the dash-mounted switch. Operation of the slider is quiet, quick and simple, and the driver never needs to take eyes off the road to adjust the opening or closing of the rear window. Ventilation has never been so easy to control!

EXTERIOR ACCESSORIES

Winch

Number one on my list of necessary accessories for an off-road vehicle that will actually be used off-road is a winch. In the past twenty years of off-roading, I have used a winch only twice to rescue myself, but in the past few years have used a winch a dozen times to rescue other people. And those were times when nothing but a winch would work. There was no possibility of digging out or using a snatch strap, because circumstances didn't allow those alternatives. So a good winch ranks at the top of my list.

One thing that must be stressed is that anyone who intends to use a

With the seat out of the truck, new carpeting can be laid, making sure it fits well over the driveline tunnel without puckers. The Ford dealer can order factory carpeting, or you can buy from aftermarket companies such as Auto Custom Carpets, where this one came from.

If you're tired of reaching over your shoulder to open or close the rear sliding glass in your truck, consider one of these slick units from C.R. Laurence Automotive Products. It's an electrically operated sliding rear window that is tinted to look good as well as to protect driver and passengers from the heat of the sun. The drive unit mounts behind the seat, and a cable leads up to the drive mechanism. A convenient dash-mounted electric switch does the rest.

winch needs to learn the proper methods of rigging and operation. A winch in the hands of an inexperienced person can be dangerous, so learn to use it the right way. Pay strict attention to the operating instructions that come with your unit. Another important point is to carry a winch accessory kit, which should include heavy leather gloves to protect the hands when working with the wire rope, a snatch block to double line-pulling power, a tree protector strap, and other items. Warn offers a complete accessory kit that includes all the essentials.

These days, the most popular winches are electric, so a lot of attention needs to be given to the truck's charging system. Dual batteries and a battery isolator are a good idea, to ensure that you don't drain down your primary battery during the winching operation. A heavy-duty alternator that is powerful enough to keep up with the electrical demand of the winch is vital. You can determine your exact electrical requirements by referring to the winch owner's manual.

In my opinion, the most useful winch set-up is one that will permit moving the winch from the front of the vehicle to the rear. To have a winch that is mountable both front and rear, it is necessary to install the winch on a platform that incorporates a hitch receiver-style bar. Then, with both front and rear receivers, the winch can easily be moved, plugged in, and operated from whichever end of the truck is best for the rescue. Rear hitch receivers are available from companies such as Reese, Eaz Lift, or Draw Tite, but front receivers are more difficult to come up with. Fortunately, Warn makes exactly what is needed — a 2-inch square receiver that bolts between the front frame rails using existing bumper mount bolt holes.

Of course, to make it all work, you need a wiring harness to power the winch from the rear position. Again, Warn comes to the rescue by supplying a 20-foot power cable that runs from the battery to the rear bumper, with a quick-connect plug at the far end. To keep the quick-connect plug from fouling with muck, a plastic cover is provided. Secure the plug beneath the rear bumper to one side of the hitch, where it will be in position for a quick-connection with the matching pigtail from the winch. Using a battery with wing-nut terminals, the rear wiring harness can be left disconnected when the winch is not in use in the rear position, and quickly hooked up when necessary.

On a truck I built using this type of winch arrangement, I didn't want the winch to have to sit out in the weather nor be vulnerable to anyone with a plan for theft, so I installed a lockable bed-mounted tool box that was bolted to the front wall of the cargo bed. This position centers the weight of the winch, rather than having it weighing down the front or rear of the vehicle. As it turns out, the box is perfectly sized for the winch and mounting platform. Actually, there was a little more room than needed, so I lined the chest with 1/2-inch plywood on the floor and walls, which served to cushion the space between winch and chest walls to prevent damage, and it keeps things quiet when bouncing over the trail.

On my most recent Ford project truck, I installed a new and different style tool box called a Sports Trunk, which is made by Landau Marketing of Fort Worth, Texas. The Sports Trunk features aerodynamic styling, rather than the more boxy styling of traditional tool chests. Items carried inside are protected from the elements by the weatherproof lid that, when open, is supported by a pair of pneumatic lifts. Pull-out drawers make it easy to organize small items. The Sports Trunk is available in either treadplate or ready-to-paint smooth aluminum.

The most convenient winch arrangement is one that can be attached either front of rear of the vehicle by utilizing front and rear mounted receiver hitch units. A dedicated wire harness is permanently routed to the rear of the truck, and the winch is equipped with a quick-connect electrical plug.

Roll Bar

Originally, roll bars were designed to provide protection in the event of an accident resulting in a vehicle roll-over. But somewhere along the line of "progress" between then and now, many "roll bars" became light bars or sport bars or some other form of cosmetic bars. Roll-over protection isn't even a consideration for some of these accessories. Not only are many of these products too flimsy to provide real protection, but the way they are installed — simply bolted to the thin sheet metal floor in the bed of a pickup — reduces protection in a rollover.

In a true protective roll bar, a double-tube design is better than a single tube. This is not only because two tubes are stronger than one, but also because with two tubes you can spread the bottom attachment points and a bipod is formed on each side for a more secure foundation. However, a double-tube or even a triple-tube system in which all the bars have a common foundation at the bottom is not much better than a single-tube roll bar. If you decide to use this type of design, make sure you include "kicker" tubes that angle rearward for diagonal support.

Street trucks with light bars don't need to pay much attention to the mounting process, but off-road trucks with real roll bars must take some extra precautions to make sure the protection will be there when needed. Rather than just bolting the roll bar footing to the thin sheetmetal of the cargo bed, there should at least be some sizable backing plates on the underside of the bed to secure the mounting bolts. But that is the minimum. For even greater protection, it is best to fabricate a system of braces that are connected to the truck's frame to provide support beneath the roll bar mounting points.

Typical of the cosmetic bars that serve mostly for carrying driving lights and adding machismo to a truck is a bar I installed on a project truck. Manufactured by Mercury Tube, the Grizzly Bar comes as five pieces that need to be assembled by using specialized rivets. Ideally, assembly should take place in the cargo box, to ensure a proper fit. With all the

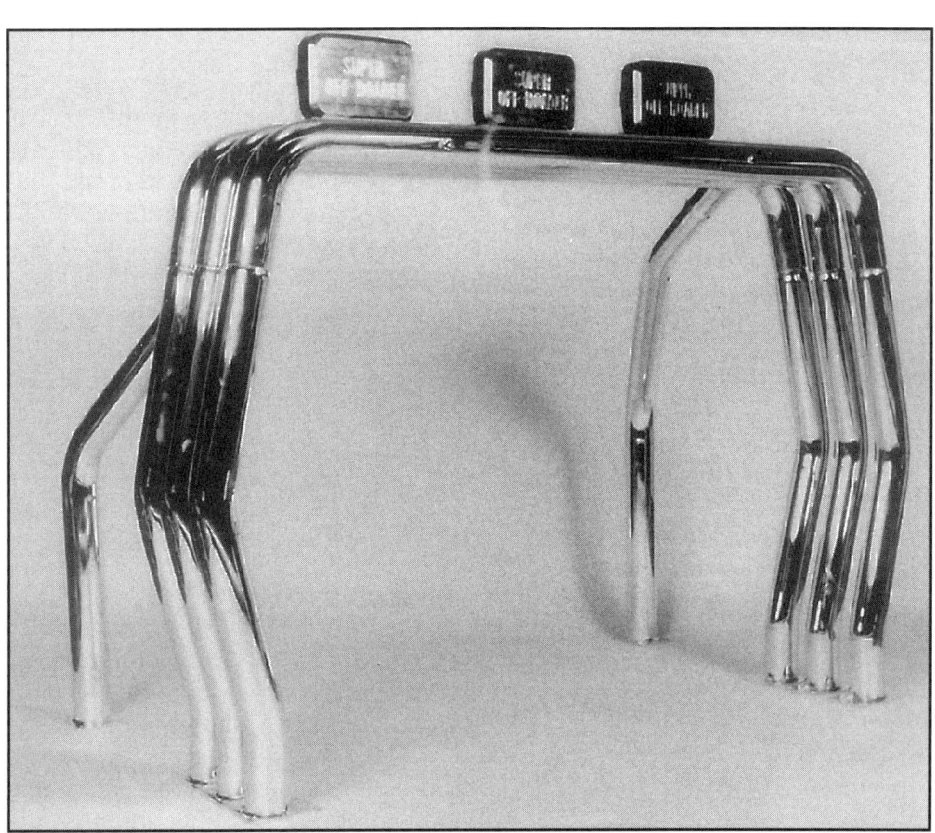

There is a vast difference between an honest-to-goodness roll bar and a light bar, when it comes to offering protection in a roll-over accident. Pictured here is a triple-tube roll bar, which is not intended for upside down use, but does an admirable job of supporting a set of driving lights.

Even though the forward edge of the cab of this F-250 was crushed somewhat by a rollover, the rollbar obviously prevented more extensive damage at the rear of the cab where driver and passenger heads are positioned. This is what a "real" rollbar is supposed to do, and a full cage would be even better.

pieces put together, holes are drilled, impact rivets inserted and smacked with a hammer, and the job is done. With this kind of bar, bolting through the cargo box floor is sufficient. You don't need to worry about going to the frame, because the bar is only for show anyway.

Driving Lights

Once a roll bar is installed, the next natural addition to the accessory list is a set of driving lights. Any auto supply store can sell you a number of different driving light configurations. But be aware that driving lights are not all created equal. Some are designed to endure the rigors of 1000-mile off-road races across the worst terrain on the planet, while others are too flimsy to hold up to that kind of abuse. Your choice of lights will depend a great deal on the type of driving you'll be doing, as well as your budget. Be realistic. Most of us never drive at night in off-road races where it is legal to take the covers off these lights and actually turn them on. If what you're looking for is the cosmetic appearance of a tough off-road vehicle, you don't need to pay to big price for the best lights. Get something that looks good and bolt them to the roll bar.

Besides the durability factor, driving lights come in a variety of power ratings and patterns of beam. High-powered pencil beam lights throw a very narrow beam for a long distance. These are not necessarily the easiest lights to use, because the beam is so narrow that when the truck bounces over the ground the beam bounces all over the sky. Serious racers use them to cut through the dark on long open stretches of desert, but you have to get used to these lights to use them effectively. Broad-beam units don't throw the light as far, but the beam pattern is wide and not so easily moved off the trail as the truck negotiates bad terrain. Many people find this pattern more usable for off-road night driving.

Driving lights don't always have to be mounted in a forward position to be useful. I like one broad beam flood light pointed aft to serve as a combination cargo bed light and powerful backup light. Factory backup lights are next to worthless for actually showing what's behind the truck. About all they do is notify other drivers that your truck is in reverse. A powerful flood light really does the job, but you should install a special switch for this light so it doesn't turn on every time you put the transmission in reverse, and blind other drivers. With the switch, you can selectively turn on this backup light only when needed.

Ditch lights are another good use for broad-beam flood lights. Ditch lights are pointed sideways from the truck so you can see clearly what is beside the trail or campground (or in the ditch, I suppose). Again, special switches for these lights allow selective use for left and right banks, and only when needed.

For my truck, I went to Warn for two different types of lights — I wanted a pair of high-intensity pencil beams pointing forward, and a single flood light pointing to the rear to serve as a super-duty backup light. Model W610 is a 100-watt quartz halogen pencil beam that is ideal for seeing a long way across the wide open spaces. Model W620 is of matching size, but has a quartz halogen bulb behind a flood lens that gives a broad beam to illuminate a wide area for a short distance. Perfect for lighting up the campsite area when you arrive after dark and need to set up the tent. Both lights are protected in a polished stainless steel housing and come with hard plastic lens covers that snap on and off quickly.

Be watchful of electrical current draw when installing lights, so you don't accidentally overtax the electrical system. The Warn pencil beam lights draw 8 amps each, and the flood light draws 4 amps, so with all the lights turned on, I would be drawing 20 amps just for that purpose. And my truck is relatively conservative from a driving light standpoint. I've seen trucks with so many lights it would take Hoover Dam to power the system. As you decide about installing lights, make sure the electrical system is designed to provide enough current to handle the number of lights you install, as well as all the other electrical accessories in the truck.

Fender Flares

Fender flares serve a dual purpose — they improve the appearance of many trucks by adding a body contour to an area that is often pretty dull, and they cover the tread of wide tires. Legally, the tread is supposed to be covered to prevent rocks and muck from getting tossed onto other vehicles, possibly resulting in damage to those vehicles, or distracting the driver and causing an accident. In some states, there are fair weather laws that permit hot rodders with fenderless roadsters to drive when the weather is dry, but you may have a hard time convincing the local constabulary that your truck is a roadster.

Aside from the statutory restraints, there are other reasons for wanting your tire tread covered. One of the best reasons is because the greatest amount of damage done by flying rocks and crud is generally inflicted on the vehicle doing the tossing. Fender flares protect the rocker panels and quarter panels from getting dinged to death and requiring frequent repair and repainting.

Bed Liner and Tailgate Net

If your truck is destined to live a functional life in pursuit of fish, game, and firewood, hauling stuff for the yard, lumber for building a patio cover, or gravel for the driveway, you should consider the benefits of installing a bed liner.

Again, several different brands are available, and the choice is yours. In my project truck, I chose a Pendaliner, which is an under-rail model that slips easily into place, using two Dual-Lock fastener clips to secure the headwall of the liner to the forward end of the cargo box. The sides of the liner fit snugly up under the side rails of the bed, preventing the liner from shifting. Installation time was literally no more than a couple of minutes, and the result was an immediate and dramatic improvement in the truck's appearance and functional utility.

Over-rail models of liners are also available, with the black plastic molded to fit over the top of the cargo bed side rails. This offers protection to this vulnerable part of the cargo box, but is not very nice from a cosmetic standpoint. If you're looking for rugged protection, that is a great way to go. But if your plans lean toward cosmetic improvement, there are other ways to protect the side rails and make the truck look even better.

Installation of a bed liner makes sense even if you aren't going to be hauling a lot of stuff in the back. Strictly from a cosmetic standpoint, the clean high-contrast appearance of a bed liner makes the truck look sharp. And from a function standpoint, you never know when you will want to load a quad-runner or motorcycle, or even just throw a flat tire in the back. The bed liner will offer protection as well as good looks.

If the truck's tailgate is to be retained, a tailgate cover will also be in order. Generally, when you buy a bed liner you get a tailgate cover as part of the package. In my case, I opted to shed the gate and install a Pro Net. The Pro Net is available in several colors, and comes from Team Tricks Co., Inc. It features stiff vertical side supports that keep the net from sagging, and strap retainers to keep the strap tails from flapping in the breeze. Installation is quick and easy, a matter of simply drilling four holes and bolting the clips to each side of the tailgate opening. Optional quick release clips allow the net to be hooked up or taken down in a heartbeat, for loading and unloading cargo. The net also helps reduce wind resistance that is created by having a solid tailgate in the vertical position.

Bed Caps and Side Rails

Finishing touches on a cargo box may involve installation of side bed caps and bed rails. Both of these accessories offer dual purpose improvement. First, they offer protection and the ability to tie down a load. Second, they are a definite cosmetic improvement over a plain cargo box. On my truck I installed a set of Putco Truck Skins wrap-around bed caps and Locker side rails.

The Truck Skins are installed first, and they are form fitted to match the contour of the cargo bed sides. Putco gives buyers a choice between polished stainless steel, black powder

Putco's Truck Skins are contoured to precisely fit the curves of the bed rail. At right is a photo of the underside of the Truck Skin, showing the 3M adhesive tape used for easy installation. The flange can also be drilled and screwed to the cargo box, if desired. The Rugged Liner bed liner added good looks as well as protection to the cargo box.

coat, and rugged Treadbrite aluminum. I chose the stainless steel, so they would complement the side rails to be installed next.

It's handy to have a place to tie down a load that is being carried in the back of the truck. My decision to install a set of side rails was directly related to the convenience they offer as a tie-down anchor that runs the full length of the bed.

Grille

One of the first things an observer will notice about your truck is the grille. Stock grilles don't do much to enhance the cosmetic appearance of a truck, so you may want to consider installing an aftermarket custom grille. Among the most popular of these are tube grilles, with both round and square tubes available. However, there are now billet aluminum grilles that, to some, are even more attractive than the tube grilles. These units are easy to install, using built-in mounting tabs that match the positions of stock mounting holes that were used to secure the factory grille.

On my own truck, I replaced the broken plastic factory grille with an attractive aluminum billet model from Stull Industries. Replacement of the stock unit was simple, and the resulting cosmtic improvement was stunning. Sixteen polished, thin, horizontal, billet aluminum grille bars replaced the blocky plastic piece that Detroit had installed as original equipment. The dress-up factor was enormous, and was immediately noticed and appreciated by all who saw the transformation.

A brush guard and grille guard assembly from Go Rhino! Products was installed as a protective measure for our new billet grille. The brush guard extends far enough to each side of the grille guard to provide protection to the headlights during off-road forays in brushy country.

Custom Body Panels

Customizing the exterior of a truck is fairly easy these days. Companies have specialized in manufacturing everything from molded running boards to fender extensions to ground effects panels. In fact, it's possible to install so many custom body panels that the original truck is hardly recognizable.

Lund Industries, Inc. manufactures a broad spectrum of easy-to-install custom body components. Their inventory list ranges from hood shields and grille screens to window nets and windshield visors, and everything else to make a truck look tough and rugged or smooth and sleek, depending upon which design direction you favor. Some of their products can be painted directly on

A full-size Ford pickup takes on a whole new appearance, with the addition of some Lund body accessories. The F-150 pictured at left features an Interceptor Wrap-Around Hood and Fender Shield, lighted MoonVisor, Fastback cab spoiler with driving lights mounted on top, and RunningMates fiberglass running boards.

Lund Truck Accessories can transform a stock pickup into a smooth custom truck. The Super Cab Ford in the photo to the right features a Screen Front grille insert, Interceptor Wrap-Around Hood and Fender Shield, MoonVisor lighted visor, Fastback cab spoiler, RunningMates fiberglass running boards, and WideSides fiberglass fender extensions over the rear tires, turning an otherwise common late-model truck into a custom show truck.

For those seeking the ultimate in off-road tough truck appearance, Lund offers a multitude of custom body panels and accessories. The Ford Ranger pictured to the left is a showcase for some of Lund's body-modifying equipment. Included on this truck are a FrontRunner Hood Deflector, Eclipse headlight covers, Screen Front grille insert, SuperStep universal truck step, Racerback cab fairing that can support driving lights mounted on top, WideSides fender extensions, and a MoonVisor lighted visor. This makes a nice looking package that is sure to turn heads wherever it goes.

the exterior to match the cosmetic scheme of the rest of the truck, and other items are clear and intended to be painted from behind. This prevents damage to the paint from gravel, mud and other things that might scratch or chip the color coat.

Ground effects consists of special skirts and dams that are patterned after similar items which were originally developed for application in the racing world to prevent air from getting under a race car, or invading the space around the tires, etc. By excluding air from beneath the undercarriage, the vehicle hugs the ground more effectively at high speed, eliminating the tendency for air to lift the vehicle. These special body panels also help channel the air around the body more smoothly, increasing aerodynamic efficiency. They allow race cars to be driven much faster than before the ground effects panels were installed. Of course, these things are important when you're

GST Industries offers several different packages for Ford trucks. Pictured above is the AeroExpress, the flagship package of the GST line. This aggressive 15-piece package includes a front air dam, side rockers, rear scoops, three sets of "finger plates," rear fender extensions, cab extender, wing and moldings.

At left is Razzi Corporation's "Lone Ranger" package. Razzi has ground effects packages for most Rangers dating back to 1982, and kits are available for Standard Cab as well as SuperCab models, and in both long- and short-bed lengths.

At left is a rear view of the "Lone Ranger" by Razzi, showing the smooth and pleasing body alteration treatment resulting from installation of their Ground Effects panels.

As can be seen below, one-piece tilt beds and hoods can be fabricated to meet the requirements of those who have special needs. Combining these tilting body units with hydraulic lifts results in a dramatic, and sometimes even useful, body modification.

going to be driving 180+ miles per hour, but at normal highway speeds the actual benefit of these panels is recognized as being generally more cosmetic than functional. Trucks that are sitting at stock ride height, or those that have been lowered are able to take maximum cosmetic advantage of ground effects aerodynamic body panels, which make a truck look lower than it really is.

Razzi Corporation manufactures ground effects kits, utilizing panels which are intended to be painted to match or otherwise complement the truck. Razzi employs a thermoset ABS material in the manufacture of their products, and installation of the one-piece panels leaves no screws or rivets visible. Razzi has Ranger Ground Effects for models dating back to 1982. In most Ranger models, they have kits available for Standard Cab and Super Cab, in both long-bed and short-bed lengths. As we went to press, the company was planning to release a new kit for F-Series trucks, but no photos were available at press time.

GST Industries, a division of Stauffer Classics Ltd., offers a full line of aerodynamic panels for your choice of mild to wild customizing. Hand-laminated cloth-backed and Kevlar reinforced fiberglass components are used in the GST line, which includes such items as front air dams, side rockers, rear scoops, rear fender extensions, cab extenders, wings and others pieces.

One-piece hood and fender combinations are popular with some, particularly racers, because of the convenience provided when it's time to work under the hood. With the hood and front fenders bonded into a single unit that tilts forward on hinges, it's possible to work on the engine without having to lean over the front fenders. The owner can virtually crawl right into the engine compartment and go to work. I have also seen many completely removable one-piece front units, which offers the ultimate in convenience. You can build a system that allows for the one-piece hood/fender combination to tilt when you want or to be completely removed when necessary. This can be accomplished by making the hinges of a quick-release design, so all you have to do is pull a couple of pins and lift the whole unit off and set it aside while you work in the engine bay. Adding hydraulic rams to a tilting body unit allows the driver to easily lift the hood or cargo box for access to engine compartment or chassis.

So, as you can see, there is almost no limit to the directions you can take in personalizing and customizing your truck, both inside and out. Let your imagination run wild.

Performance Modifying Ford Trucks

Paint & Body

Unless you happen to be a die-hard off-roader who just doesn't care that his truck is occasionally scratched by close encounters with brush, rocks and other trail obstacles, chances are you will want to dress your dream truck up in something more than just a factory paint job. In fact, there are many hard-core off-roaders who, with full knowledge of what will happen on the trail, still put a lot of money and time in making the truck look good — regardless of how fleeting the cosmetics may be.

But the question is, "How do you go about getting a really show quality paint job?" The answer to that question is that the very best paint jobs don't rely on paint alone to make the truck look great. To make a truck look its best, it is necessary to spend some time dealing with some of the body glitches that come right out of the factory. A brand new truck, right off the assembly line, will have areas of the body that need to be worked on to spell the difference between a show winner and just another shiny truck.

None of this is absolutely necessary. You can have a pretty paint job sprayed on without going to all the trouble I'm about to describe. But if you want to win the hearts of the show judges, or if you just want to be able to take exceptional pride in your truck, you may want to consider going this extra mile.

All car show judges will know where to look at a vehicle to see if the builder has really done the job the right way. Most folks walk past a truck and say, "Boy, that's a pretty truck!" and wonder why it didn't win the blue ribbon. The dividing line between a show winner and an aver-

Paint & Body **123**

Depending upon the body condition, it may be necessary to replace entire body panels. This truck eventually became a real show vehicle, but not until it received new door panels, a new hood, and a new cargo box side.

age truck cannot be seen by looking at how fancy the paint is on the outside, or what the graphics look like.

Seams, where body panels are welded together, are areas of concern. When the sheetmetal is assembled at the factory, body panels are held in jigs while welding takes place. After the pieces are joined, there are gaps and globs all along the welded joints, and these are just painted over. If you are thinking about preparing a truly fine truck to enter in shows, even if they are only local shows held at the city park, you'll want to take care of these nasty body seams.

Making seams disappear is not as difficult as you may think. The first step is to minimize the gaps. You can do with by simply using body filler, or by glassing over the seams with thin strips of fiberglass. Or you can go all the way and either have the seams leaded or weld thin strips of sheetmetal across the gap the length of the seams and the follow up with body filler to eliminate the seams completely.

Depending upon the original condition of the truck you're working with, you may need to focus some attention on more than just body seams. If there are areas that have rusted through, there are various means to make repairs. Fiberglass can be shaped across rust-outs to make a temporary fix. Or for a more permanent repair, sheetmetal patch panels can be welded in where the old corroded metal has been cut out. When removing rusted areas, be sure to get all of it. Cut away the old panel until you are all the way back to healthy metal, because rust that is left behind will spread to adjacent metal and eventually rot it away.

After welding in new patch panels, or sheetmetal strips to conceal body seams, it is necessary to blend in the new metal with the old, so there is no visible evidence that a repair has ever been made. There are several different approaches that can be taken, but some are better than others.

If you can find a true master sheetmetal man who knows how to use lead as a body filler, that is the best and most permanent solution. But these craftsmen are rare. You may find one if you ask around at a custom car show, because custom cars require a lot of sheetmetal work that hides seams or the restoration of old rotted metal.

Another approach is to use fiberglass and body filler. The problem with fiberglass and filler is that these are subject to separation and cracking, especially if the truck is used hard or there is a lot of vibration as a result of your driving habits.

Regardless of which approach you take, eventually you will end up working with body filler, grinders, and sandpaper. Before body filler is even considered, the area should be worked as much as possible to minimize the amount of filler that will be needed. Some master body men can almost completely dismiss the need for filler, but the rest of us live in a world where some filler is going to be necessary. However, filler should not just be loaded into a gap like pudding in a dessert dish. For the best results, the area should be prepared in such a way that only a minimum of filler is needed.

Body filler is easy to use. Normally, only small amounts of filler are mixed at one time, because it must be applied and blended into the gaps and dents before the setting agent kicks and the stuff hardens. Filler is one of those things where you put on 5 ounces and grind off 4 ounces. Then you sand off another half ounce. Ideally, only the merest layer of filler remains, just enough to eliminate any hint of a variation in the surface of the body panel.

It may be that your truck has had a hard life, and some of the body panels are ready for the scrap pile. In cases like this, it may be best to simply remove entire panels and replace them. This can be done with door panels, hoods, fenders, cargo box sides, etc. Depending upon the age of the truck, it may be possible to find replacement panels in an auto wrecking yard, or you may opt to purchase brand new panels from Ford or another supplier. Be aware that there is a big difference between Ford factory-produced panels and those that come from suppliers other than Ford Motor Company. Quality differences occur not only in metal gauge, but also in fit. Check with a trusted body shop before you buy panels from anyone other than Ford.

Even though you buy brand new body panels from the factory, it may still be necessary to do some preliminary body work to eliminate minor flaws that can originate at the factory or develop during shipment of the panel. The point of all this is to finish with a truck that you can drag a nylon stocking across, and it will never snag.

The key to an excellent paint job is preparation, and the preparation should not stop with the exterior. To build a true show quality truck, strip the entire vehicle, inside and out, and prepare every square inch of sheetmetal, as if a show judge would run his hand over every part of the truck. Door jambs and underhood areas are commonly judged, both by sight and by touch, so make sure there are no flaws to be found.

To ensure that your truck ends up with a high-quality paint job, make sure the person who applies the paint is top notch. You can find out a lot about the quality of work being put out by a paint and body shop by asking for references, then go and have a look at the paint jobs this shop has applied on other vehicles. If there are several painters working at a shop, find out which one is best, and insist on having that person do the spraying. This will give youthe est chance of coming out of the shop without sags, runs, orange peel, or other common problems.

Use only the best materials, because primer and paint are, in the long run, the cheapest part of a high quality paint job. As long as you're investing so much in the experienced labor of a true craftsman, don't skimp on the materials. Modern two-part paints are durable and beautiful, but require special preparation and consideration when spraying the material on the truck. Some of these products are so highly toxic that the painter must wear what amounts to a space suit for personal protection. If you are looking for a painter to spray one of these exotic products on your truck, you'll know if the guy is experienced by asking to see his protective suit. If he has none, he may have no experience with these paints. Or he's not conscientious enough to make sure his safety equipment is up to snuff. That may tell you something aobut the type of care the painter takes with his work. You should look elsewhere to find a painter who knows what he's doing and cares enough to make sure everything is right.

When all is said and done, it's taking the time to do the nit-picking detail work, using quality materials and locating an experienced paint and body shop that make all the difference in how a truck looks. Spend the time and money to get the best your budget can afford, and you won't be sorry.

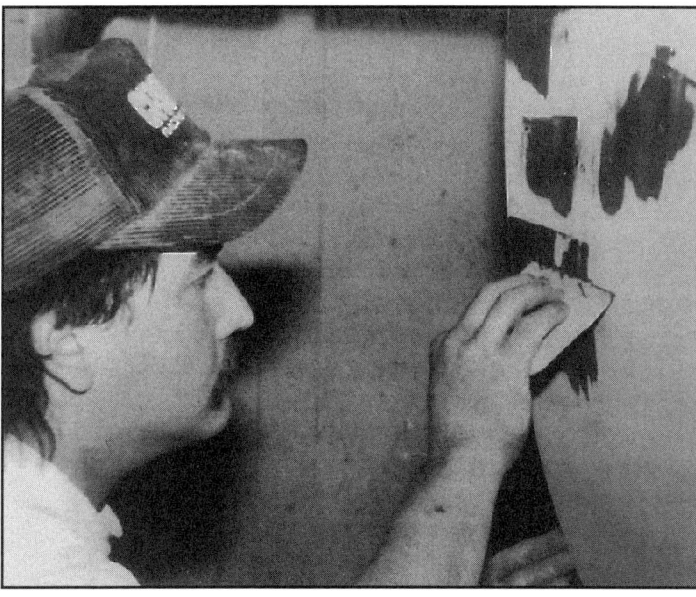

After the entire body has been worked on, a true paint and body craftsman will go back with glaze to fill all the pin holes or other flaws that may exist in the surface of the body filler or the metal itself. Little things like this mean a lot when preparing a show truck.

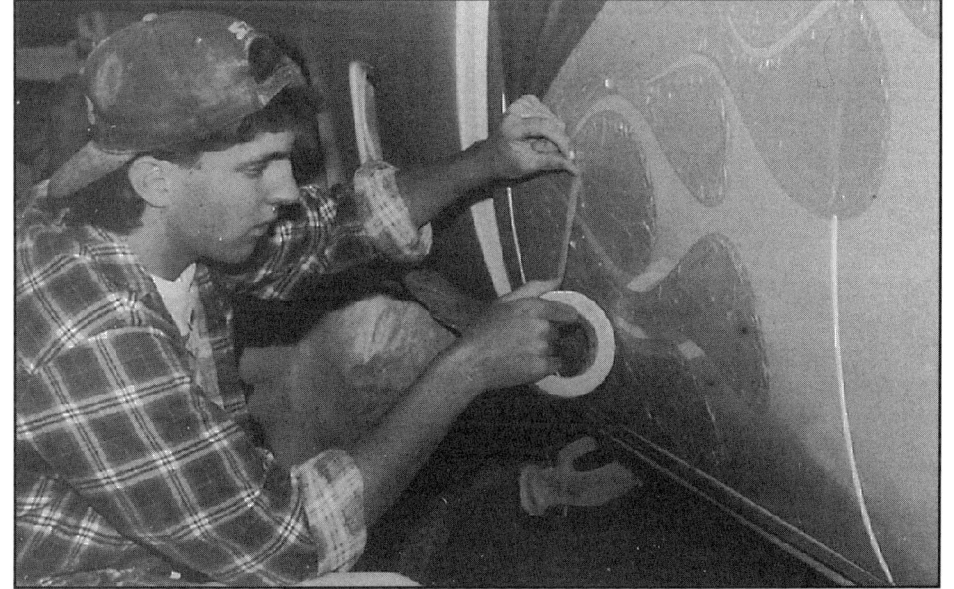

The quality of the finished product will depend upon the careful preparation for paint and graphics. Here, the pattern for flames is being taped off before painting. Work like this is tedious and expensive, but it makes the difference between an average truck and a real show stopper.

The marketplace is huge, which is both good and bad. It's good because you have an almost endless supply of stuff to choose from. It's bad because the challenge of knowing where to locate parts and pieces for a performance build-up of a truck can be confusing.

But, never fear, we're here to help you. Following is a list of sources that should help make your search somewhat easier. Many of these companies publish catalogs that you can order. Some are elaborate, while others are simple and small. But all contain information about performance components that may fit into your plans for buillding a performance Ford truck.

To make life easier, we've organized our source list in alphabetical order.

ARB Air Lockers
1425 Elliott Avenue West
Seattle, WA 98119
(206) 284-5906

Advance Adapters Inc.
335 Santa Bella
Paso Robles, CA 93447
(805) 238-7000

Air Lift Company
P.O. Box 80167
Lansing, MI 48908-0167
(800) 248-0892

Amptech
2305 Montomery St.
Fort Worth, TX 76107
(800) 364-9966

Art Carr Performance Transmission
10575 Bechler River Ave.
Fountain Valley, CA 92708
(714) 962-6655

ASAP
Automotive Specialty Accessory Parts, Inc.
P.O. Box 1907
Carson City, NV 89702

Auburn Gear Inc.
400 E. Auburn Dr.
Auburn, IN 46706
(219) 925-3200

Auto Custom Carpets
P.O. Box 1167
Anniston, AL 36202
(205) 236-1118

BBK Performance Parts
1611 Railroad Street
Corona, CA 91720
(909) 735-2400

B&M Racing & Performance Products
9142 Independence Ave.
Chatsworth, CA 91311
(818) 882-6422

Bell Tech Inc.
2822 East California Ave.
Fresno, CA 93721
(209) 445-1602

Bilstein Corp. of America
8845 Rehco Rd.
San Diego, CA 92121
(619) 453-7723

Borla Performance Industries
5901 Edison Dr.
Oxnard, CA 93033
(800) 927-5129

Brake Man
2455 Blanchard Rd.
Camarillo, CA 93012
(805) 491-2185

Bushwhacker Inc.
9200 N. Decatur St.
Portland, OR 97203
(800) 234-8920

By Cobra Inc.
1843 Floradale Ave.
South El Monte, CA 91733
(818) 443-4197

Centerforce Clutches
7171 Patterson Dr.
Garden Grove, CA 92641
(602) 771-8422

C.R. Laurence Co., Inc.
P.O. Box 21345
Los Angeles, CA 90021
(800) 421-6144

Cutler Induction Systems, Inc.
19595 NE 10th Ave., Suite A
N. Miami Beach, FL 33179
(305) 653-9098

Deflecta-Shield
1800 North 9th Street
Indianola, IA 50125
(800) 247-2400

Dee Zee Inc.
P.O. Box 3090
Des Moines, IA 50316
(515) 265-7331

Dutchman Motor Sports
7937 N.E. Alberta
Portland, OR 97220
(503) 257-6604

Edelbrock Corporation
2700 California St.
Torrance, CA 90503
(310) 781-2222

Explorer Pro Comp
3552 Fowler Canyon Road
Jamul, CA 91935
(800) 776-0767

Federal Mogul
P.O. Box 1966
Detroit, MI 48235
(810) 354-7700

FEY Automotive Products
15854 Ornelas St.
Irwindale, CA 91706
(800) 345-8476

Ford Motorsports Performance Equip.
44050 N. Groesbeck Highway
Clinton Township, MI 48036-1108
(313) 337-1356

Gale Banks Engineering
546 Duggan Ave.
Azusa, CA 91702
(800) 438-7693

Go Rhino! Products
591 West Apollo Street
Brea, CA 92621
(714) 257-0330

GST Industries
815 Stewart St.
Madison, WI 53713
(608) 271-5339

Holley Replacement Parts
11955 East Nine Mile Road
Warren, MI 48089
(502) 843-8630

Hooker Industries
1024 W. Brooks St.
Ontario, CA 91762
(909) 983-5871

Introspect
8851 Lakewood Blvd.
Downey, CA 90240
(310) 861-4519

Jardine Performance Exhaust
4257 S. Highway 89
Jackson Hole, Wyoming 83001
(307) 739-0818

K&N Engineering, Inc.
P.O. Box 1329
Riverside, CA 92502
(909) 684-9762

Keiper Recaro Seating Inc.
905 W. Maple Road
Clawson, MI 48017
(313) 288-6800

Landau Marketing
5440 Davis Blvd.
Fort Worth, TX 76180
(817) 498-2875

LeCarra U.S.A.
15850 W. 6th Ave.
Golden, CO 80401
(303) 279-5181

Level 10 Products
188 Route 94
Hamburg, NJ 07419
(201) 827-1000

Lock Right Powertrax
245 Fischer Ave., Bldg. B-4
Costa Mesa, CA 92626
(800) 562-5377

Lund Industries, Inc.
911 Lund Boulevard
Minneapolis, MN 55303
(800) 328-5863

Mercury Tube Ind.
1802 Santo Domingo Ave.
Duarte, CA 91010
(800) 253-2859

Mickey Thompson Performance Tires
4670 Allen Rd.
Stow, OH 44224
(330) 928-9092

Moser Engineering
1616 N. Franklin St.
Portland, IN 47371
(219) 726-6689

Mr. Gasket Company
8700 Brookpark Rd.
Cleveland, OH 44129
(216) 398-8300

MSD Ignition
1490 Henry Brennan Dr.
El Paso, TX 7936
(915) 857-5200

Nitrous Oxide Systems, Inc.
5930 Lakeshore Dr.
Cypress, CA 90630
(714) 821-0580

Novak Enterprises, Inc.
13321 Alondra Blvd. Unit C
Santa Fe Springs, CA 90670
(213) 921-3202

Optima Batteries
5 East Mississippi Ave.
Denver, CO 80210
(303) 340-7440

Paxton Superchargers
1260 Calle Suerte Ave.
Camarillo, CA 93012
(805) 987-5555

Penda Corporation
P.O. Box 449
Portage, WI 53901-0449
(608) 742-5301

Putco
216 W. First St.
Story City, IA 50248
(800) 247-3974

Rancho Suspension
6925 Atlantic Ave.
Long Beach, CA 90805
(310) 630-0700

Razzi Corporation
1050 Branch Drive
Alpharetta, GA 30201
(800) 235-6087

Reese Products
P.O. Box 1706
Elkhart, IN 46515
(800) 359-5505

Rugged Liner, Inc.
P.O. Box 230
Mt. Braddock, PA 15465
(412) 430-2065

Sanderson Headers
202 Ryan Way
So. San Francisco, CA 94080
(800) 669-2430

Simpson Race Products
2415 Amsler Street
Torrance, CA 90505
(310) 320-7231

Speed-O-Motive
12061 Slauson Ave.
Santa Fe Springs, CA 90670
(310) 945-2758

Speed Pro
100 Terrace Plaza
Muskegon, MI 49443-0299
(616) 724-5200

Spicer Axle Dvision
Dana Corporation
P.O. Box 1209
Fort Wayne, IN 46801

Street & Performance
#1 Hot Rod Lane
Mena, AR 71953
(501) 394-5711

Stull Industries, Inc.
12155 Magnolia Ave. #5
Riverside, CA 92503
(909) 343-2181

Summers Brothers Inc.
530 So. Mountain Ave.
Ontario, CA 91762
(714) 986-2041

Summit Racing Equipment
P.O. Box 909
Akron, OH 44309-0909

Superior Spindles
1522 N. Indiana St.
Los Angeles, CA 90063
(800) 640-3767

Suspension Techniques
13546 Vintage Place
Chino, CA 91710
(909) 465-1020

TCI
One TCI Dr.
Ashland, MS 38603
(601) 224-8972

Team Tricks Companies, Inc.
1099 N. Batavia
Orange, CA 92667
(800) 942-9910

Thermo Tec
P.O. Box 946
Berea, OH 44017
(216) 243-9997

Tractech (Detroit Locker)
11445 Stephens Dr.
Warren, MI 48090
(810) 759-3850

Trans-Dapt/Hedman
9599 West Jefferson Blvd.
Culver City, CA 90232
(310) 921-0404

The Turbo Shop
940 West Manchester Blvd.
Inglewood, CA 90301
(310) 215-0147

U.S. Gear Corp.
9420 Stony Island Ave.
Chicago, IL 60438
(312) 375-4900

Vortech Engineering
5351 Bonsai Ave., Suite 3
Moorpark, CA 93021
(805) 529-9330

Warn Industries
13270 SE Pheasant Court
Milwaukie, OR 97222
(503) 659-8750